Drawing Parallels

Drawing Parallels expands your understanding of the working process of architects by looking at their work from an alternative perspective. The book focuses on parallel projections such as axonometric, isometric, and oblique drawings. Ray Lucas argues that by retracing the marks made by architects, we can begin to engage more directly with their practice as it is by redrawing the work that hidden aspects are revealed. The practice of drawing offers significantly different insights, not easily accessible through discourse analysis, critical theory, or observation.

Using James Stirling, JJP Oud, Peter Eisenman, John Hejduk, and Cedric Price as case studies, Lucas highlights each architect's creative practices which he analyses with reference to Bergson's concepts of temporality and creativity, discussing the manner in which creative problems are explored and solved. The book also draws on a range of anthropological ideas including skilled practice and enchantment in order to explore why axonometric drawings are important to architecture and questions the degree to which the drawing convention influences the forms produced by architects.

With 60 black-and-white images to illustrate design development, this book would be an essential read for academics and students of architecture with a particular interest in further understanding the inner workings of the architectural creative process.

Ray Lucas is senior lecturer in architecture at the University of Manchester, where he served as head of department from 2014 to 2018.

Lucas has a PhD in social anthropology from the University of Aberdeen on *A Theory of Notation as a Thinking Tool*. From 2014 to 2018, Lucas was an associate researcher and external advisor for the ERC Advanced Grant Knowing From the Inside which worked among the disciplines of anthropology, fine art, design, architecture, and others in order to interrogate how we know our world.

ii *Drawing Parallels*

Lucas is author of *Research Methods for Architecture* (Laurence King, 2016), *Anthropology for Architects: Social Relations and the Built Environment* (Bloomsbury 2019), and is coeditor of *Architecture, Festival and the City* (Routledge 2018). Lucas's current research includes 'graphic anthropologies' of marketplaces in South Korea and urban festivals in Japan, as well as an interest in sensory design, film and architecture, anthropology and geometry, and further research into drawing.

Drawing Parallels
Knowledge Production in Axonometric, Isometric and Oblique Drawings

Ray Lucas

LONDON AND NEW YORK

First published 2019
by Routledge
2 Park Square, Milton Park, Abingdon, Oxon OX14 4RN

and by Routledge
52 Vanderbilt Avenue, New York, NY 10017

Routledge is an imprint of the Taylor & Francis Group, an informa business

© 2019 Ray Lucas

The right of Ray Lucas to be identified as author of this work has been asserted by him in accordance with sections 77 and 78 of the Copyright, Designs and Patents Act 1988.

All rights reserved. No part of this book may be reprinted or reproduced or utilised in any form or by any electronic, mechanical, or other means, now known or hereafter invented, including photocopying and recording, or in any information storage or retrieval system, without permission in writing from the publishers.

Trademark notice: Product or corporate names may be trademarks or registered trademarks, and are used only for identification and explanation without intent to infringe.

British Library Cataloguing-in-Publication Data
A catalogue record for this book is available from the British Library

Library of Congress Cataloging-in-Publication Data
A catalog record has been requested for this book

ISBN: 978-1-4724-1283-6 (hbk)
ISBN: 978-1-315-57804-0 (ebk)

Typeset in Sabon
by Cenveo® Publisher Services

To Morag, for being wonderful.

Contents

	Acknowledgements	viii
	Illustration list	x
1	Introduction: Parallel projection, mimesis, and intersections	1
2	James Stirling's axonometric traps	23
3	Scale and Gesamtkunstwerk in JJP Oud	43
4	Occlusion and deliberately hidden lines: Hejduk's Wall House	64
5	Indeterminacy and transfiguration: Hejduk's multiple projections	83
6	Axonometry as theoretical instrument: The case of Eisenman	100
7	Cedric Price's 'In Action' drawings	120
8	Cognition, image, and embodiment	141
9	Conclusion: The purpose of axonometric drawing	164
	References	193
	Index	200

Acknowledgements

This book presents research initiated in the Canadian Centre for Architecture's Drawing Collection in 2011, and was supported by the MIRIAD research centre at Manchester Metropolitan University and generous research leave from the University of Manchester. I would like to thank MIRIAD (Manchester Institute for Research in Art and Design) for their financial support, and Renata Guttman and the CCA archivists for their invaluable assistance. Financial support for the illustration reproduction rights comes from the Department of Architecture at the School of Environment Education and Development, University of Manchester.

Further thanks must go to my academic peers across a range of conferences and research projects where I have rehearsed the arguments presented here. The most significant of these is Tim Ingold's *Knowing from the Inside* research group from 2013 to 2018. Whilst all of the flaws in the book are my own, several elements of the argument were established during my time with Tim as a PhD candidate in Aberdeen. The KFI group, consisting of my fellow associate researchers—Anne Douglas, Stephanie Bunn, Amanda Ravetz, Mike Anusas, and Emilia Ferraro, co-investigator Jo Vergunst and the project's research fellows Jen Clarke, Caroline Gatt, Rachel Harkness, Elizabeth Hodson, and Griet Scheldeman deserve thanks for providing such a fertile academic family over the last five years. The wider group also deserves sincere thanks, and represent a broad network of participants across disciplines. My colleague Stephen Walker must be singled out for gratitude, giving his time to review the manuscript and offering feedback helpful in rounding off some of the harder edges of my draft. All errors do, of course, remain my own.

Informal discussions with colleagues have also informed my thinking on the topics presented here, perhaps in a way that those responsible are unaware of. Particular thanks must go to Liz Hallam, who has always been encouraging of my work and provided invaluable advice on publishing. In this, the patience of my editor, Aoife McGrath, at Routledge has been greatly appreciated, and I would also like to thank Val Rose who originally commissioned this book at Ashgate.

Chapter 8 is an expanded reworking of material presented originally as: Lucas, R. 2017. "Why a Drawing Is Not an Image (and Why That Might Not Be a Problem)" in Hodson, E. (Ed.), *Imaginations Interiors Surfaces*. Aberdeen: Knowing from the Inside. This book also contains material from a paper presented at the Royal Anthropological Institute conference in June 2018: "Why All Drawings Are Failures," *RAI 2018: Art, Materiality & Representation*, panel *Notions of Failure in Art and Anthropology* convened by Alana Jelenick and with Jen Clarke as discussant.

Chapter 9 is a reworking of material from my PhD thesis presented originally as: Lucas, R. 2006. "Bergson, Duration and Drawing" in *Towards a Theory of Notation as a Thinking Tool*. Aberdeen: University of Aberdeen, pp. 150–186.

I continue to be in debt to my parents, Sandra and Andrew Lucas, whose unwavering support of my early research career is in evidence in the pages of this book, with my growing fascination with axonometric drawing beginning early in my academic life at the University of Strathclyde, further articulated once I began my PhD thesis, which forms an early version of some of the arguments presented here. Thanks are also due to my informal coauthors Omar and Odessa (two rather large Maine Coon kittens) have provided company and distraction in equal measure whilst writing the draft chapters.

The final and most important thanks must go to my wonderful wife, Morag Fyfe, whose support throughout the entire project has been crucial. Her patience with the considerable angst and frustration during the rather protracted production of this manuscript has been considerable, particularly through the period when I was the head of department at Manchester, when progress was slowed to a crawl due to endless committees and meetings. Thank you for propping me up, hearing me out, and getting me through it!

Illustration list

Unless otherwise stated, illustrations are the work of the author.

1.1	Example of a cube drawn in axonometric projection	3
1.2	Example of a cube drawn in isometric projection	3
1.3	Example of a cube drawn in oblique projection	4
1.4	Example of a cube drawn in reverse-angle axonometric	4
1.5	Examples from the series *A Graphic Anthropology of Sanja Matsuri*	11
2.1	Redrawing of AP140.S2.SS1.D67.P7.0140-249, sketches of the Latina Library project showing the gable facade development	26
2.2	James Stirling (Firm), axonometric drawing for British Olivetti Headquarters, Milton Keynes, England, 1970–1974; ink on paper, 47 × 47.8 cm; AP140.S2.SS1.D40.P23.6, James Stirling/Michael Wilford fonds, Canadian Centre for Architecture	31
2.3	Diagrammatic representation of the picture plane of worm's eye and bird's eye views	32
2.4	Diagrammatic example of standard worm's-eye and bird's-eye axonometric drawings	33
2.5	Diagrammatic example of a frontal worm's-eye axonometric drawing	35
2.6	Redrawing of AP140.S2.SS1.D52.P11.2	37
2.7	Axonometric drawing for Staatsgalerie, Stuttgart, Germany, 1977–1984; pen and ink, graphite and coloured pencil on tracing paper 28.5 × 27 cm; AP140.S2.SS1.D52.P11.2, James Stirling/Michael Wilford fonds, Canadian Centre for Architecture	38
3.1	Redrawing of DR1984:0142, chair designs for Metz & Co. by Oud (1933)	51
3.2	Redrawing of DR1984:0063-069, interior study for MJI de Jonge van Ellemeet's office, Rotterdam City Hall	52
3.3	JJP Oud, axonometric drawing for furniture for MJI de Jonge van Ellemeet's office in Rotterdam City Hall, Netherlands, 1930–1931; graphite on tracing paper, 46.8 × 52.6 cm; DR1984:0067, Canadian Centre for Architecture	53

Illustration list xi

3.4 JJP Oud, Elevations, plan and axonometric for a kitchen for terraced housing, Weissenhofsiedlung, Stuttgart, Germany, 1927; pen and black ink on linen, 63.5 × 77.7 cm; DR1984:0070, Canadian Centre for Architecture — 54

3.5 Redrawing of DR1984:0070 and DR1984:0552, composite sheets of drawings and blueprints describing the kitchens of Oud's Wiessenhof houses for Stuttgart (1927) — 55

3.6 Redrawing of DR1984:0561, isometric drawing of director's office in the Shell Building, The Hague (1938–1949) — 56

3.7 Redrawing of DR1984:0376, axonometric drawing of school project including the porter's house — 57

3.8 Redrawing of DR1984:0379, axonometric drawing of the porter's house — 58

3.9 Redrawing of DR1984:557, axonometric drawing of Blijdorp workers' housing (1931–1932), Rotterdam — 59

3.10 Redrawing of PH1984:1098, axonometric drawing of the new Stock Exchange Building, Rotterdam (1926) — 60

3.11 Redrawing of DR1984:0361, axonometric drawing of Vredenburg Square Project — 61

4.1 Redrawing of some examples of the nine-square grid problem as presented by Hejduk (1971) — 65

4.2 Demonstration of a form drawn first in axonometric projection without hidden lines (x-ray), and the same form drawn using dotted lines and then using hidden lines — 68

4.3 John Hejduk, north axonometric for North East South West House, 1978–1979; pen and India ink with coloured pencil over graphite underdrawing on translucent paper, 58.4 × 86.1 cm; DR1984:1517; John Hejduk fonds, Canadian Centre for Architecture, gift of Elliott and Carolyn Mittler — 70

4.4 John Hejduk, Axonometric for Wall House 1, 1968–1974, ink on translucent paper, 93 × 93 cm; DR1998:0077:026, John Hejduk fonds, Canadian Centre for Architecture — 72

4.5 Redrawing by Ray Lucas of DR1998:0077:025, axonometric drawing for Wall House by John Hejduk — 75

4.6 Redrawing by Ray Lucas of DR1998:0077:026, axonometric drawing for Wall House by John Hejduk — 76

4.7 Redrawing by Ray Lucas of DR1998:0077:027, axonometric drawing for Wall House by John Hejduk — 77

4.8 My 'missing drawing' of Wall House by John Hejduk. This drawing by the author is set at 45° in order to show the scheme more clearly; noting that this was not Hejduk's intention for the project — 79

4.9 The Sumiyoshi Pine at Katsura Rikyu, a tree planted specifically to deny a view of the complete garden — 80

xii *Illustration list*

5.1 *John Hejduk*, Soundings: Thoughts Upon an Uccello Painting, *1991; ink on paper 22 × 28 cm; DR1998:0129:076, John Hejduk fonds, Canadian Centre for Architecture* — 96

5.2 *Redrawing of DR1998:0129:076,* Thoughts Upon an Uccello Painting — 97

6.1 Redrawing of DR1994:0134:527, showing collage drawing of overlapping gridded cubes. Note the projection here is down at 45° from a 90° set plan drawing — 108

6.2 Redrawing of DR1994:0139:001-008 showing the el-form and its deformations, combinations, and collisions — 109

6.3 Redrawing of DR1994:0134:458 showing initial simple experiment with el-form — 110

6.4 Peter Eisenman, axonometric sketch for House VI, Cornwall, Connecticut, 1973; graphite with coloured pencil on translucent paper 23 × 26 cm; DR1994:0134:458, Peter Eisenman fonds, Canadian Centre for Architecture — 111

6.5 Redrawing of DR1994:0139:283; sectional axonometric of House 11a — 112

6.6 Peter Eisenman, axonometric for House III, Lakeville, Connecticut, between 1969 and 1975; black ink on vellum mounted on wove paper 55.9 × 55.9 cm; DR1994:0131:212, Peter Eisenman fonds, Canadian Centre for Architecture — 115

6.7 Redrawing of DR1994:0131:203-215, studies for House III showing developments in the geometry of the design — 116

7.1 Redrawing of DR1995:0212:014 and DR1995:0212:016, Donmar Warehouse axonometric drawing — 123

7.2 Cedric Price, axonometric interior view with figures and furniture for the Donmar Theatre, London, England, 1963; black ink, graphite and black pencil on wove paper 38 × 71.6 cm; DR1995:0212:014, Cedric Price fonds, Canadian Centre for Architecture — 124

7.3 Comparison of two cubes in parallel projection. The first is a conventional drawing showing all of the vertical elements. The second shows how Price tends to draw, allowing the upper surface to carry the description of the form and omitting the vertical edge nearest the front. This economy of line extends further to unfinished vertical elements and sometimes also horizontal lines. The determining factor is whether another plane can do the work of describing the work. If so, then lines can be suggested or indicated rather than actually described and drawn — 125

7.4 Cedric Price, axonometric drawing for Fun Palace, ca. 1964; ink, coloured pencil, and adhesive film on translucent paper 38 × 69.1 cm; DR1995:0188:128, Cedric Price fonds, Canadian Centre for Architecture — 126

Illustration list xiii

7.5 Redrawing of DR1995:0280:651:001-2. These drawings show the way in which construction was considered as a practical reality of architecture, not abstracted out from the work of the designers 130

7.6 Cedric Price, Assembly, stage 8 for Generator, Yulee, Florida, 1967–1979; electrostatic print on paper with red ink stamp, 29.7 × 21 cm; DR1995:0280:651:001:008, Cedric Price fonds, Canadian Centre for Architecture 131

7.7 Redrawing of DR1995:0280:263. The application of conventions to describe the swing of doors demonstrates both the complex geometry possible with the Generator (necessitating the programmed instructions to ensure access), but also adds an unusual layer of notation to parallel projections 136

8.1 Mitch Miller's studio in axonometric projection, Ray Lucas, 2017 144

8.2 Failed drawings of Namdaemun market stall (a-c) followed by the 'final' version (d). Ray Lucas, 2016 145

8.3 Drawings of Sanja Matsuri ephemera. Ray Lucas, 2017 149

8.4 Extracts from *A Taxonomy of Lines* sketchbook 150

8.5 Axonometric drawing of a mikoshi, Ray Lucas, 2017 151

8.6 Examples from the graphic anthropology of Sanja Matsuri, 2017, and the graphic anthropology of Namdaemun Market. Ray Lucas, 2016 156

8.7 Examples of market carts drawn in axonometric. Ray Lucas, 2016 160

8.8 Material enthusiasm: collaborative live drawing exercise with Jen Clarke and Sekimoto Kinya in Gallery Turnaround, Sendai, Japan, Ray Lucas, 2015 161

9.1 *Examples from* Graphic Anthropology of Namdaemun Market *(2014–2017) by the author depicting a variety of found pieces of architecture from around the general market site* 173

9.2 *'Completed' axonometric drawing from* Getting Lost in Tokyo 178

9.3 Establishing the centre of the square and dividing the square into four 179

9.4 Establishing the centre of the square and dividing the square into four 180

9.5 Working down to the corner 181

9.6 Establishing the corridor framework 182

9.7 The jumble of pencil lines prior to inking 183

9.8 Inking lines in order 184

9.9 Selective inking 185

1 Introduction: Parallel projection, mimesis, and intersections

1.1 Parallel projection: a history of the form and a taxonomy of types

This book is the result of research into how we might understand inscriptive practices such as drawing as a form of knowledge production forming an alternative to the written text. This alternative status is understood to have two key facets: firstly, that drawing, diagramming, and notation are equivalent to extended discourse in writing; and secondly that they offer significantly different insights, not easily accessible through textual models of discourse analysis, critical theory, or observation. It is important to my broader project to position this study within the catch-all term of *inscriptive practice* to group forms of graphic representation together while maintaining the separate identities of practices such as sketching, notation, diagramming and draughting.

This idea has been under development for some time, grounded in my PhD research which established a theory of notation as a thinking tool, responding to the anthropologist Tim Ingold's discussion of knowledge production as a practiced activity, and the necessity to understand the processes of creativity rather than addressing only the end result or artefact. This broad turn towards practice can be seen in a wide range of disciplines, with an interest in the making of things, the nature of the

2   Introduction

creative impulse, and the social conditions under which these activities are undertaken. As such, this book intends to be an account of some of the possibilities available to a draughtsperson making drawings in one of the conventions of parallel projection.

To this end, I have investigated inscriptive practices with reference to the conflation of creativity and temporality in the work of Henri Bergson. Bergson, and later Gilles Deleuze both characterise creative practices in terms of the quality of their temporality—the manner in which problems are explored and solved. Simply stated, the conventional understanding wrought through architectural histories and theories only gives a part of the story. By retracing the marks made by five selected architects, we can begin to engage more directly with their practice. Understanding the drawings as scores to be reenacted is one way of describing this process: It is only by performing the drawing that aspects of it are revealed. This recalls aspects of Nelson Goodman's thesis in *Languages of Art* (1976), where the discussion of inscriptive practices is afforded by comparison: a sketch can be described when contrasted with a notation, for example. In Goodman's language, the process engaged with here transforms the autographic mark of Hejduk's drawings to the allographic drawing—as a script which produces meaning through practice.

This book emerged from a research project, *An Anthropology of/with Architectural Drawings,* the aim being to understand the ways in which drawing practices inform their home disciplines. In this case, the focus is architecture and the use of parallel projection. By positioning the study as anthropological, certain forms of argumentation are opened, focusing on the nature of the creative practice as a fundamental human activity and exploring the relationship between creativity and practice. This relies upon my reading of each drawing, shown through copying and description, the intention is to show each drawing as a part of a larger social system of communication through common conventions. Over a short period, I redrew works held by the Drawing Collection at the Canadian Centre for Architecture, focusing on the axonometric as an under-theorised form of representation which lies between orthographic and perspective drawing conventions. The redrawing project was conducted in graphite on two A4 skechbooks with dot-grid paper. A variety of pragmatic concerns emerged, and the categorisation of different parallel projections became important:

> Axonometric (planometric) refers to those drawings where the horizontal plane is true: none of the angles are distorted on this plane, but often rotated as this shows wall details most clearly. This rotation is often wilfully rejected, however, to enhance the geometry of occlusion (figure 1.1). The vertical plane is projected upward, so that walls are distorted and skewed, the angle between uprights and ground plane most deformed.

Introduction 3

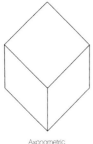

Figure 1.1 Example of a cube drawn in axonometric projection.

Isometric is a rather different procedure to axonometric, despite looking similar (figure 1.2). The horizontal plane is distorted, opening the elevations out. Right angles on an isometric drawing are drawn at 120° rather than 90°. Variations on this include trimetric, where the angles differ between north and south faces of a cube and the east and west faces. Another variation is dimetric, which is similar to isometric, but with different angles of distortion. These are used to prevent elements from overlapping.

Oblique drawings are somewhat rarer, and come in a variety of forms (figure 1.3). Variations are called *cabinet projection* or *cavalier projection*, where the distances of the deformed plane can vary. One plane is true, parallel to the picture plane. This might be an elevation of a plan, but the projection of the opposite plane is heavily skewed, often by 45° to the vertical and horizontal.

Worm's eye (reverse angle) drawings demonstrate a certain virtuosity in drawing, and are used to describe volumes and ceiling details (figure 1.4). Most often used with axonometric projection, these drawings are difficult to read as well as to draw, but give a great deal of information missing from other projections.

In the most practical, straightforward language, I examined the archival drawings and sketchbooks closely, and produced my own sketched versions of these, producing 100 pages of drawing in total. By re-enacting, each quality of the original works is revealed to hold significance. The projections, angles, relationships, and line quality are all shown to convey meaning and content. These might look in places to be hesitant or even unfinished works, but they contain great complexity and sophistication of

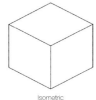

Figure 1.2 Example of a cube drawn in isometric projection.

4 *Introduction*

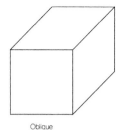

Figure 1.3 Example of a cube drawn in oblique projection.

thought. This is despite the apparent childlike quality of some of the lines in late Hejduk, the International Style line erasing the labour of Oud's hand, the sparse economy of Price's representation, or the showy complications of Eisenman and Stirling.

1.2 Some history of parallel projection

This book does not present a comprehensive history of parallel projection but is instead an investigation into some of the potential of these conventions by discussing some of the ways in which it was used by a selection of 20th-century architects. It is important to trace some of the history of the drawing convention and its use within architecture. This will, however, be limited in scope and bears the marks of some of the difficulties in pinning down a precise period when parallel projection is 'invented'.

There remain some issues with nomenclature, as Booker notes in his 1963 work *A History of Engineering Drawing*[1]. Here, we see discussions continuing until the mid-20th century over the use of *axonometric* or *planometric* drawings, the invention of new terms such as *axometric*, and the desire for one term to cover a range of projections including isometric, dimetric, and trimetric (1963:207).

As a genre of engineering drawing, it is clear that parallel projection solves certain problems of representation. Parallel projection shows a three-dimensional image whilst being measurable, making it an easier working drawing than a perspective, for example. Parallel projections in an oblique convention are used in the West from the Middle Ages in both

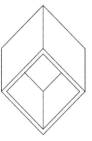

Figure 1.4 Example of a cube drawn in reverse-angle axonometric.

Introduction 5

mathematical treatises and military engineering[2] (Lefevre, 2004:184), coming to particular prominence in the 16th century when it was eventually supplanted by perspective. Some variations of parallel projection have been used historically without a stable convention, not being codified until textbook writers in the 19th century turned their attention to making the rules explicit (Booker, 1963:211). Of these, Gaspard Monge's *Descriptive Geometry* of 1798[3] is often seen as a source for contemporary drawing practices, particularly as it had such wide circulation through relatively swift translation into other European languages. The development of these ideas after Monge's introduction to England is discussed by Lawrence[4] where the further development of isometric drawings by William Farish (1820) and Peter Nicholson's *Parallel Oblique System* (1822).

By far the most comprehensive account of the history of parallel projection is Massimo Scolari's *Oblique Drawing*[5]. According to Scolari, there is evidence in the West of parallel projection as far back as the fourth century BCE, and it has a more consistent history of use throughout China and Japan than the alternating use in Europe where it falls into and out of fashion several times. When describing the need for axonometric and parallel projection, the aim of practicality is reinforced by Scolari:

> Bartolomeo Romano described a spherical perspective in which the 'measured parts shall give the right distances, which the oval form would not do because of the foreshortening its parts produce.' Goivan Battista Belici (Belluzi), who was firmly convinced that 'the soldier must also be a theoretician,' used parallel representation because 'we need to see the thing whole, distinct, clear; one can find the truth precisely with compasses.' He favoured axonometry over perspective. Because in war 'one single view does not serve, since the whole has to be shown.' (2012:9)

Further exploration of the nomenclature of parallel projection is explored by Hilary Bryon[6] who differentiates between oblique and axonometric forms of parallel projection in terms of the *projectors* (2008:337). In perspective, the projectors converge at a vanishing point, distinct from parallel projection where they never meet. Oblique, as one would expect, uses projectors which are oblique to the plane of projection, where axonometric projectors are perpendicular to it.

A similar picture is given by mathematician Vlasta Moravcova[7], noting the predecessors of Monge's work in producing rules for parallel projection. One of the most important is the painter, Albrecht Dürer whose treatise of 1525 still contains some errors (Moravcova puts these down to Dürer's expectation of how certain forms such as ellipses ought to look), corrected by Monge's more accurate, later work. Cavalier projection emerges as a dominant form for military purposes between 1500 and 1600, also described as *transoblique perspective*[8] and grounded firmly in the solution of pragmatic

6 Introduction

problems of representation. Alonso-Rodríguez and Calvo-López (2014:565) note that Le Corbusier and other early modernists were strongly influenced by Choisy's use of parallel projection[9] and setting the ground for the architectural drawings discussed here.

1.3 Copying, mimesis, and innovation

Recent work in fine art and anthropology has rehabilitated the idea of copying the work of acknowledged masters both as a way of learning about that work and about the act of drawing itself. There is a long tradition in architecture of drawing from buildings as a way of understanding them more closely. This moves beyond the production of sketched perspectives and towards redrawn plans, and other projections in order to analyse a work. This is proposed by writers such as Simon Unwin[10] who also maintains that you can know a building better by examining the drawings than by visiting it. Whilst I do not hold to this provocative view, his method of understanding architecture through drawing respects the means of the discipline and produces deep knowledge of precedent consistent with the practice of design.

Many similarities can be found in Sudnow's account of learning not only to play piano but learning to improvise jazz piano as a member of a band[11]. His work is written in the mode of an anthropologist in the field, but complicated by the deep implication and close participation in the work under examination. This discussion of practice from within is increasingly common in anthropology, where the conventional idea of discussing 'creativity' as a topic is inextricable from the practices themselves. Somehow such discussions have been one of the last bastions of scientific notions of maintaining distance in anthropology as opposed to the more direct engagement of participant observation and beyond into autoethnography and reflexivity.

The discussion of art and creative practices has, problematically, been restricted to the outcomes and product of creative practices: the art-object (such that categories of art are even valid in all cases). Influential works such as Gell's *Art and Agency* have compounded this with discussions of the social pressures which build up to the production of a work, but never the making itself.

Notable works on the anthropology of creative practices have of course moved significantly away from this position, including Küchler's *Malanggan*[12] which discusses the cycle of making as something entirely separate from the consumption of funerary sculptures by Western connoisseurs and collectors. Küchler's account of how motifs find their way from everyday life into decorative sculpture speaks to the acts of translation undertaken in creative practices.

More pertinent still are two writers who examine the act of copying within this context. The first of these is Fuyubi Nakamura, who writes on contemporary Japanese calligraphy practices[13] (2007). This paper challenges the foundation of art and creative practice by the nebulous criterion of originality. The aura, so challenged in the aesthetic theory of Adorno and appreciated by Benjamin, appears to be alive and well in discussions of art, particularly from outside the actual practice of art. Nakamura instead locates art and creativity in skilled practice. This again recalls the notions of autographic and allographic works noted by Goodman, further challenging the notion that these are fixed states. Perhaps such states are rather more fluid and contingent than might at first appear.

The presence of the model in Japanese calligraphy is well established, but this is different from absolute copying. In a manner akin to the pianist approaching a score, the calligrapher, through practice and training, becomes more and more competent to the point of virtuosity with regard to the originating model: surpassing it whilst still referring to it. Western art history is similarly littered with referential works. The ruptures of modernism still cast back to their predecessors, Picasso working with compositions and themes from Manet's *Lunch on the Grass* as well as a number of others.

Nakamura problematises the idea of the copy, preferring to talk about reproduction with reference to Benjamin's essay on *The Work of Art in the Age of Its Mechanical Reproduction*[14]. In the reproductive practice, Nakamura contends, the aim is to understand more than what is on the paper:

KEIRIN: First stage, focusing on the mechanics of brush technique.

IRIN: Second stage, interpreting the spirit and intention of the work.

HAIRIN: Third stage, reproduction from memory without looking at the model.

adapted from Nakamura (2007:82)

Some forms of inscriptive practice have more in common with musical performance, where the trace is the result of a set of gestures. Ingold (2007:72–75) contends that in many cases, the trace can be regarded as incidental, and that the trace is what is important. This idea is explored in depth in other projects, notably *Gestural Artefacts* (see Lucas 2009).

The second key writer on copying is the painter and researcher Patricia Cain[15]. Cain discusses the idea of reenacting a drawing in her experiential account of copying a drawing, *Glass*, by Richard Talbot (2010:134–143, 155–247). The account is told through text, journals, and stages of the drawing, a precise and complex pencil drawing comprised of elliptical planes cut through a bulb-shaped object in perspective projection. Cain, after making an initial copy, in the *Keirin* stage, then moves towards what Nakamura identifies as *Irin*, where a series of further diagrams are produced to interrogate the intent and decision-making process behind Talbot's originating work. Finally, the *hairin* stage is also engaged with, where Cain produces a series of large scale drawings which interpret the engagement with Talbot's drawing, but by allowing a conversation to emerge with her own practice.

8 *Introduction*

The account reveals many of the struggles, risk, and uncertainty in producing a drawing as well as the possibility for understanding through copying, retracing, reenacting, or using a work as inspiration.

Further explorations of copying in a Japanese context are given by Rupert Cox in the introduction to his edited volume on the practice[16]. He discusses mimesis as 'the faculty to copy, absorb, and become other' (2008:4), and notes that it has become associated with a notion of the 'primitive' mind in Western thinking dominated by social Darwinism. The issue is with the nature of the copying engaged in more than the notion of the copy itself, and that machines can produce better, more accurate copies. Japanese examples show that the picture is much more complicated, both in that context and outside of it.

Cox develops a position whereby the *original* and *originality* are open to question. Identifying an original is important when copying, and it is clear that ideas of originality are socially constructed. In our case, the original is clear, but originality opens questions of influences, of the stacks of drawings which might have been destroyed or discarded whilst engaging in a design process. The drawings I copy from are 'originals' but might themselves be copies or final iterations of a long sequence of decision making. In the same volume, Irit Averbuch (in Cox 2008:21) discusses body-to-body transmission in the copying tradition of Kagura performance[17]. Drawing on Schechner's theory of theatre, performance becomes an issue as a repeated operation of copying. This duplication, repetition, or reproduction is a special condition for actions: We understand performances differently as both performers and as audience members. We often know innately when an action is being copied, and when this is appropriate behaviour. Note the childhood game of repeating precisely what someone else has said and how they act—out of context, this behaviour is disruptive, humorous, or annoying; in an appropriate context, it can become a religious incantation or meditation, a process of understanding, or rote learning. This 'twice-behaved behaviour' accumulates significance from being seen as worthy of this repetitious engagement—in the way that I am arguing that the sometimes incidental drawings I copy are similarly worthy of deeper consideration.

This is imperfect copying, however, and Averbuch identifies these small variations and errors as one distinction between such performances and the fine arts, where a script may be performed either deliberately different, or perfectly in accordance with the score. This is a temporal and intentionality based distinction. There is a desire within this process to make our way back to the starting point, as the transmission of works (in Averbuch's case, generationally), leads to a frustration that the original, authentic version can never be returned to. Transmission is one question for us to address in the copying process: What are the means by which this transmission is achieved, where are its imperfections, what does it afford?

There is often a presumption within the more obviously performative art forms of dance and theatre, that the problems of transmission can be solved through either notational transcription or audio/video recording. This leads to some issues, however. Film introduces an additional mediation, casting the observation through the strategies of the film-maker and positioning the record in the position of an audience and missing elements such as the forces exerted by performers, whilst notations often carry with them the interests of the notational scheme's originator—a theory which determines what is important and what is redundant. Averbuch argues that the generational body-to-body transmission of Kagura, whilst imperfect in some ways, allows for some continuity of performance.

> The fact that Kagura survives is perhaps due to this dynamic technique of 'creative copying'. The dancers copy while repeating, repeat while variegating, but still maintain their essential style ... in their attempt to reconstruct the strived-for ideal performance, they have developed this copying wisdom, and indeed become the masters of the 'creative copy', the 'dynamic copy', which can preserve a constant, through repetitious variation. (2008:32)

Much of this can be applied with little adaptation to the copying of drawings, and indeed there is a case to be made for the relationship between dance and architecture or drawing[18].

Writers such as Marcus Boon[19] have called for a return to copying, highlighting the variation and invention possible within the practice. He restates arguments from rhetoric (2010:47), that there is scope for *inventio* or the selection and editing of elements; *dispositio*, the general disposition or arrangement of those selected elements; and *elocutio*, pertaining to the manner of their presentation. Similarly to the copied drawing, there are aspects elided and removed from the account, arrangements and collections of these pieces, and the specifics of just how they are portrayed.

This places the copy in the realms of being a rhetorical figure, superseded by the Cartesian focus on method and measurement, the persuasive nature of rhetoric as a skilled form of utterance became somewhat suspect and lacking in evidence. Copying is understood, however, to be a very human act. Learning by copying is one manifestation, representing the order back to itself in a symbolic or satirical form during festival periods is another. Performance is once again implicated in copying as a process, the presence of the copy suggests the practice which was engaged in to make it.

One of the foundational texts in the discussion of mimesis is a short essay by Walter Benjamin[20]. Here, Benjamin traces the origins of our heritage in mimicry, finding the roots of culture and language within imitation of the natural world and the behaviour of others.

> 'To read what was never written.' Such reading is the most ancient: reading before all languages, from the entrails, the stars, or dances.

10   *Introduction*

> Later the mediating link of a new kind of reading, of runes and hieroglyphs, came into use. It seems fair to suppose that these were the stages by which the mimetic gift, which was once the foundation of occult practices, gained admittance to writing and language. In this way language may be seen as the highest level of mimetic behaviour and the most complete archive of non-sensuous similarity: a medium into which the earlier powers of mimetic production and comprehension have passed without residue, to the point where they have liquidated those of magic. (Benjamin 1997:162–163)

The use of language is understood as a distant form of mimesis, making sense of what a person finds in the environment beginning as onomatopoeia. Copying drawings is a way of deepening your understanding of them. If there is a relationship between language and imitation, the copied drawing allows it to enter into a dialogue. It becomes open to discussion, it is a linguistic operation of meaning and interlocution. The copy is a conversation with the original.

We learn about the world by mimicking it. We learn language by imitating the sounds, and we learn to draw by copying drawings, reenacting their moves before improvising and making traces of our own intentions. Returning to the copied drawing opens it up and unlocks its hidden intentions. It is not possible to unpack every intention, the copy is limited in what it teaches us, but it allows the copyist to create a new meaning, a new interpretation, and a new version of the original.

Several theorists have tackled the concept of mimesis more thoroughly. Michael Taussig's work, *Mimesis and Alterity*[21], presents an account of copying that implicates the body of the copyist in reenacting a phenomenon or work. Taussig does this by ascribing a tactility to the eye[22]. This is not a call to synaesthesia so much as the process by which the copyist processes the connection between their body and the work being perceived. By copying, you are engaging your own body—making sense of the original drawing in this case by moving. This kind of knowledge, deploying the muscle memory of drawing, has a significant difference in kind from other forms of engagement. This sensuous engagement offers access to theorisation by means appropriate to architecture:

> Here is what is crucial in the resurgence of the mimetic faculty, namely the two-layered notion of mimesis that is involved—a copying or imitation, and a palpable, sensuous connection between the very body of the perceiver and the perceived. (Taussig 1993:21)

Taussig continually reinforces a tactility for the eye in this mimetic scenario, justified by a range of writers and conforming to his own notions of the senses: That when the eye is looking to copy, it acts in a similar way to physical contact. Benjamin uses the term *aura* to describe this process,

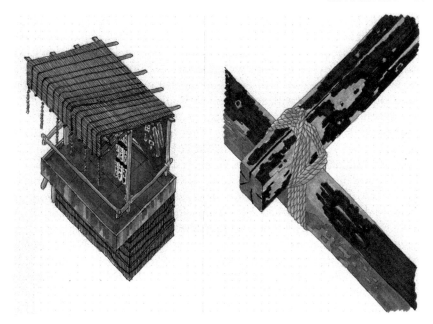

Figure 1.5 Examples from the series *A Graphic Anthropology of Sanja Matsuri*.

creating 'physiognomic aspects of visual worlds' (1993:24) whereby percepts from one sense are translated into another. Architecture is used as an example of this physiognomic knowledge, that there is an embodied element to how we remember our way around a building which is first based in visual understanding. In this construction of space, the eye, seeking stimulation, is an extension of the body precisely in the manner of premodern optics, where light was presumed to be a ray cast out *from the eye* rather than received by it. This is also discussed by Ingold (2000:254-8), who prioritises *looking* over seeing, the act of being in the environment.

By discussing mimesis within this framework of sensory translation, bringing the external world in to the actions of the body, and embedding the idea of copying into a wide range of perceptual activities. There is a complex perceptual, material and social machinery at work when attending to the world and making it available as a drawing. In the first instance, we know the world by re-presenting it, putting our own inflection upon it. When drawing an axonometric drawing, for example, of an object found in the field as in Figure 1.5, there is a sophisticated act of producing geometry from fragmentary experiences, photographs, and multiple views. Here, we have mimesis as a process of understanding. The conventions of orthographic and parallel projection can be understood to constitute very specific forms of mimetic machinery.

12   Introduction

The aim is similarity, bearing some of the qualities of something else. Those qualities might be inexact in some ways, imprecise and estimated, but a sense of the similar needs to remain. Taussig makes a comparison with sympathetic magic (1993:44), whereby items with qualities in common can be said to act upon one another over some distance (noting that magic tends to be conceptualised *either* as contact with something with special qualities or as *similarity* over distance). Distance is a useful description for the errors and alterations made when copying. My sketchbooks of re-drawings use different materials and support to the originals, often missing colour and texture; have the assistance of a grid of dots; and are at a different scale to the originals.

The copied drawings can be considered as extended quotations, recasting the idea of citation not merely as a form of acknowledgement for prior work and intellectual context, but much deeper: to include the idea that by quoting, one might be rewriting and re-understanding the text cited. This brings us into contact with writers such as Nelson Goodman, who, in *Ways of Worldmaking*[23] presents the idea that perception without some form of mediation (expressed as *conception* in his framework) is understood as blind. The reverse, of conceptual thinking without perception, is empty (1978:6). We *make* worlds by our perceptions and concepts of it working in concert, much as Ingold would have in the coproduction of environments and people. Engaging with Goodman suggests that the reenacted, copied, or mimicked drawing can be understood as a fresh performance of the same underlying score. Whilst there is no explicit score in existence for producing the drawings in question, and I am mindful of making too great a claim for what can be found out through making copies, there is an aspect of this argument which rings true—an underlying score which can be performed over and over again, often necessitating some translation into different media, but from a fundamentally similar source.

Goodman's argument is that there is no *a priori* world to be found, that we *make* that world every time we encounter it, making sense of perceptions. Taussig supports this with the idea that:

> To exercise the mimetic faculty is to practice an everyday art of appearance, an art that delights and maddens as it cultivates the insoluble paradox of the distinction between essence and appearance. (1997:176)

The *appearance* is important, more than the superficial. This is the quality of evocation, the power to return your experience to the original or to highlight certain pertinent aspects of it. It can, in the manner of a good photograph, throw light upon the subtle beauty of the world, moments which resonate with us, but which pass largely unobserved. Taussig describes how, in mimesis, 'we come to feel those movements as sensations in ourselves' (1997:200) something which might usefully be applied to the copied drawing. Much in the way that the copyist reenacts and retraces the steps of the original, the observed practice and action opens the process up to the observer as a second-order tactility, removed from the experience sedimented in memories of making and handling materials—the embodied knowledge of the hand.

There is a distinction between the copy made by eye and the one made by tracing. Tracing is not appropriate for the use of archival materials such as the drawings this book has been based on, but the idea of the trace does have some presence: in the stacks of tracing paper used in the practices of James Stirling for example, where iterations and alternatives are explored using a common base drawing. The trace is a copy by contagion, by direct touching, according to Taussig's account. Tracing is relatively easy, where copying involves some of the skills involved in the production of the original. Is there a morality to the manner of the copy? Tracing produces a more accurate copy but less of an understanding.

There is an accusation, given the topic of mechanical drafting and hand drawing, of having a sense of the nostalgia for recently obsolete things. This investigation into axonometric drawings sits firmly within this impulse: a regret for lost skills. There is more to it as there is continuing value in the process of understanding gained through the use of the convention. The aim is to restore the axonometric drawing and other parallel projections to the status of design drawings, developmentally important alongside plans, sections, and elevations.

The idea that the copy influences the original, outside the confines of Taussig's study of magic (1997:250), is important to the study: that the process of crafting a copy simultaneously edits and reproduces key features of the original. Something new is produced that dialogue with the original, and offers insights because of this. Mimesis is a process used in the production of culture. Mimesis is a process of coming to an understanding of a thing, and of communicating that understanding with others, it is an imitative reenactment of the original.

There are dangers, however, of excessive citation, and of seeing culture as a closed unit where the only option is to repeat traditional forms endlessly. This is where the beaux arts came to its end, starting with laudable aims, it ended up as a replication of patterns from the past without due consideration of the contemporary condition. Adorno identifies this as a tool of repression (1997:254), leading many modernists to reject any form of mimesis or copying, to the detriment of their creativity. This is hugely important to address, and useful for our overall project here: The trap of academic copying as 'civilising' art production and architecture in the beaux arts, to the extent that innovation became impossible; there are more dangers to mimesis when deployed unwisely.

1.4 Five architects

This book considers the work of five 20th-century architects and their use of parallel projection. They represent a sample of architectural production during the century, and following the trajectory of modernism.

14   Introduction

Each of the five has a literature associated with them, different in character from one architect to another, producing some interesting biases in the material available. Each of the architects has a relationship with publication, with Oud's association with De Stijl, initially a magazine before it came to mean the group who produced it; Stirling used publication to promote his practice and secure his place in architectural history; whilst Eisenman and Hejduk both used publication to further their ideas of architectural theory. Price published in an entirely different way, seeking to sway public opinion through the nonprofessional press (in order to get his grand projects of the Fun Palace and Potteries Think Belt funded), and acting as a provocateur within periodicals aimed at fellow architects. The selection is all male, European and American, as the profession is skewed strongly in this direction during this period; something very resistant to change and only just showing modest improvements at the time of writing. Whilst in a number of cases, it should be written that *the office of* Stirling or Eisenman produced a certain drawing, I have used the convention throughout of using the lead architect's name. This is not to denigrate the efforts of the wider office and the various junior architects and partners involved in each scheme (many of whom have independently significant careers beyond the scope of this volume), but simply an expedient convenience for which I feel the need to offer an acknowledgement to the collaborations present in each of these architectural firms. Such interactions are better served by contemporary ethnographic field work, again, beyond the scope of this work[24].

As a member of the Dutch modernist movement De Stijl, JJP Oud (1890–1963) is the first of the architects, chronologically speaking. His work is placed within the wider territory of the modern movements across Europe, and his output is often placed within that of the movement most associated with modernism in the Netherlands. In many ways, he is portrayed as a player in a political history of architecture: never figuring as strongly as more prominent members of De Stijl such as Cornelis van Eesteren, Piet Mondrian, Theo van Doesburg, or Gerrit Rietveld. His is a solid, workmanlike architecture, moving with the times from early architecture influenced by Berlage and Dudok, his membership of the influential De Stijl group represented best by Café de Unie in Rotterdam (1925), and towards the International Style championed by Philip Johnson. Oud fell from favour, however, with a return to ornamentation in his Shell HQ Building for The Hague between 1938 and 1948, for which he was largely ostracised from modernism's elite, although this can be argued to have prefigured the postmodernist return to ornament later in the century. Oud was unapologetic over the building and argued that the ornamentation was an essential, and not retrograde, aspect of the architecture.

The remaining four architects worked during the postwar period, and represent alternative strains of avant-garde and postmodern production. James Stirling (1926–1992) is one of the most important British

Introduction 15

architects of the 20th century. The literature surrounding Stirling's work is a combination of the appreciation of fellow architect theorists and conventional art histories. Stirling's work, in partnership with James Gowan from 1956 to 1963 and Michael Wilford from 1971 until his death in 1992, is particularly suited to the art-historical mode, as it is loaded with references to other architects including Denys Lasdun, Karl Friedrich Schinkel, and Le Corbusier. Stirling is best known for his university buildings and museums.

Czech architect John Hejduk (1929–2000) is best known as an educator, having been the dean of the Cooper Union school of architecture in New York from 1964 until 2000. His practice included illustration, such as for a copy of *Aesop's Fables*[25]; poetry which was published in collections including *Architectures in Love*[26]; a small number of built projects including Wall House II, constructed after his death in Groningen; and installations such as *The Collapse of Time* which figured in his many paper projects. The literature around Hejduk echoes his poetic use of image and text, the power of suggestion and openness to interpretation is important, as are his influential educational approaches.

Whilst each of the figures discussed in the book can be said to have been big personalities, Cedric Price (1934–2003) is rather renowned for this quality. A famed raconteur, some of the literature around his work focuses on this aspect of his biography, perhaps to the detriment of the deeply felt social conscience at the heart of the work. This is in part due to the playful and provocative nature of his public persona, where he would prod and provoke both the profession and the academy to consider whether building anything at all was appropriate, and vehemently opposing the preservation of his own work, which he argued could be made obsolete, and make room for something else when it was no longer needed.

Finally, Peter Eisenman (1932–) is an established architect who has maintained a strong interest in architectural theory throughout his career. This parallel of architecture and its theory comes together in his explanations of his own work, and also in large volumes dedicated to the analysis of the work of other architects. Given the linguistically oriented nature of Eisenman's theory, the literature around his work has a similar quality, often densely argued critical theory questioning the possibility of an autonomous architecture, and its ability to convey content or meaning.

Four of the architects' works intersect in some seminal publications, allowing some correspondences and distinctions to be drawn. The best known of these publications is *Five Architects*[27] which gave us the loose grouping known as the *New York Five*. The five architects presented in the book were Peter Eisenman, Michael Graves, Charles Gwathmey, John Hejduk, and Richard Meier, two of whom are covered in the present volume. Architectural critics Kenneth Frampton and Colin Rowe provided a theoretical underpinning at a time when modernism was seen to have failed,

16   *Introduction*

but a successor school was not apparent. There is an idea that these architects had rejected subsequent fashions such as the townscape movement, brutalism, and the clean classicism of Mies van der Rohe, instead capturing the spirit of 1930s modernism[28]. This is perhaps a loose connection back to the work of Oud, but it remains an important one: the group was uninspired by the International Style, and saw—at this stage of their careers at least—a return to the potential of modernism when it was emerging and full of possibility, as the way forward. Claims made at the time for the five to represent a movement were somewhat overstated, but it did spark a debate within architecture around the issue of context versus formalism[29].

In *Five Architects*, Peter Eisenman is represented by *House I* and *House II*, the built examples from his series of theoretically informed houses, accompanied by his two-part essay *Cardboard Architecture*. Here, Eisenman outlines his opposition to writers such as John Summerson, who saw modernism's purpose lying in its social engagement, to be found in the programme of the building. Eisenman argues that this pushes architecture towards typologies, which do not contain enough information to determine form, and that it is form which provides the greatest opportunity for meaning to emerge in architecture. As such, his house projects are an attempt to think about architecture where the form is created for its own sake, as the intention of the work. Hence his *Cardboard Architecture* is a call to think of the forms created as we think when making a model from plain, undifferentiated cardboard: masses, planes, columns all made from the same conceptual material. The process is one of differentiating between forms which are informed by programme and those which are not, and unloading any meanings which have accumulated and been ascribed to the forms being used.

John Hejduk, at this stage of his career, was working on a similar numbered series, presenting *House 10* (1966), the *Bernstein House* (1968), and *One Half-House* (1966) in *Five Architects*. These projects are presented with little by way of contextual information: a brief note of the *program*, treatment of the *surfaces*, and a few words on the *idea-concept* in each case. For Bernstein House, he diverges a little from the pure white aesthetic of the other proposals and presents a distinctive De Stijl inspired colour scheme for the exterior: primary yellow with red and blue details, drawn in a flat frontal 90° axonometric drawing of the compact, square composition. *House 10* is a precursor to the later *Wall House* and *North South East West House* we shall discuss later, and the plan is dominated by an elongated corridor with carefully arranged diamond, square, circular, and sinuous free-form rooms coming off it.

A second exhibition brings another combination of architects together. Published as *Houses for Sale*[30] this catalogue presents a series of house plans ostensibly for sale and intended to be built by the buyers of the plans. The architects here included Emilio Ambasz, Peter Eisenman, Vittorio Gregotti, Arata Isozaki, Charles Moore, Cesar Pelli, Cedric Price, and O. M. Ungers. Again, two of the architects in question are also brought into contact in

Introduction 17

this volume. Drawing on Gaston Bachelard's influential writings on the phenomenology of the home, editor B. J. Archer writes:

> A house is *first* a geometric object of balanced voids and solids to be analyzed rationally—an object that should be able to resist metaphors that include the human body and the soul. However, when considered as a place for the pursuit of happiness and intimacy, the house immediately becomes an object of poetic speculation, its geometry surpassed by the act of inhabiting. (Archer 1980:xi)

The drawings produced were intended to be designs for a family house, each architect working to the same brief to occupy an acre and cost no more than $250,000. The drawings themselves were for sale in the gallery, part of a historical move to value the architectural drawing outside of its use value within the design and construction process[31]. Eisenman's contribution, *House El Even Odd*, was presented in 45° diamond shapes applied directly to the wall, each cut away carefully to reveal the drawings. The form of this scheme is explicitly axonometric, projecting the form of a drawing of a cube in parallel projection onto the plan, a series of skewed forms are excavated from the earth.

Cedric Price's contribution to *Houses for Sale* is accompanied by a text, *Platforms, Pavilions, Pylons, and Plants*, where the architect presents his work as 'sufficiently boisterous yet loose' (Price, in Archer 1980:88) as to allow for some delight to emerge. His argument is that the house does not contain human activity but ought to be able to respond to it, a 'twenty-four hour living toy' (1980:88). The drawings are in an unusual convention for Price, who uses isometric and axonometric more often: an oblique projection with the plan drawn at 90° and true, whilst the vertical planes are projected down and deformed to 45° angles.

A third combination is provided by the architect Rafael Moneo in a collection of lectures published under the title *Theoretical Anxiety and Design Strategies*[32], the work of both James Stirling and Peter Eisenman were included alongside Robert Venturi and Denise Scott Brown, Aldo Rossi, Alvaro Siza, Frank O. Gehry, Rem Koolhaas and Herzog & De Meuron. The preface to the book gives a good account of Moneo's selection procedure: that the eight had an impact upon 20th century architectural education in particular. The aim is to illustrate connections between architectural theory and practice, with a trajectory from the accepted canon of modernism mined by Stirling for inspiration to the later fragmentation into a multiplicity of positions with Eisenman, Venturi & Scott Brown, and Koolhaas. The end of this time-line has a tacit rejection of explicit theory, with Herzog & De Meuron's lighter touch celebrating materials and sensory experience of architecture without an explicit theoretical framework or manifesto.

Moneo makes reference to Rowe's comments on Stirling—that there is an absence of facade in his work, and perhaps this can be seen most

18   *Introduction*

keenly in the axonometric drawings. The facades are omitted from the reverse-angle interior spaces described which appear to prefigure some of Bernard Tschumi's *Screenplays* projects and the *Manhattan Transcripts* where there is a narrative embedded within the city. The section of Selwyn College (after Stirling's 'walled city' concept for Churchill College—the wall becomes the architecture) is accompanied by an axonometric drawing of the entire scheme showing how it curves across the site forming a barrier. Interestingly, Moneo chooses to define the section as the key moment in the development of Stirling's Engineering Building for Leicester University. The axonometric drawing which so clearly communicates the design's clarity is ignored completely, even as the drawing is reproduced. Sectionally, the building is an accumulation of rectilinear volumes. I would argue that it is in axonometric that the compositional elements of this building come alive.

It is evident throughout his chapter on Stirling that Moneo is keen to focus on section. This is despite the evidence he presents himself of axonometric drawings which demonstrate the commitment of the practice to this form of representation: its importance is shown—not to the detriment or exclusion of other drawings—but it has a strong presence in the process as well as in the presentation of works. The section is unarguably evident in the project for Queen's College Oxford: The buttressed amphitheater form surrounding a raised courtyard is clearly expressed in a section which wraps around the public space, but this still needs its accompanying axonometric drawing to make any sense. The relationship with the river and the square is clearly demonstrated by the parallel projection.

Turning his attention to Eisenman, Moneo gives an interesting account of his drive. In contrast to Stirling, who effaced himself to an extent, Eisenman is continually present within his works, and he argues that his mission was to complete the unfinished business of modernism, which had been arrested in its development:

> Eisenman's mission was to recover for architecture the ideals of modernity. Modern architecture had never been fully executed, it had never come to incarnate the true spirit of modernity, because of distractions with questions of style and because it made functionalism its banner. (2004:147)

The idea of Eisenman's architecture as bereft of *place, function, building systems,* and *all* external referent is an incredibly purist position, one which makes him an anti-anthropological architect, perhaps prefiguring some of our contemporary posthumanism debates. Moneo makes a useful observation about the way in which Eisenman numbered his houses in this early period: akin to the way in which a composer would simply number their symphonies. This 'assert[ed] the abstract character of his work' (2004:149). Eisenman introduces 'process' in Moneo's account as a way of distancing himself from the product of his endeavours, as there is an implication that when so much has been stripped away and abstracted in avoidance of any

Introduction 19

connotation of architecture's traditional and conventional modes of production, that the *architecture* is therefore equivalent to the *architect*. In order to depersonalise it, he mobilises 'process' although you could argue that this has some roots at least in architectural tradition.

1.5 The structure of this book

Chapters 2 to 7 of this volume discuss the architects in question; these are followed by two chapters discussing the theoretical implications of parallel projection. Chapter 2 looks at the work of James Stirling, with a particular focus on his use of the 'worm's eye' or reverse-angle axonometric projection, a notoriously difficult drawing to both draw and to understand. The thrust of this chapter is to look at the way in which Stirling uses drawing as a tool to communicate and also as a way of enchanting or entrapping the potential client. The complexity of the drawing completed with absolute virtuosity is almost a test of his qualities as an architect, instilling confidence in his work through his abilities as a draughtsperson. Following this, in Chapter 3 is the work of JJP Oud, a member of the De Stijl group who produced designs across a range of scales. This issue of scale returns us to the discussion of mimesis in this chapter: what are the limits for verisimilitude when dealing with everything from furniture and door handles to entire urban quarters using the same drawing conventions?

Chapters 4 and 5 discuss the work of John Hejduk. Hejduk's work undergoes a significant change from his early career producing perfect modernist houses with strong cubist and constructivist influences, to his later allegorical work exploring narrative and memory. In Chapter 4, the focus is upon Hejduk's *Texas Houses* and *Wall Houses* series, the former being based strictly on a nine-square grid (later used extensively in teaching), and the latter distributing elements of the house along thin elongated walls: deliberately drawn against the tendency of axonometric, in order to hide, occlude, and reveal themselves gradually. Chapter 5 considers Hejduk's later works might, at first glance, appear to be abstract or expressionistic in quality, but which are careful and intelligent works which work at the edges of drawing conventions, and shift in projection over the course of a page. The hand of the architect is present, and Hejduk draws himself into the page with these narrative works.

The theoretically informed work of Peter Eisenman is the focus of Chapter 6. Drawing on his *House I—House X* series (along with *House XIa, El Even Odd* and other explorations of form), the chapter explores how Eisenman developed his theory of an autonomous architecture separated from external referent through the use of axonometric drawings, collages, and, even in one instance, a model. Parallel to this is the use of axonometric drawing by Eisenman to analyse the work of others—a practice he began with his PhD thesis and continues to this day with the publications *Ten Canonical Buildings, Guiseppe Terragni,* and *Palladio Virtuel.*

20   Introduction

Chapter 7 is the final chapter on individual architects and considers the work of Cedric Price, who produced projects with a social conviction underpinning them. His work sought to rethink the postwar cultural consensus in Britain with large-scale projects including the *Fun Palace* and *Potteries Thinkbelt*, proposing adaptable, transformable architecture with an eye to their eventual obsolescence. Price makes greater use of human figures than any of the other architects under discussion, working in sequences to show how his projects would be constructed, how they transform whilst in use, how people can actually make use of the space in different ways, and finally how they would be dismantled.

Chapter 8 draws these themes together, having established that there is an inherent form of knowledge production in architectural drawing, and that the conventions used generates a particular kind of knowledge about form and geometry. This draws on the literature around skilled practice in anthropology, noting that knowledge is embodied and as present in the hand and eye as it is in the mind.

Concluding, Chapter 9 is a meditation both on how to draw an axonometric drawing and answers the question of why it is still pertinent to do so. This final chapter is a rewritten account from my 2006 PhD thesis which included an exhibition of a series of drawings of the Tokyo metro rendered in a coded axonometric drawing. The drawings are understood through the lens of Henri Bergson's philosophy of creative practice and its relationship to temporality. Taking the reader through this process step by step illuminates the process of hiding and revealing lines, the construction underpinning the simple geometry of the corridors being drawn, and the knowledge gained by doing so. Contemporary drawing practices privilege the production of a complete CAD model from which the desired views can be taken. This removes some of the architect's agency from the production of the desired drawing, meaning that many of the elements best developed by drawing and sketching in parallel projection are missed out of the design process in preference for the problems solved best by plans and digital models. This is not intended to be a luddite narrative of reclaiming old ways of making architecture. After all, history teaches us that such projections are socially and historically contextualised, passing in and out of use, but recurring because they remain incredibly useful tools for thinking with. This research seeks to understand the utility of axonometric drawings, allowing the reader to come to their own conclusions about its continuing usefulness within their own practices. Importantly, the drawing convention is understood as a way of producing knowledge, either as a descriptive drawing or as a projective one: delineating the world around us and proposing interventions into it within the consistent and communicable framework of a shared drawing convention. In addition to this, the examples within this book show that ideas of historical quotation and material reinterpretation; adaptability

Introduction 21

and agency; spirituality and poetry; meaning and form; pragmatism and totality; can all be developed and communicated through axonometric drawing. The examples range from the most utilitarian to the esoteric, austere and symbolic. It is the commonly understood conventions of parallel projection that allows these to be compared and contrasted with one another, showing a remarkable flexibility in accommodating the desires of the draughtsperson.

Notes

1. Booker, Peter Jeffrey. 1967. *A History of Engineering Drawing.* London: Chatto & Windus.
2. Camerota, Filippo. 2004. "Renaissance Descriptive Geometry" in Lefevre, Wolfgang (Ed.). *Picturing Machines 1400–1700.* Cambridge, Massachusetts: MIT Press, pp. 175–208.
3. Monge, Gaspard. 1798. *Géométrie Descriptive, Leçons Donées aux Écoles Normales.* Paris: Baudouin.
4. Lawrence, Snezana. 2003. "History of Descriptive Geometry in England" in *Proceedings of the First International Congress on Construction History,* Madrid.
5. Scolari, Massimo. 2012. *Oblique Drawing: A History of Anti-Perspective.* Cambridge, Massachusetts: MIT Press.
6. Bryon, Hilary. 2008. "Revolutions in Space: Parallel Projections in the Early Modern Era" in *Architectural Research Quarterly,* Vol. 12, Issue 3–4. pp. 337–346.
7. Moravcová, Vlasta. 2014. "History of Descriptive Geometry with an Emphasis to the Boom of Descriptive Geometry in Austro-Hungarian Empire in the 19th Century" in *Technical Transactions/Czasopismo Techniczne,* 1 NP (7), pp. 160–176.
8. Alonso-Rodríguez, Miguel Ángel & Calvo-López, José. 2014. "*Prospettiva Soldatesca*: An Empirical Approach to the Representation of Military Architecture in the Early Modern Period" in *Nexus Network Journal: Architecture and Mathematics*, Vol. 16, pp. 543–567.
9. Choisy, Auguste. 2018 [1899]. *Histoire de l'Architecture.* Paris: Hachette Livre-BNF.
10. Author of a number of sophisticated textbooks on architecture which, whilst presenting fundamentals in an accessible manner, have a depth of engagement which emerges from a great deal of research. Unwin, Simon. 2007. "Analysing Architecture Through Drawing" in *Building Research & Information,* Vol. 35, No. 1, pp. 101–110.
11. Sudnow, David. 2001. *Ways of the Hand: A Rewritten Account.* Cambridge, Massachusetts: MIT Press.
12. Küchler, Suzanne. 2002. *Malanggan: Art, Memory and Sacrifice.* Oxford: Berg.
13. Nakamura, Fuyubi. 2007. "Creating of Performing Words? Observations on Contemporary Japanese Calligraphy" in Hallam, Elizabeth & Ingold, Tim (Eds.). *Creativity and Cultural Improvisation.* Oxford: Berg.
14. Benjamin, W. 2008. *The Work of Art in the Age of Mechanical Reproduction.* J. A. Underwood (Trans.). London: Penguin Great Ideas.
15. Cain, Patricia. 2013. *Drawing: The Enactive Evolution of the Practitioner.* Bristol: Intellect Books.

22 Introduction

16. Cox, Rupert (Ed.). 2008. *The Culture of Copying in Japan*. London: Routledge. This interest in copying in Japan is further developed in Jordan, Brenda G. & Weston, Victoria (Eds.). 2003. *Copying the Master and Stealing His Secrets: Talent and Training in Japanese Painting*. Honolulu: University of Hawaii Press. Similar issues of transmission, creativity, and skill are raised. More obliquely, Yanagi discusses the contrast between seeing and knowing, privileging *seeing* as crucial to any aesthetic activity—in this case ceramics. Yanagi, Soetsu. 2003 [1972]. *The Unknown Craftsman*. Tokyo: Kodansha International, pp. 109–113.
17. A form of Shinto performance, with dances tied to the seasons and having both folk and imperial variations.
18. In my own work, this is explored with reference to Laban notation: Lucas, Raymond. 2006. *Towards a Theory of Notation as a Thinking Tool*. Unpublished PhD Thesis, Aberdeen: University of Aberdeen. See also Spier, Steven. 2005. "Dancing and Drawing, Choreography and Architecture" in *The Journal of Architecture*, Vol. 10, No. 4, pp. 349–364; and Eisenstein, Sergei. 1946. "How I Learned to Draw (A Chapter About My Dancing Lessons)" in de Zegher, C. (Ed.) 2000. *The Body of the Line: Eisenstein's Drawing*. New York: The Drawing Center.
19. Boon, Marcus. 2010. *In Praise of Copying*. Cambridge, Massachusetts: MIT Press.
20. Benjamin, W. 1997 [1933]. "On the Mimetic Faculty" in *One-Way Street and Other Writings*. London: Verso, pp. 160–163.
21. Taussig, Michael. 1993. *Mimesis and Alterity: a Particular History of the Senses*. London: Routledge.
22. For more on this tactility of vision, see the following: Pallasmaa, Juhani. 1996. *The Eyes of the Skin*. London: Academy Editions. Marks, Laura. 2000. *The Skin of the Film: Intercultural Cinema, Embodiment and the Senses*. Durham, North Carolina: Duke University Press.
23. Goodman, Nelson. 1978. *Ways of Worldmaking*. Indianapolis, Indiana: Hackett Publishing.
24. Houdart, S. & Chihiro, M. 2009. *Kuma Kengo: An Unconventional Monograph*. Paris: Editions Donner Lieu. Yaneva, A. 2009. *Made by the Office for Metropolitan Architecture: An Ethnography of Design*. Rotterdam: 010 Publishers.
25. Hejduk, John (Illustrator). 1991. *Aesop's Fables*. New York: Rizzoli.
26. Hejduk, John. 1995. *Architectures in Love*. New York: Rizzoli.
27. Eisenman, P., Graves, M., Gwathmey, C., Hejduk, J., Meier, R. et al. 1975. *Five Architects*. New York: Oxford University Press. The book is a catalogue for an exhibition of the same name, curated by Colin Rowe and Arthur Drexler for the CASE Group (Committee of Architects for the Study of the Environment) meeting at the Museum of Modern Art in New York in 1969. Pubished initially in 1972, with the 1975 edition gaining greater traction within the profession.
28. As proposed by the Museum of Modern Art's architecture curator at the time, Arthur Drexler.
29. See Kauffman, Jordan. 2018. *Drawing on Architecture: The Object of Lines, 1970–1990*. Cambridge, Massachusetts: MIT Press. pp. 12–13.
30. Archer, B. J. (Ed.). 1980. *Houses for Sale*. New York: Rizzoli. Also discussed in detail in Kauffman (2018:171–200). The book's editor was a pseudonym for Barbara Jakobson, an art collector and important patron of modernism in New York.
31. A historic move detailed in Kauffman (2018).
32. Moneo, Rafael. 2004. *Theoretical Anxiety and Design Strategies in the Work of Eight Contemporary Architects*. Cambridge, Massachusetts: MIT Press.

2 James Stirling's axonometric traps

2.1 Stirling and the interchangeability of material logics

As the first case study, James Stirling is perhaps the most conventional. What is important to note, however, is the way in which axonometric drawing informed his architecture. Many of the working and presentation drawings by Stirling and his office were produced in axonometric projection, perhaps characterised by their careful execution and the use of worms-eye or reverse-angle axonometric, demonstrating complex and compound geometry and showing the interior volume in more detail.

Such drawings are not only difficult to produce, but they are challenging to read as well. The main thesis of this chapter is that the drawing convention was, a significant driver for the formal characteristics of James Stirling's work. Redrawing not only completed buildings but also sheets of sketches showing serial variations on a theme, the chapter identifies motifs and explores the relationship of geometry to axonometric drawing.

Stirling's work offers us an opportunity to consider the role of virtuosity in architectural drawing. The manner of Stirling's drawing invites wonder, and reinforces the expert character of the architect. Whilst Stirling and his partners selected the materials of their buildings carefully, there are several interesting attitudes towards the interchangeability of materials when Stirling discusses his first scheme with James Gowan: housing at Ham Common.

In a long discussion of the influence of Corbusier's Maison Jaoul on the project of three 2- and 3-storey residential blocks, Amanda Reeser Lawrence (2012:45–47) pays particular attention to the brickwork. The buildings are constructed from London bricks, concrete with shuttering marks visible, and prefabricated timber window casings. Reeser Lawrence establishes that this scheme is not so much influenced by Corbusier's postwar project, as a built critique of it. Rather than a scathing attack, however, it is a sympathetic response which looks to redress some of the issues Stirling found with Jaoul. In Corbusier's example, the bricks in particular, are treated as a surface rather than as a pattern. They could have been any material at all whilst maintaining the same overall effect, the junctions between timber,

24 *Stirling's axonometric traps*

concrete, and brick are flush and smooth. The effect is a continuity expressing structural logic of mass concrete, modular brick, and planar timber, but the overall geometry remains the key image of the scheme.

Stirling also leaves his bricks exposed, partly down to the English vernacular, but also to establish the interchangeability of these materials, that the geometric effect can be achieved just as well through a rough and imprecise module with deeply engraved mortar accentuating the effect. The crucial critique is that the junctions between key materials are carefully managed to allow each to be expressed clearly. The effect is to bring materiality to the abstract machine aesthetic of Corbusier in more ways than the exposed shuttering so characteristic of brutalism.

The materiality of the construction is used to articulate Stirling's collaged assemblages, carefully articulating the elements. Reeser Lawrence (2012:96–97) notes that the identity of each element of the design is maintained within the swirl of the composition through an appropriate material logic applied to the lecture theatres, engineering shed, and office tower in his Leicester project. Rather than attempt to unify through the construction details, a deliberate move in the design keeps the various programmatic elements distinctive from one another and legible at all times. In this way, the materiality of the architecture once again generates the geometry. In the developing oeuvre of Stirling and his partners, materials lose their interchangeability in this scheme, surpassing the architectonics of Le Corbusier with his expressive use of multiple building technologies.

Axonometric drawings can be argued to contribute to this interchangeability of materials[1]. Taking the Leicester Engineering Building as an example. Peter Eisenman's description of the scheme in *Ten Canonical Buildings*[2] underlines this materiality. The manner in which Stirling's drawings communicate the material strategies of the building is discussed, in particular the inversions whereby glazed elements are read as solid rather than transparent.

> 'What was seen in modernist abstraction as transparent, planar, and void is now to be read as more opaque, volumetric, and solid. A fourth change involves the actual material solids. In the drawing, these are rendered accurately, denoting the difference between the ceramic and running bond brick. All the surfaces which run vertically (denoting their nonstructural condition) are rendered in the drawing with vertical hatching, while the bearing-wall brick surfaces are rendered with horizontal hatching.' (2008:160)

The axonometric drawings in Eisenman's analysis depict the project as a kit-of-parts: the drawing is understood almost as a substitute for a model. This attitude allows the elements to be discussed as discrete parts with their own material logic. They can then be moved, rotated, placed into and out of relationship with one another; all in a sea of white paper—the context is relatively unimportant in Eisenman's analysis. We know from other accounts that the environment was crucial to the development of Stirling's schemes. The disinterest in context here is Eisenman's.

The act which Eisenman identifies as most important in the design is the strategy which takes the glazed elements away from being planar and towards solidity through cutting and chamfering: this demonstrates the volume of the form.

The account given by Mark Girouard (1998:193) from interviews with one-time Stirling employee Leon Krier suggests that the practice's axonometric drawings had a larger role in the *publication* of the architecture than in the design process itself, noting that whilst two key monographs were commissioned earlier in his career, it was not until a fallow period in the early 1970s that Stirling's office turned to the production of the 'black book' and the 'white book' charting Stirling's career from 1950–1974 and 1975–1992 respectively[3]. These were essentially advertising for a struggling practice as well as an attempt by Stirling to position himself as Le Corbusier's heir.

The office redrew earlier schemes for publication, and deliberately selected and omitted images in order to construct an identity. The early influence of Frank Lloyd Wright was missing, and Stirling's small sketches used in the design process were also absent, generally treated as disposable and not retained in the archive. This selection and redrawing process constructed a mythology around Stirling, erasing the labour of architectural production and focusing on the final scheme as built. This is symptomatic of the era: processes and practices of design were not seen as being of primary interest, and the office represented an individual genius figure rather than a collaborative effort by a collectivity.

The pages of sketches within the collections at the CCA including those redrawn in Figure 2.1 run counter to this narrative, however: drawings were clearly used developmentally as well as for profession- and client-facing activities[4]. This is reinforced by the analysis of Amanda Reeser Lawrence once again:

> Stirling's use of the axonometric drawing here bears mention as more than simply an arbitrary choice of representational technique and instead as a reifying of his conceptual strategy of 'articulation' or 'piece-by-piece' composition. As the early drawings make clear, Stirling designed the project in axonometric drawing. To say that somewhat more forcefully, the drawing technique wasn't an after-the-fact means through which to represent the building as it had been conceived; it was the means through which Stirling arrived at and tested design ideas. Leicester is a built axonometric. Robin Evans famously argued that drawing always precedes building in architecture, and that there is a necessary translation, a gap, between drawing and building. But in Stirling's case, and particularly at Leicester, it's as if that gap is missing. He simply 'records' the drawing with the architecture.' (2012:95)

26 *Stirling's axonometric traps*

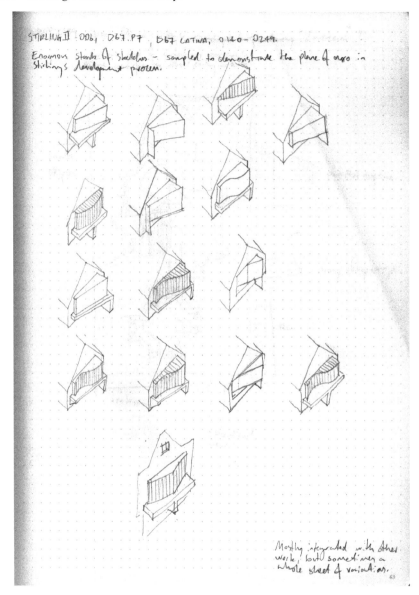

Figure 2.1 Redrawing of AP140.S2.SS1.D67.P7.0140-249, sketches of the Latina Library project showing the gable facade development.

Stirling, Wilford & Associates worked on a public library for the Italian town of Latina. The site, in a Mussolini-era new town development, lacked identity and the depth of history a person might expect of Italy, so this project for a public library had an interesting role to play in the life of the town. The main features of the design are two drum-shaped reading rooms, treated differently—the reading rooms are designed for the lending library and reference collection respectively[5].

A series of sketches demonstrate something of the working practice within Stirling & Wilford's studio at the time[6]. The focus here is the gable end of the library, and a series of sketched axonometric drawings explore various designs for a first-floor level window. Seriality is an oft overlooked quality of drawing, with conventional wisdom discussing drawings as singular and unique objects. There is a challenge to this in the repetition and iterative variation within a series.

2.2 Alfred Gell's notions of entrapment and enchantment

The anthropologist Alfred Gell's work on entrapment[7] and enchantment is pertinent to the virtuosity with which Stirling produced drawings. As noted in the introduction, publication was pursued by Stirling for the good of the business: to demonstrate what the practice was capable of. Alongside this was a desire to communicate within the profession and to reinforce a position of expertise. One way in which this can be achieved is through gaining the confidence of clients by showing the rigours of the design, presented most often as drawings.

By using drawings which were often difficult to read alongside those of a high level of finish and sophistication, Stirling was looking to both entrap his clients and to draw them in to the beauty of the work.

Anthropologists gives us a great many insights on the ways in which images can be used, and Alfred Gell's work is particularly useful in this regard. Rather than focusing entirely on visual representation, Gell presents the idea that a trap can be thought of as an *image* of the animal it is designed to capture as well as of its creator (1999:200). This is different in nature to a representation or depiction of that animal, where the visual representation of the features of the animal would be transferred into another material with a degree of accurate observation. The image is instead a reflection of the behaviour of the animal concerned—its feeding patterns, the way it moves. A successful trap must take account of these behaviours, understanding the ways in which the target observes its environment and which actions to expect given a stimulus, translating these habits into a physical form. The trap is therefore indexical to the animal, taking account of how its behaviour unfurls over time as much as the overall physiology of the creature.

Given the dual nature of the trap as the extension of the hunter, and as a 'lethal parody of the animal's *Umwelt*' (1999:201), how might this relate to the drawings in question? The drawing serves as a form of prosthesis to the draughtsperson, a way of extending or distributing their presence. As a substitute for the presence of the architect, it represents not only their intentions, but speaks of their character at the same time. Standardised languages and codes for drawing have not resulted in an erasure of the

28 *Stirling's axonometric traps*

autographic mark. An observer can still tell the forms preferred by one architect from another, their handling of material and the choices made in communication. The architect remains present within their drawings, something we return to in Chapter 5 with John Hejduk's later works.

The second notion is perhaps more controversial: that the drawing is a trap. This is not used in a pejorative sense, to suggest that something underhanded is going on, but that drawings are designed to entrap their target audience. Gell suggests a similar position: that there is a strong kinship between post-Duchamp artworks described in his paper and the traps designed around the behaviour of various animals. It might be uncharitable to suggest that the art world is trapped by conceptual art as detailed by Gell, but it can be argued to have come about due to the art market conditions of their time. Stirling's drawings are, therefore, images of the architectural commissioning process during his lifetime.

Gell's work on enchantment and captivation develops this theme further, perhaps in less controversial language. Gell draws a comparison between the Kula exchanges of Trobriand Islanders with the process of viewing a Vermeer painting in an art gallery. The economic exchange of the Trobriand Islands is conducted on highly decorated flotillas of canoes, the prows of which are given particular attention. The intent is to dazzle their trading partners into losing their senses and exchange goods for less than they are worth (Gell 1997:69).

Gell describes a *demoralisation* that he feels when viewing the artwork which he cannot reproduce. The spectacle's virtuosity is beyond the scope of the viewer, who has 'an inability mentally to rehearse the origination' of the work. This ties in to the overall theory of artworks which Gell is proposing: that such works have agency in the manner of a sentient being or person, that they have the ability to act and effect the world through that action.

Architectural drawings, and those of Stirling in particular, are produced to have this intention: to act within the world, sometimes independently of the architect's presence. The virtuosity demonstrated by Stirling is such that they are designed to dazzle the client, to give them confidence in his abilities as an architect, and that they eventually have greater ownership of their understanding of the architecture as the works are presented as a puzzle to be solved[8].

2.3 The absence of facade

It is noted by several commentators including Colin Rowe, Anthony Vidler, and Amanda Reeser Lawrence (2012:89–90) that Stirling's architecture is often designed with little regard for the facade. Reeser Lawrence finds this to have its origins in the Leicester Engineering Building, which, similar to other campus-based architecture, lacks the urban context that might have made a conventional elevation more relevant.

The design of Leicester is volumetric rather than planar, with study models and the development of the scheme through axonometric drawings demonstrating the process as a series of blocks which can be stacked and manipulated in different ways through the process. One stated aim of Stirling was to move away from architecture where diverse programmatic needs were contained within a simple box, but towards an architecture where each element—in this case the flexible shed, lecture theatres, stack of offices, and water tower—were all to maintain their identity and assembled into a coherent composition on those terms.

Reeser Lawrence notes an important distinction between Stirling's approach and that of Lasdun or Corbusier: whilst each element of the programme is clearly articulated, Stirling moves away from an upwardly extruded plan and towards a more sectionally complex assembly:

> The key distinction between these earlier projects and Leicester was that Le Corbusier's and certainly Lasdun's assemblages were essentially plan-based. The pieces, in other words, were assembled on the ground plane and then extruded vertically. Although the geometry of the pieces was more complex in Le Corbusier's projects than in Lasdun's—particularly at Centrosoyuz—the basic operation of arranging the pieces on a more or less flat plane was the same. At Leicester, by contrast, the assemblage is fully three-dimensional and more sectionally complex; the articulated volumes are arranged centripetally around both vertical and horizontal axes, and most—including the towers and lecture halls—never touch the ground plane. (2012:93)

Whilst this is described as a sectional logic, the centripetal composition has much in common with De Stijl manifestoes and architectures: and the logic is one of axonometry rather than section. What is clear from the material documenting the development of the project is that axonometric drawing plays a role in the process of design, not merely as a flourish of representation at the conclusion of the project or reinterpretation for a professional audience, but the testing and iterative composition is at least in part achieved through a series of axonometric studies.

In this case, the affordances of axonometric are a freedom from flat orthographic representation, presenting programmatic elements as discrete and solid blocks. This carries its own issues of course, and is not presented as superior to other forms of inquiry or design, simply one which allows certain kinds of composition to be revised and tested swiftly. Once the forms of the elements are settled (and this compositional process relies on that decision being made early on, perhaps to the detriment of that element's design), their arrangement becomes a simpler matter.

The collage logic emerges once again. Not in the sense of a flat homogenising surface, but as an underlying logic allowing juxtaposition to drive the process.

30 *Stirling's axonometric traps*

Crucially, Stirling's project continues to develop after this compositional stage: the elements are refined in different ways. The 45° angled roof light structure, so famously accommodating the need for both the orientation of the site and the brief's requirement for north lighting, features in the design early on, whilst other features articulating and expressionistically developing each of the programmatic blocks, comes later.

Competing notions of movement are presented here—with Rowe commenting on the lack of a facade to the Staatsgalerie project:

> Anthony Vidler writes, 'Without a face or façade, Rowe believed a building lost any frontality, and thus any "metaphorical plane of intersection between the eyes of the observer and what one might dare to call the soul of the building (its condition of internal animation)"' (Vidler 2008:103). Rowe's concept of movement, in other words, remains picturesque and classical, while Stirling's incorporates more subtle forms of dynamism and duration.'

The conventional wisdom that a clear facade is needed to communicate something about the building precludes its potential to hide and reveal itself gradually. This is the aim of Stirling's development of the architectural promenade: it is an explicitly experiential or even phenomenological design.

2.4 The worm's eye, down, and reverse-angle axonometric drawing

Conventionally, parallel projection drawings are taken from the point of view of an observer high above the picture plane. By the logic of perspective drawing, this observer can be understood to be at an infinite distance as described by Robin Evans (1995) and Louise Pelletier and Alberto Perez-Gomez (1997)[9].

> We should recognise that isometry derives from a perspective construction in which the converging points are postulated at infinity, so that parallel lines can remain parallel. (Pelletier & Pérez-Gómez 1997:308)

Pelletier and Pérez-Gómez note that parallel projection required the introduction of standardised units of measurement before it could become widespread, and that its use could be understood as a technological development. The 19th-century treatises from Farrish and Jopling introduced some useful aspects to the discussion, particularly the notion of the 'residual' observer referring to the orientation of the drawing. Starting with a presumed cuboid form, isometric drawings could be observed with any of the six faces presented, alternating between excavated voids and descriptions of volume, a multiplicity of views are, therefore, made possible. This speaks to Pelletier and Pérez-Gómez's position that the distinction between

Stirling's axonometric traps 31

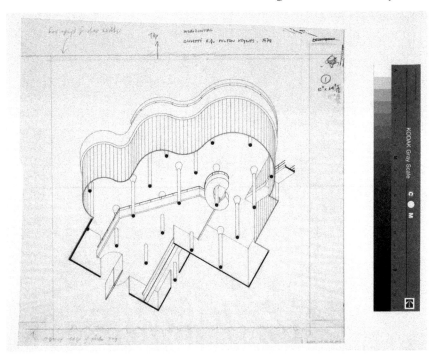

Figure 2.2 James Stirling (Firm), axonometric drawing for British Olivetti Headquarters, Milton Keynes, England, 1970–1974; ink on paper, 47 × 47.8 cm; AP140.S2.SS1.D40.P23.6, James Stirling/Michael Wilford fonds, Canadian Centre for Architecture.

perspective as subjective and axonometric as objective has been overstated somewhat (1997:317).

The nomenclature of this kind of drawing varies from one source to another: often referred to as 'worm's eye' and 'bird's eye' respectively, other terminology includes 'reverse-angle' and—as is preferred in much of the literature on Stirling and his partners—'up' and 'down' axonometrics (figure 2.2). Here, I will, for the sake of clarity, work with the worm's eye axonometric drawing as it leaves no room for uncertainty. The gaze is an important part of this definition, and engaging the zoomorphic imagination in order to describe the act of looking upwards from the ground has a certain everyday poetry to it (see figure 2.3).

The worm's eye drawing complicates axonometric projection significantly, and takes a degree of skill on the part of the viewer to read it accurately. Rather than looking down on the building, revealing the external form and roof, the worm's eye is an interior view: showing the ceiling rather than the roof, and expressing the articulation of walls as they undulate. Clearly a standard bird's eye view with a sectional aspect to it, cutting through horizontally to reveal the interior, can achieve this interior quality, so it is the reveal of the ceiling that really sets the worm's eye view apart.

32 Stirling's axonometric traps

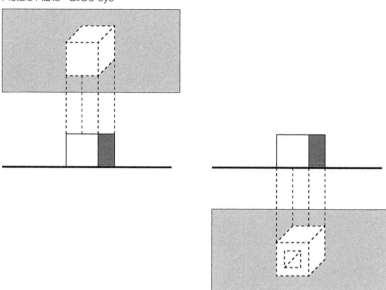

Figure 2.3 Diagrammatic representation of the picture plane of worm's eye and bird's eye views.

This view prioritises spaces such as interior courtyards and atria, expressing the qualities of these elements in great detail. The drawing of a worm's eye axonometric is clearly an attempt to show the viewer a holistic view of the interior of the building with the spatial composition of a plan and the three-dimensional data of a standard axonometric. The architecture expressed is not a spectacle in the usual sense but a series of chambers which invite the viewer in, to imagine how they might occupy and move through the space. This sequentiality is something we shall return to later. An initial difficulty in establishing how to understand the drawing can be quite an obstacle, however: it is a geometric feat requiring a spatial imagination on the part of both the draughtsperson and the viewer.

This difficulty could be said to serve a purpose, however. As discussed earlier in this chapter, the idea of *enchanting* the audience is a powerful one, and is achieved partly by rewarding some effort on the part of the observer in working the drawing out. The drawing does not give up its secrets easily, but does reward the investment with a comprehensive understanding of the interior of the structure (see figure 2.4). This has some similarities to the way in which a film spectator is stitched in[10] to cinematic action through identification, or by being given elements of the plot just ahead of a detective protagonist whilst holding other elements back[11]. Such filmic theories give

Stirling's axonometric traps 33

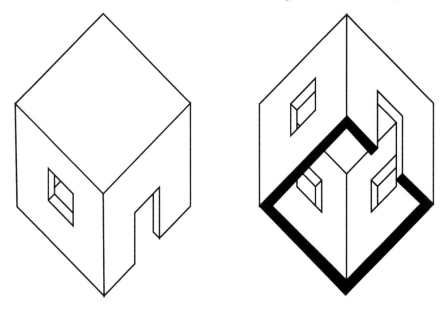

Figure 2.4 Diagrammatic example of standard worm's-eye and bird's-eye axonometric drawings.

further opportunities for interrogating the narrative of a drawing[12], how the spectator is manipulated, and how connections made by a viewer are stronger than the obvious ones given directly by a more immediately legible drawing. This is an approach adopted by Satter (2012)[13], who argues that Stirling's place in rehabilitating early modernism's interest in movement—a unity of spatial and temporal movement—is one way to work with the ideas presented by Deleuze's *Cinema 1: the Movement Image* and *Cinema 2: the Time Image*.[14]

> His projects posit a density of signs and an archaeological palimpsest that obfuscate the boundaries between landscape and building, natural and constructed, past, present and future, acting as a critical reflection on the nature of difference over identity, maintaining a unitary and singular concept that accommodates a multiplicity of events in what Deleuze calls 'the affirmation of all chance in a single moment.' (Satter 2012:57)

Whilst Satter's focus is naturally on the buildings themselves, these intentions can also be read in the drawings. Writing of the Leicester Engineering Building, he notes that the preference for so-called 'expressive' modes of drawing allows for full exploration of the sequential nature of the spaces proposed for each project (Satter 2012:61–62).

34 *Stirling's axonometric traps*

What is important here is the sequencing of space suggested by Satter: highlighting the power of alternative drawings (assuming a normative position for the plan) and notations to demonstrate vertical compositions as well as horizontal ones. This idea of flows and circulation with reference to the Staatsgalerie is discussed by Stephen Cairns (2012:462), describing its handling of conventional ideas of circulation as both 'aggressive' and 'experimental'. Satter insists that, in alternating between smooth and striated space:

> Stirling's architectural strategies, which express, rather than represent, the force of events as organisational intensities, and imbricate, without immobilising, time, space and their potential. (2012:70)

The confidence of the borrowings in the Staatsgalerie, and its reliance on 'accident' (Moneo[15] in Satter 2012:66) is evident in the drawings for the scheme, which have a collage quality and logic, alternative views hide and reveal different aspects of the same element (as in the case of the frontal worm's eye axonometric drawing discussed by Jencks and mentioned later).

I argue, in this case, that the choice of such a complex form of representation as the worm's eye axonometric has two audiences: the architectural profession and the client. Both constituencies are reading these drawings differently, and that is the intention of the practice in their production: the deliberate construction of a consistent oeuvre akin to Le Corbusier (and a curated one at that), on whom Stirling based himself to a degree. The mythology of the practice and the individual genius of the lead architect was an important driver behind the production and projection of a public image through drawings. It was important to Stirling that he impress the profession, that he influenced a generation of architects.

Other drawings are even more unusual in their projection (see figure 2.5): eschewing the usual 45° angle of axonometric projection in favour of a flat, elevational projection (as we shall see later with John Hejduk's work, this convention hides as much as it shows). This, coupled with a worm's eye viewpoint, mimics the act of walking alongside a building with a richly articulated surface with projections, niches, overhangs, and colonnades.

In his analysis of some of Stirling's presentation drawings for the Staatsgalerie (notably signed by Stirling rather than produced by his office), Charles Jencks notes the frontal axonometric drawings accentuate the dualism present within the ornamentation and detailing of the scheme:

> These coloured drawings clarify the design intentions behind the museum and theatre. Above all, they accentuate the dualisms inherent in the design, the juxtaposition of rectangle and circle, frontality and rotation, axiality and diagonality, and also the attitude of collage, the idea that new buildings should both support and contrast with the existing urban fabric. (1982:51)

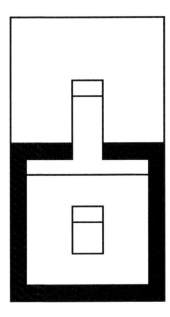

Figure 2.5 Diagrammatic example of a frontal worm's-eye axonometric drawing.

Jencks is clearly establishing a connection between the drawings and the aims of the architecture. Without overplaying the instrumentality of the drawing convention, the suggestion is that the drawing at least follows the aims of the architecture in playing both old and new simultaneously. The uncertainty is described as a collage: without citing Colin Rowe and Fred Koetter's influential work on late modern urbanism[16] directly, the same concerns and solutions are indicated: that the tabula rasa of pure modernism is moderated for a more harmonious urban environment through a patchwork or collage approach where a range of eras coexist and respond organically to one another. Jencks takes issue with this (1982:53) in Stirling's case, arguing that collage relies upon the jarring effect of juxtaposition, and the harmoniously arranged borrowings found in Stirling are quite different to collage. That aside, the collage logic of these 'frontal' drawings is to deny as much as possible, the three-dimensionality of the surface in order to highlight how elements are assembled into a composition.

The use of axonometric conventions to add further detail to elevation drawing demonstrates an interest in the ceiling plane, with the canopies of the building entrances depicted from alternative angles, the coloured steel against a flush sandstone/travertine-clad wall. Rather than show the articulation of the vertical surfaces, the drawings accentuate their flatness: almost wilfully—playing against the affordances of the convention. Such conventions are a creative constraint within these drawings: conformity to convention and working within the scaffold provided is one valid option, but there are ways of denying or working against the expectations of a convention to depict the structure in a particular way. In this case, the canopies

36 *Stirling's axonometric traps*

are famously crucial to the architecture, and the designers are well aware of this, to the extent that they control and channel the narrative with their choice of representation.

The worm's eye drawings show a concern for the interior: architecture as experienced, rather than as an external image. Interior elevations are described, rooms and the thresholds between them are elaborated, and the architectural promenade is fully considered.

2.5 The drum drawing

This promenade is at its most fully realised in the project for the Staatsgalerie extension in Stuttgart. The drum of the sculpture courtyard exemplifies the approach of the practice to drawing. Through a number of variations and alternative abstractions, the following is produced to show the colonnade around the perimeter of a drum. A ramp climbs the side of the space, the walls punctured by arched openings. Every one of these moves appears designed to be difficult to represent in this projection, but the impression is given of standing within the space looking upwards, seeing the connections it has to the other parts of the project (see figures 2.6 and 2.7).

A great deal of intellectual labour is spent tracing Stirling's influences and sources. Geoffrey Baker[17], in common with other commentators[18], finds Schinkel's Altes Museum to be of particular importance.

By way of example for the eclecticism in Stirling's influences for form and detail, Baker draws some explicit comparisons with Schinkel's work as a direct source for the drum in the design and the Italian town of San Gimignano as the source of the architectural promenade or sequence of spaces. Accompanying a reproduction of the axonometric drawings, in particular the reverse angle drawing, shows:

> Stirling revels in the way a route can connect spaces to introduce a myriad of volumetric and spatial perceptions... If San Gimignano is organic, a growth over time that has accommodated each addition with a sensitivity specific to Italian hill towns in the Middle Ages, and if the New State Gallery is a carefully controlled and precise rendition of twentieth century rational thought, each makes its presence manifest by an architectural language of mass that resonates beyond its time. They each have arcuated gateways, views that offer unexpected vistas, and each is penetrated by routes that are narrow and which take us from one part of the town to another. (2011:234).

Baker goes on to discuss how axonometrics describe the building, alternately bringing attention to the overall composition, or to the kit-of-parts from which the architecture would be assembled. This recalls the engineering roots of the convention, and manuals for stripping down and maintaining engines, which would have been familiar to Stirling. The lack of distortion

Stirling's axonometric traps 37

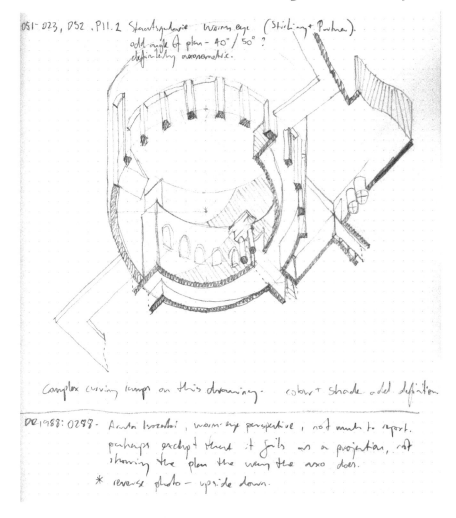

Figure 2.6 Redrawing of AP140.S2.SS1.D52.P11.2.

in the projection chosen is important, even as the choice of unconventional and difficult forms of representation such as the worm's eye view began to feature more prominently in his output. In describing the work as explicitly sequential and temporal, the flow from one space to another is described, the experience of being in the space is articulated carefully, and the staging of the spaces is considered with a great deal of attention.

This temporality is a function of the trap discussed earlier. Traps function by drawing their victim in, giving a hint at a reward and conforming to some of their known behaviours. The result here is rather less sinister, and I am interested in the role of the drawing as a trap rather than the eventual architecture: the effect here is to exploit the subjective possibilities

38 *Stirling's axonometric traps*

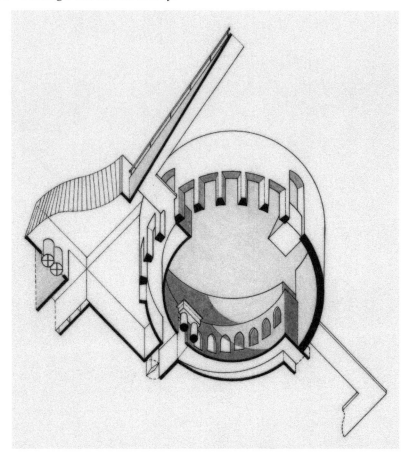

Figure 2.7 Axonometric drawing for Staatsgalerie, Stuttgart, Germany, 1977–1984; pen and ink, graphite and coloured pencil on tracing paper 28.5 × 27 cm; AP140.S2.SS1.D52.P11.2, James Stirling/Michael Wilford fonds, Canadian Centre for Architecture.

of axonometric drawing, presumed by some to be a much more objective form of architectural representation but containing the possibility for placing the observer mentally within the structure presented. This requires a greater act of imagination than more directly illusionistic drawings such as perspectives, but it is possible to generate this response. The viewer must imagine themselves as a part of the drawing, projecting an avatar of sorts into the spaces described and further exploring these by moving that character about[19].

The practicality of showing these elements makes facades difficult to represent, and this aspect of Stirling's architecture was something of a point of consternation from contemporary writers such as Colin Rowe. Competing notions of movement are presented by Satter[20] with reference to Rowe's comments about the lack of a facade in the Staatsgalerie project:

> In other words, architecture operates via intensities before it ever materialises. The smooth and the striated are conceptually adept at negotiating these dynamics, treating architecture as assemblages linking content and expression, concrete without being functionally reductive and expressive without being naively utopian. Intensities posit architecture as metastable entities that can be lessened or augmented but cannot be divided, subtracted from or added to without qualitatively changing. (2012:60)

The conventional wisdom that a clear facade is needed to communicate something about the building precludes its potential to hide and reveal itself gradually. This is the aim of Stirling's development of the architectural promenade: it is an explicitly experiential or even phenomenological design, and the use of axonometric drawings is crucial to the development and eventual articulation of this position. This is underlined by Joseph Bedford[21] whose paper on the influence of Corbusier on Stirling's facades explores the relationship Stirling has with the idea of facade and elevation versus axonometric forms. Rather than focus on Stirling's interpretation of precedents, however, it is more important for our purposes to underline the dynamism of his aesthetic: against the picturesque tradition of Rowe and towards one which implicates the movements of building users as part of the architecture's motive.

The theme of hiding and revealing through axonometric projection will be developed further in Chapter 4, where John Hejduk explicitly manipulates our expectations of the convention in pursuit of an experiential architecture. What is clear here is that axonometric drawings were a crucial tool in Stirling's work, co-producing the architecture both allowing and determining aspects of his formal compositions. The drawing convention is not solely responsible for the architecture, of course (he uses the full range of architectural drawing conventions), but it does contribute to it. Axonometric drawings are particularly suited to Stirling's interchangeable materiality; interior promenades; and collages of blocky elements. The drawings are in evidence both as working process and final post-construction re-presentation of his works to establish the importance of his architecture, enchanting potential clients into hiring the firm.

Notes

1. It is worth noting here that in his discussion of Stirling (Moneo, R. 2004. *Theoretical Anxiety and Design Strategies in the Work of Eight Contemporary Architects*. Cambridge, Massachusetts: MIT Press, pp. 8–49), focused on the shift from plan to section, Rafael Moneo does not mention axonometric or other forms of parallel projection used by Stirling. I argue that this is

40 Stirling's axonometric traps

something of an oversight, and that what he writes off as mere 'extrusions' are, in fact, sophisticated volumetric manipulations central to the development of Stirling's designs.

2. Eisenman, Peter. 2008. *Ten Canonical Buildings 1950–2000*. New York: Rizzoli.

3. Stirling, James. 1996 [1975]. *James Stirling: Buildings and Projects, 1950–1974*. London: Thames and Hudson
Stirling, James. 1994. *James Stirling: Buildings and Projects, 1975–1992*. London: Thames and Hudson

4. See also Reeser Lawrence's account of the drawings (2012:95), where she asserts that the choice of axonometric is far from accidental, and represents a deliberate part of Stirling's design process which allowed for overall composition and articulation of individual elements. Leicester was designed *in axonometric*, and was not post-rationalisation as suggested by Krier.
Similarly, Baker (2011:xv) notes from his discussion with Stirling's partner Michael Wilford, that drawing was crucial to communication within the office, that it formed the starting point of discussion and allowed for the design process to be shared amongst members of the team. Drawings come first, a large series of sketches are made, until something emerges that is worth continuing. It is only then that any kind of reflection or intellectualisation takes place. Stirling would work in isolation to begin with, taking it to others in the office once he was happy with how far it had developed.

5. See Maxwell, (1998:108–111) for a brief account alongside drawings; Girouard (1998:231) notes that the eventual failure of the scheme came at a bad time for the practice, losing out on both the Getty Center to Richard Meier, the Sainsbury wing of the National Gallery in London to Robert Venturi (partly on political grounds), and made Stirling wary of further projects in Italy.

6. The role of tracing paper in architectural drawing practice is discussed in relation to this project's variations in Lucas(2017b:116–137).

7. Gell, Alfred. 1999. "Vogel's Net: Traps as Artworks and Artworks as Traps" in *The Art of Anthropology: Essays and Diagrams*. London: London School of Economics Monographs on Social Anthropology, Athlone Press, pp. 187–214.

8. Elsewhere, Gell (1998:84) discusses examples of how complex patterns are understood to act upon the world, providing a variety of wards from evil in different circumstances. One instance is given of Celtic knotwork patterns, complex overlapping cords which are carved in stone and said to be so enticing to devils and demons that they are immediately attracted to them, seeking to solve the puzzle of how the knot works. Gell describes this process as 'demonic fly paper'.

9. Evans, Robin. 1995. *The Projective Cast: Architecture and Its Three Geometries*. Cambridge, Massachusetts: MIT Press.
Pérez-Gómez, Alberto & Pelletier, Louise. 1997. *Architectural Representation and the Perspective Hinge*. Cambridge, Massachusetts: MIT Press.

10. See Lucas (2002:4.3) for more on the intersections between theories of suture and architecture. The cinematic theory of suture (borrowed from a medical term, simply 'to stitch up'), considers the means of stitching the spectator into the action at hand. The relationship between narrative and spectator is the essence of suture; the codes which stitch the spectator *into* the narrative. In classic fiction film, certain methods are used. The system of shot/reverse-angle shot is a primary means of suture. The first shot, through a matching of eye lines, positions the spectator as the one looking, from character A to character B. The next shot, the reverse shot, positions the spectator as character B. We adopt the position of what our initial character looked at. The off-screen space is visualised; it comes into view, an illusion of space beyond that which

we see on screen is constructed, thereby placing us within the text. The shot/reverse-shot also returns us to the subject of the return of gaze. It is worth noting the similarity in language between the regular axonometric drawing and the *reverse-angle* often used to describe worm's eye drawings.

11. See Lucas (2002:3.9–34) for more on the intersections between narratology and concepts of retardation in architecture. The story can actively block events through retardation, slowing the reveal of information; this is the means by which it serves the story to occlude the viewer from certain story events, such as the developing details of a suspense story. These are kept from the viewer until such a time as the protagonist discovers them or reveals their findings to another character.

    Retardation prevents a situation of totality, allowing the story to unfold in a carefully controlled manner, building the expectations of the audience and operating to either reinforce or to surprise through use of this expectation. Every story employs the strategy of impedance/retardation to postpone the world in some way. This allows the story to develop over time. Generally, the denouement, is kept from the viewer. The controlled construction of the story world by retarding certain plot events is the means by which most narratives are constructed, rather than attempting to achieve a simultaneous presentation of all events of the time and space. An excellent example of this occurs in Christopher Nolan's *Memento* (2001) in which the world is created and recreated according to the protagonists' neurological condition; according to which he cannot make new memories.

    Film theory is also explored as a way in to Stirling's architecture by Jerome Todd Salter, who explores the theory of image and temporality in Deleuze's (1992, 1994) *Cinema* books with relation to Stirling: Salter, Todd Jerome. 2012. "James Stirling's Architecture and the Post-War Crisis of Movement" in *Deleuze Studies*. Vol. 6, No. 1, pp. 55–71. Salter's argument rests on Deleuze's concept of a crisis of movement in 20th-century aesthetics. The focus for Salter is the ramp as a figure, placing it between Deleuze and Guattari's smooth and striated spaces (1998), as was intended by the authors; an intermixed rather than dialectic condition where the space is understood as a framing device by the building user, but a destabilising one. The paper is rather limited in its understanding of the drawings themselves, however, relegating some to 'representational' strategies: plans, elevations; whilst secretions and axonometrics are described as 'expressive' in a similarly limited description. The argument can, regardless of the naivety regarding drawing practices and their place in architectural design, discourse, and theory, be applied successfully to the drawings themselves.

12. We shall see further applications of montage theory in Chapter 7 when discussing the work of Cedric Price.

13. Satter, T. J. 2012. "James Stirling's Architecture and the Post-War Crisis of Movement" in *Deleuze Studies*, Vol. 6, No. 1, pp. 55–71.

14. Deleuze uses cinema to build a taxonomy of images in this two-volume work. See Chapter 7 for more on this.

15. Moneo, Rafael. 2005. *Theoretical Anxiety and Design Strategies in the Work of Eight Contemporary Architects*. Cambridge, Massachusetts: MIT Press. see also Satter (2012:55–71).

16. Rowe, Colin & Koetter, Fred. 1978. *Collage City*. Cambridge, Massachusetts: MIT Press.

17. Baker, Geoffrey H. 2011. *The Architecture of James Stirling and his Partners James Gowan and Michael Wilford: a Study of Architectural Creativity in the Twentieth Century*. London: Routledge, p. 234.

42 *Stirling's axonometric traps*

18. See for example: Jencks, Charles. "A Note on the Drawings", in Stirling, James et al. 1981. *James Stirling: Architectural Design Profile.* London: Academy Editions/St Martin's Press, pp. 50–55, where he reads the buildings as combining the contextual Schinkelesque ground of stone—rendered as a 'veneer' of alternating travertine and sandstone; with De Stijl references in the powder-coated steel canopy in its bright colour and angular geometry.
19. This is a relatively common form of representation in video games, from arcade games such as *Zaxxon* (Sega 1982) and *Q*bert* (Gottlieb 1982) to ZX Spectrum games such as *Knight Lore* (Ultimate 1984) and a more recent example of a mobile app like *Monument Valley* (Ustwo Games 2014) which exploits the parallel projection to create puzzles.
20. Satter (2012:55–71).
21. Bedford, Joseph. 2010. "Stirling's Rational Facade: Self-Division within the Reading of Garches and Jaoul" in *Architectural Research Quarterly (ARQ)*, Vol. 14, No. 2, pp. 153–164.

3 Scale and Gesamtkunstwerk in JJP Oud

3.1 Oud's relationship with De Stijl and International Modernism

Whilst axonometric drawing predates the Modern era, it was the 20th century which saw the greatest proliferation of this convention. JJP Oud is used here to discuss the modernist preference for axonometric drawing more generally before moving on to discuss the substance of his contribution: the variety of scales at which he was comfortable working.

As an architect of the De Stijl movement, Oud is immersed in discussions of the totality of the work of art, as shown in his projects, which range from district-scale urban design projects all the way down to furniture designs.

As such, this chapter explores the historical context of the axonometric drawing and its affordances. Following from this is the fundamental idea of scale. Oud was a proponent of standardisation in architecture, seeing the potential efficiency of common detailing as well as larger architectural elements—but always with an eye to the spiritual role of building and dwelling.

Throughout his output, Oud draws in parallel projection,[1] the axonometric drawing is more than a presentation drawing for Oud, but clearly part of his thinking process in arranging geometries, assembling discreet parts, and composing his largely asymmetric plans. Iterations of drawings can be seen throughout his work, where variations are produced serially on tracing paper, becoming ever more detailed throughout the very rational process. There is, throughout his career, a variety of projections: isometric, axonometric, and oblique are each used when necessary—this is never a stylistic decision, but one of pragmatism related to which planes or faces are primary in each case. The use of axonometric drawing, which became the more or less settled style of modernism over time, had not yet been decided, meaning that each drawing was the result of a decision process over precisely which form of parallel projection was the most appropriate.

In examining Oud's work, it is important to explore why he is the focus rather than one of the better known members of De Stijl. One answer is simple: Oud's architecture is worthy of examination in its own right, and it

44   Scale and Oud

affords a discussion of a crucial theme within this work—of scale. This is an issue not explicitly explored by Gerrit Rietveld and Theo van Doesburg, but one which I was keen to address within this volume. In short, other members of De Stijl are reserved for a future volume where their planar vortices and use of colour will feature strongly.

> To Oud it was gospel truth that a building was, as the Germans say, 'einmalig', that it could occur only once, for whatever purpose it might be intended. Therefore every commission demanded his whole and undivided attention. (1965:5)[2]

This specificity and contextuality goes some way to explaining the interest which Oud gave his projects across a full range of scales.

Ornamentation is a concern within Oud's work, a source of much controversy in his later career. Despite the prevailing opinion in early modernist circles, Oud does not take as hard a line as the likes of Adolf Loos, who devoted some consideration to the idea of *Ornament and Crime*[3]; even before the notorious example of the Shell Building (1938–1949) in his later career, Oud experimented with fully architectonic means of adornment, using detailing around doorways to convey a sense of decoration without the application of traditional figurative sculptural form (1965:10).

Oud's early work brought him into contact with Willem Marinus Dudok and Hendrik Petrus Berlage, under whose influence he drew inspiration from Frank Lloyd Wright, although he was critical of his 'picturesque' compositions in the country house projects. It was under Berlage that Oud began to develop his position regarding the monumental in architecture, a concern for this chapter regarding scale as we shall see.

His friendship with Theo van Doesburg introduced him to the wider group of artists of De Stijl, with Oud lending a greater understanding of architecture to van Doesburg. The aim was to develop a language of abstraction through the collaborations of different creative practitioners, eventually eradicating the boundaries between those disciplines and also, famously, between art and life in general. Oud's trajectory is a little different from the core De Stijl group, and whilst there is a significant move towards planar geometry, his work remained faithful to both Wright and Berlage and working as a Rotterdam city architect, at the scale of districts and neighbourhoods as well as individual units.

Giedion, in his history of the modern movement[4] (2008:426) makes this connection between Frank Lloyd Wright and De Stijl, with Berlage and Dudok adopting some of his ideas in 1910, this forms a basis for Oud and De Stijl, with van Doesburg also writing an early article introducing Wright's work to Europe. He is a stimulus for new thinking, a kind of catalyst, rather than an influence. He argues that rather than borrow directly from Wright's approach, for De Stijl, it suggested potentiality for self-realisation rather than direct adoption of his organic architectural principles, so distinct from European modernism of the time. Giedion's continued discussion of De Stijl's debt to Wright, discusses it as stripped of his ornament, and the group borrowed his organisational strategy of 'the house as a flowing space bounded by vertical and horizontal planes had been fully taken and understood' (2008:590).

In 1936, Oud's international esteem was at its apex[5], he was so highly thought of that he was offered the post of the chair of architecture at Harvard University, a post that was later (famously) to go to Walter Gropius. This was part of Philip Johnson's campaign courting Oud, and offering him work in the United States. Rejecting the academic post, Oud was more interested in remaining as a professional architect and turned his attention more and more to urban issues, large housing estates such as Bijdorp. His process came to the conclusion that there needed to be more order to the schemes than merely an accumulation of individual units.

This was in the context of CIAM's move towards a 'scientific' model of city planning, but whilst Oud was resistant to this development, he acted as a moderating influence, arguing that there was a lack of space for the artistry and associated emotion in city planning if this were to be the only model pursued. Giedion (2008:800) notes Oud's use of courtyards as a way of 'humanising' the blocks indicated on plans such as those prepared by Berlage for South Amsterdam, and his contribution to the Wiessenhof project alongside Mies van der Rohe and Le Corbusier demonstrated a modesty of approach, with delicately detailed row houses for workers designed for the project showcasing the housing of the modern movement at the time. Giedion associates Oud with the rebirth of the idea of town planning, the example of Amsterdam and the Netherlands more broadly is taken further by the others within the modern movement, but this association with the town and city as much as with the individual units is a key move which Oud is representative of, and which is, therefore, crucial in terms of discussing his scaled drawings, ranging from furniture and detailing through to complete neighbourhood plans.

> Oud saw in urban planning the emancipation of the statistical survey. In 1935 Oud argued for a method of urban planning that would use the possibilities found within the modern city to dramatise the contemporary cityscape, such as high-rise construction, rowhousing, viaduct overpasses, and the American parkway. An argument for the cityscape as foundation of visual and emotional experiences. It is within this urban-planning perspective that Oud, throughout the 1930s, concentrated in the significance held by the 'monumental' building for the cityscape. (Taverne & Broekhuizen, 1995:100)[6]

It was in this context that the Shell (originally BIM) building in The Hague was developed: critiquing the Amsterdam extension plan by van Eesteren of 1934 and submitting his proposal to the Amsterdam City Hall competition,

46 Scale and Oud

where his entry was judged very harshly by Le Corbusier. This might be a contributory factor to Oud's return to more classically composed and decorated architecture with the Shell Building: a response to the gatekeepers of modernism combined with a regard for the urban design of his architecture, a combination which earlier supporters such as Johnson were to feel as a betrayal of his values.

His was an alternative way of achieving the aims of Mondrian and van Eesteren and van Doesburg, whose *Neoplastic Architecture* and *contra-constructions* respectively pursued a 'spatial image consisting only of coloured planes and proportions' (1995:116); Oud's approach is to underline the differences between architecture and the other arts and to ground his work in the architectonics of Berlage: the wall has significance, and has a surface treatment with appropriate levels of articulation, but the wall is different from the plane, even if he was to borrow from the palette of De Stijl, in an applied rather than abstract fashion.

Still, the modernist establishment rounded on the building, with Johnson, who had helped Oud financially at times, such was his regard for him, echoed the disappointment which Giedion expressed for the building, perhaps more wounding to Oud given the personal nature of their relationship (1995:124). Johnson read it explicitly as a return to Dutch tradition in the manner of Berlage, rather than 'International' as Oud had claimed for his architecture. This was, as Taverne and Broekhuizen note, symptomatic of a larger crisis in international architecture in the 1940s: what did modern architecture mean in the postwar period? It could be argued, however, that the contextual and regional architecture under revival here prefigured later movements in postmodernism and critical regionalism: ways of reconciling modernism with its immediate environment, its historical context. The furore caused in the international architectural press appears to have been stylistic in nature: that modernism had become a style of architecture with its own orthodoxies to follow.

Given that his reputation appeared to rest on the response to this hostile coverage, Oud, taking time, responded to his critics by firmly stating the principles he attended to in the design of the Shell Building. Responding to the editor of the US-based periodical, *The Architectural Record,* in 1946, Oud eventually articulated his position in 1951:

> the significance of architecture as a symbol, symmetry as the foundation of form, and emotion as the ultimate objective of the architectonic creation. The first argument refers to the social status of the commission; the second pertains to architecture as a craft and a science; the third theme involves the role of the architect in modern society. (1995:144)

Oud rejects the postwar desire to see architecture as social engineering, and holds on to the idea of architecture as art, architect as artist.

3.2 Gesamtkunstwerk and scale

The idea of the Gesamtkunstwerk has its origins in the aesthetic theory of Richard Wagner. Architecture has had its engagements with this idea of the total work of art, emerging from a period of crisis as described by Mari Hvattum[7]. Here, it is related to German romantic philosophy and the concept of the zeitgeist or spirit of the times. The desire for a step change in artistic thinking and production required a kind of breakdown—crises described by cultural critics of the time including Semper.

> The *Gesamtkunstwerk*, as envisaged by Wagner, was simultaneously a manifestation and an actualisation of modern society, sublimating the modern era into an aesthetic totality. (2013:8)

Hvattum notes that these total works inevitably fail to resolve the outstanding issue, and, in time, revert to being considered as styles with rules and common features. This is, as noted previously, happened when an orthodoxy emerged within modernist architecture, with Oud falling foul of this when he stepped outside of the accepted parameters. Dalibor Vesely[8] expresses the term as a synthesis of the arts, producing a unity of experience. Citing Gadamer, Vesely problematises the direct relationship between Gesamtkunstwerk and decorative arts, noting that the introduction of the term coincided with a move towards a more holistic aesthetic understanding: arts working in concert with one another rather than embellishing one another. The argument takes us toward the idea of architecture itself, and Goethe's proclamation, prefiguring Eisenman as we shall see in Chapter 6, that architecture has the status of an 'autonomous art' (Vesely, 2004:330–331).

> This is a point of departure for a better understanding of modern attempts to restore a sense of wholeness, particularly in the sphere of architecture. The failure of these attempts is manifested in the repeated effort to establish a collaboration between architecture, sculpture, painting, and other arts in the form of *Gesamtkunstwerk* and in the more recent effort to simulate a concrete human situation in the context of virtual space. (2004:331)

The relationship between Oud and De Stijl can be complicated in terms of this ambition, as this totality runs counter to the idea of the fragmentary. Vesely argues for a continuity between the total work and the romance underlying the fragment, and that the mental act required to reconstitute the whole from a series of fragments is an important intuition, a 'restorative mapping and articulation of the world' (2004:334).

Oud's approach to architecture had something of the Gesamtkunstwerk to it, however, as he engaged in the single-minded design of each project

48   Scale and Oud

at a range of scales. This engagement consumed Oud to the extent that he would only take on a single project at a time, and never return to unsuccessful projects as the root of a new proposal—each piece of work had its own place and time. Discussing Oud's relationship with Mondrian, Alan Colquhoun[9] notes that the intended collaborations between the arts central to De Stijl were fraught with difficulty and friction. Mondrian made claims for painting as superior to architecture, as architecture retained its status as a form of representation, architecture could not yet free itself from reality (a feature which Oud found to be both true and fundamental to architecture in a more positive sense). In Jean-Louis Cohen's account of Oud's work[10], it is rather tellingly titled *Oud and Rietveld, from Furniture to House Design*. This shift in scale is important to our discussion of Oud here—that his work exploits a broad range of scales in the interests of producing a 'total work of art'.

To this end, Oud had a close working relationship with Gerrit Rietveld as well as producing his own furniture designs. These are incorporated into the projects naturally alongside the general plans and elevations, urban settings and interiors. The building was to be designed as a complete unit, with everything belonging to it. Furniture was, of course, an important aspect of De Stijl, with Rietveld's influential *Red and Blue Armchair* of 1918 being a particularly clear expression of the planar design principles of the group. Rietveld describes the chair as being 'made to the end of showing that a thing of beauty, e.g., a spatial object, could be made of nothing but straight, machined materials.' (Rietveld in Cohen 2012:142). Rietveld made his own transition from being described as the 'cabinetmaker' of De Stijl to one of its most important architects, designing the Schöder House in 1924.

Oud and Rietveld maintained a close friendship[11] and partnership in the 1920s and 1930s, with Oud asking Rietveld to produce furniture for his housing projects as well as producing his own designs. This is reinforced by accounts of designs commissioned for Spangen in Rotterdam (1918–1919) (van Zijl, 2010:37). By the time of the Wiessenhof projects (1927), Rietveld was better known as an architect than a cabinetmaker (earlier periods of his career were marked by difficulties with clients, leading him to declare that for now, he would rather design chairs). Oud wrote to Rietveld on the Szekely House:

> I will always find your "inventions" immensely attractive, as you are well aware, but it sometimes bothered me that they seemed so terribly like a "model" or were so much more like sculpture than architecture. Here...you are a true architect. We were enchanted by the beautiful, light house and by the simple way you are now going to be doing things. (in van Zijl, 2010:124)

Together with the earlier discussion of Oud's reinstatement of town planning as a concern for architecture, we can see a broad approach in each scheme, an interest in each room and its contents, the arrangements of those rooms as a compositionally sound piece of architecture, and how it works in arrangement with other buildings and districts. Colquhoun notes of the drawings produced by De Stijl that:

> In these drawings [*counter-construction ii*, 1924 and *Hôtel Particulier*, 1923], axonometry is more than a useful graphic tool. it is not only the method of representation that does not privilege one part of the building over another (for example, the facade over the interior). In 'real life', the only way to recall such a house in its totality would be to trace and retrace its interior spaces in times, as in the case of Loos's *Raumplan* houses. Axonometry converts this temporal, semi-conscious process into an experience that is instantaneous and conscious. For van Doesburg these drawings seem to have symbolised his techno-mystical vision of an architecture identical with the flow of lived experience. They were idealised representations of the ineffable. Axonometry was also fundamental to van Doesburg's attempts to represent four-dimensional space. (2002:118)

Whilst Oud's work is at the less radical end of De Stijl, his work still adheres to the group's manifesto: in particular, the equality of elements within each drawing, and across the set of drawings from detail through to site context. He retains some of the influence of Dudok and Berlage as well as Wright throughout his career, and a pragmatism in the face of the more idealist wing of De Stijl and international Modernism results in a nuanced career which develops towards later movements of Postmodernism and Critical Regionalism.

Scale in architecture tends to be treated more as tacit knowledge than as a theme for research. Moore and Allen[12] give an account which outlines some useful areas for consideration with reference to Oud. Finding that the term is subject to a wide range of meanings within architecture (much less tackling any other disciplines which use the term), Moore and Allen find a common root in the ways in which scale is used within architectural language:

> whenever the word is used, something is being compared with something else. The large-scale housing development is large in comparison to an average housing development. The scale of the architectural drawing notes the size of the rendered building in comparison to the real thing. (1976:17)

The importance of comparison in the discussion of scale offers us a way to understand its varieties. Size, to Moore and Allen, is quite distinct from scale in that scale is *relative* size, always subject to comparison with something else. This relationship can be in terms of various forms

50   *Scale and Oud*

of comparison, and the authors provide us with a number of these possibilities:

> *Relative to the whole*
> *Relative to other parts*
> *Relative to the usual size*
> *Relative to human size*

Whilst this might appear to be self-evident and not worthy of consideration, it is an often overlooked element of our architectural culture: that scale is spoken of a great deal and passed down from one architect to another without really questioning the usefulness or operation of the term. The term can be argued to date back as far as Alberti, as Rykwert et al.[13] note in their glossary on the terms used in their translation of the classic work. Their translation of *modus* as *scale* already contains the possibility for discussing the proportions of things as well as the reduction in size required for a drawing of a city block to appear on a sheet of paper.

Oud's work clearly demonstrates a broad range of working scales, meaning that his projects are deeply contextual and consider the day-to-day operation of the building. This interrelationship of scales is embedded within his working process, much more evident than the more radical members of De Stijl with whom he was working. There is a pragmatism at the root of his working across scales, and a method of single-mindedness which prevented him from working on more than one project at a time. The interiors have a clear regard for the relationship between architecture and the human scale, even in a large building, the points of contact such as balustrades, door handles, and furniture, were every bit as important to Oud as the interactions of buildings within an urban context. By establishing this web of relationships through his series of design investigations, he can work to a common approach across each of these concerns, allowing human comfort to have its place in the urban scale, and efficiency manifesting in the interiors.

3.3 Oud's interiors

Starting with Oud's drawings of furniture and interiors, we can see that there is a desire to present the interiors together with the furniture; that the chairs and tables designed by Oud were often produced with certain arrangements in mind, and not as a 'kit of parts' to be arranged as desired.

Oud's 1933 collaboration with Metz & Co. resulted in a small run of furniture manufactured largely in steel, a material new to the fairly traditional furniture company, which had to outsource the production of the work to another company (annotations on the production drawings suggest that a German firm was selected for this work). Oud felt compelled to address the expectations people might have for comfort in chairs in a press release defending the springiness and lightweight nature of the steel

Scale and Oud 51

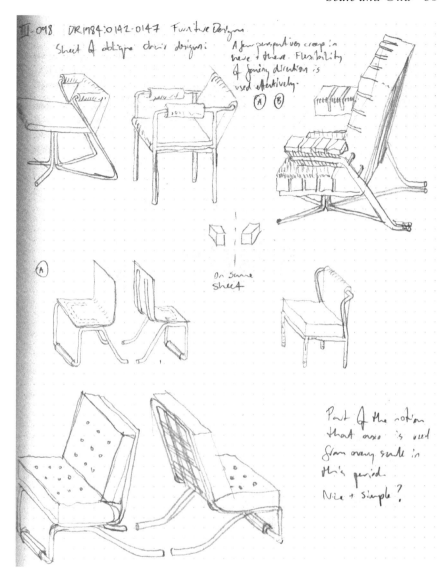

Figure 3.1 Redrawing of DR1984:0142, chair designs for Metz & Co. by Oud (1933).

construction—quite different in nature to the norm of heavy, solid frames which would remain in place.

These designs[14] are prepared in oblique projection, with the vertical plane (elevation) as the primary face, rather than maintaining the horizontal plan as the undistorted face (see figure 3.1). A form of cabinet projection is used, describing the range of armchairs with suggestions of materiality throughout (thinner bent planes suggesting plywood, conventional upholstery

52 Scale and Oud

indicated by buttons and quilting on thicker pieces, and tubular steel used throughout). The angle of projection shifts on the page using a range from 30°, 45°, and 60° left to the same angles on toward the right, sometimes showing the rear of the chair with its webbing support. Some of the designs left this support completely exposed—a move towards complete honesty in the materiality of the furniture.

Figure 3.2 Redrawing of DR1984:0063-069, interior study for MJI de Jonge van Ellemeet's office, Rotterdam City Hall.

The variability of the projection is entirely practical for these illustrations, which were indications of the furniture to be produced rather than detailed specifications. There are some repeated motifs, such as the way the steel pierces the padded seat materials, the wrapping of wooden cylinders around the foot of two examples, used as armrests, and on the elongated horizontally sloping legs. Bakelite was also used in some of the models, which, like the applied timber elements, allowed for some experiments in colour. Two designs make use of a central support consisting of four steel members which bend up from the floor, and the continuous linearity possible with the steel is used to aesthetic effect.

Drawn in measured axonometric, Figures 3.2 and 3.3 is typical of Oud's interiors. The angle of the drawing is 60/30°, and the series is drawn on tracing paper, with a clear progression showing that these are design

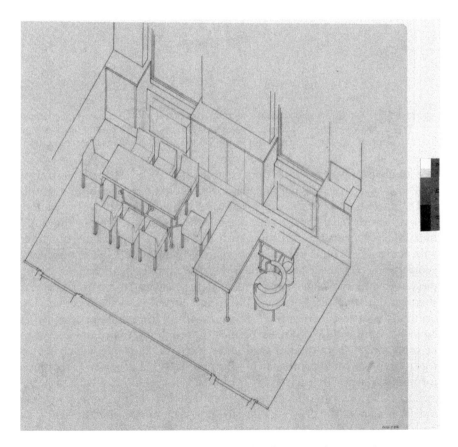

Figure 3.3 JJP Oud, axonometric drawing for furniture for MJI de Jonge van Ellemeet's office in Rotterdam City Hall, Netherlands, 1930–1931; graphite on tracing paper, 46.8 × 52.6 cm; DR1984:0067, Canadian Centre for Architecture.

54 *Scale and Oud*

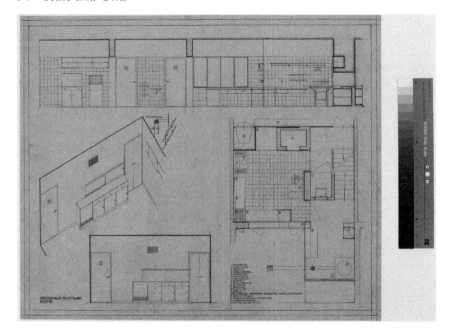

Figure 3.4 JJP Oud, Elevations, plan and axonometric for a kitchen for terraced housing, Weissenhofsiedlung, Stuttgart, Germany, 1927; pen and black ink on linen, 63.5 × 77.7 cm; DR1984:0070, Canadian Centre for Architecture.

development drawings rather than client-facing works. The room is drawn in schematic detail showing the positions of doors, the fenestration details and cabinets built in to the walls. The arrangement is for an L-shaped desk (complete with wastepaper basket and telephone, the side table having additional shelves for storage) with an armchair for the client and a meeting table with six seats. Various possibilities are tested, and subtle alterations in the geometry of each piece tested alongside some quite radical changes: examples show chunky wedge-shaped chairs alongside circular forms, rectilinear shapes, and composites bringing linear and curved elements together. The armchair is different from the meeting furniture in each case, designed to be more comfortable for longer periods. Throughout, the chairs appear to be supported by bent tubular steel again, including the table, which has six legs in a complicated arrangement of supports with a crossbar at foot level forming a Y shape on each end.

The variations often coexist with one another on the same page, the indeterminacy of the drawing allowing it to remain open for further adaptation. A rounded backrest formed from padding wrapped around a semicircular steel section is terminated in different ways in one example, testing how much it needs to remain open and what the possibilities for extending around the sitter would be. Several sheets include plan drawings and further sketch perspectives in order to resolve some issues with the geometry,

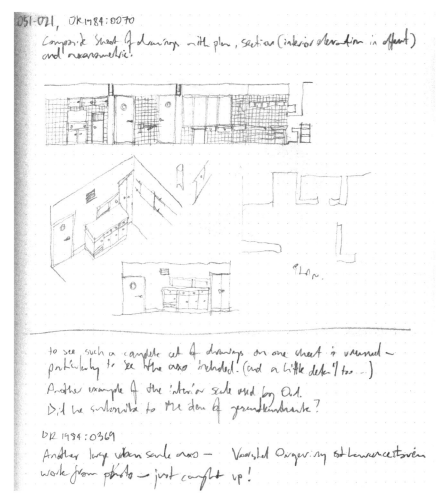

Figure 3.5 Redrawing of DR1984:0070 and DR1984:0552, composite sheets of drawings and blueprints describing the kitchens of Oud's Wiessenhof houses for Stuttgart (1927).

but notably no people ever appear to occupy the seats; they are suggested, and scale indicated by the chairs, but never explicitly.

The combination of drawings on one sheet (figures 3.4 and 3.5) efficiently conveys many of the features of the row housing interiors, with the kitchen bearing a distinctly Corbusier-inspired aesthetic with its porthole windows and simple, clean, tiled walls. The single axonometric shows more subtle detail and speaks to the attention to detail Oud was known for in his single-mindedly designed work. Informed by the interest in hygiene in early modernism, Oud's kitchen is tiled carefully on the floors and walls in order to be easier to maintain, and the drawing includes details such as

56 *Scale and Oud*

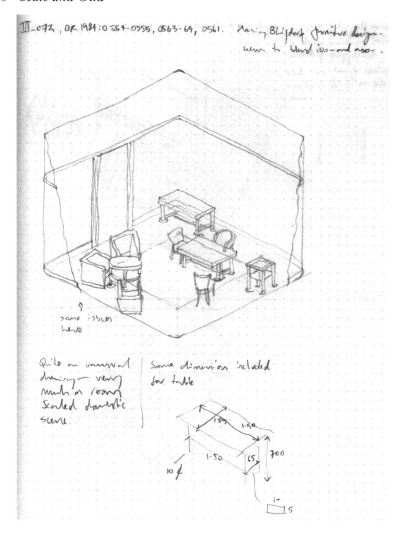

Figure 3.6 Redrawing of DR1984:0561, isometric drawing of director's office in the Shell Building, The Hague (1938–1949).

the thickness of the applied tiling with its small curved tiles, which handle the transition from floor to wall, and pot hangers, draining boards, and cupboard doors are all fully described[15].

The director's office for the Shell Building (figure 3.6) consists of an annotated reprographic copy of the original drawing, the annotations showing the profiles of several elements in detailed cross-section, and including some measurements for the table. As noted earlier, the Shell Building represented a shift in Oud's style, and this extends to these details: the furniture has timber supports and metal fittings are now decorative, the character of

Scale and Oud 57

the furniture is much heavier, but still gives details of the room some prominence. The curved edge to the corners of the room along with the simple banding decoration on the walls suggests an almost art deco approach.

3.4 Oud's exteriors

Two drawings of Oud's scheme for the Second Liberal Christian Lyceum (1949–1956) in The Hague (figure 3.7) demonstrate some of his work at an intermediate scale, for a large school. The first of these drawings shows the overall composition with its asymmetrical arrangement of four primary volumes offset by the small house.

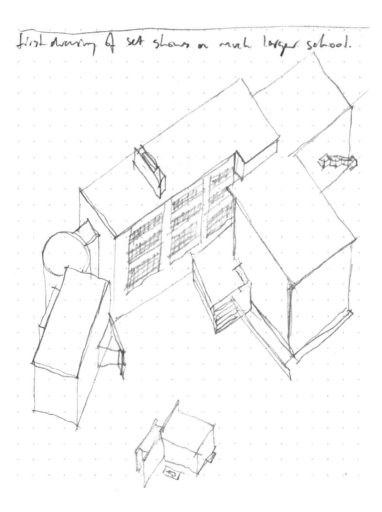

Figure 3.7 Redrawing of DR1984:0376, axonometric drawing of school project including the porter's house.

58 *Scale and Oud*

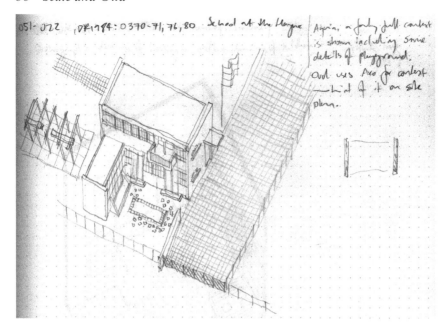

Figure 3.8 Redrawing of DR1984:0379, axonometric drawing of the porter's house.

The volumes, an *L* shape, large rectilinear block, connecting drum, and smaller block set off at an angle of around 30° to the others are fully articulated with large glazed areas and stepped entries. Unusually for Oud, there is no other context to this drawing, something restored in the second drawing, which shows the school's generously scaled porter's house in greater detail (figure 3.8), including external paving, a small garden with pool and stone slabs, a trellis area with seating, and some of the external fencing for the school.

Again, the organisation of volumes is important to Oud, the enclosures of the garden, the address of the house to the main approach with a simple visual cue of a protruding slab over the house's door. The two-storey house has an additional single-floor addition, a secluded and overlooked garden with a balcony overlooking it. There is an attention to detail which can be read in the drawing, presenting a very civilised vision of an educational establishment.

Oud was better known for his housing projects, and this unrealised scheme (figure 3.9) demonstrates many of his strategies. The project had stalled before Oud replaced the original architects, producing a large-scale plan for over 300 dwellings arranged as a perimeter block with row houses on the interior. An additional set of homes for retired people were proposed, but the scheme eventually failed due to disinvestment in housing by the government of the time. The same attention to external surfaces can be observed in this drawing.

Scale and Oud 59

Figure 3.9 Redrawing of DR1984:557, axonometric drawing of Blijdorp workers' housing (1931–1932), Rotterdam.

One way of handling the scale whilst retaining sufficient detail in the drawings is to provide typical fragments of detailing which would be repeated throughout the entire project. This way, we are presented with axonometric drawings of incomplete objects, representing elements which were typical—exemplars and proof of concept for the project as a whole.

60 *Scale and Oud*

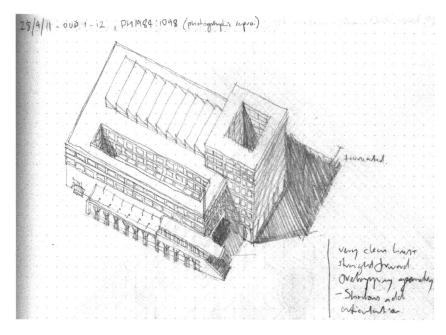

Figure 3.10 Redrawing of PH1984:1098, axonometric drawing of the new Stock Exchange Building, Rotterdam (1926).

Oud has a consideration for the placement and composition of elements within his buildings, as developed and demonstrated by his design and presentation drawings respectively. Some buildings, such as the Rotterdam Stock Exchange competition entry (figure 3.10) do present the building in isolation, absent of any wider contextual information.

The tight, compressed composition of perimeter blocks is given mass by the use of shadows, and scale through the description of the fenestration. The asymmetry typical of Oud's work is in evidence here, with a factory aesthetic emerging from the repetitive nature of the facades. At this scale, Oud's concerns for the totality of the design remain in evidence, however, the ground floor is treated differently to the upper storeys, robbing the repetition of its evenness of value, the entrance is marked clearly with a raised pier covered by a projecting slab. Oud's *monumentality* in architecture is very much in evidence here, not through the sheer scale of the building but through the use of purely architectonic means to convey aspects of the design clearly and plainly to the user.

Oud's redevelopment proposal for Berlage's 1919 Vredenburg Square in Utrecht (figure 3.11) sought to resolve issues with traffic flow and the relationship with the nearby Jaarbeurs Exhibition Complex unanticipated by the original architects. Whilst unbuilt, the project shows some of the ways in which Oud handled urban schemes.

Scale and Oud 61

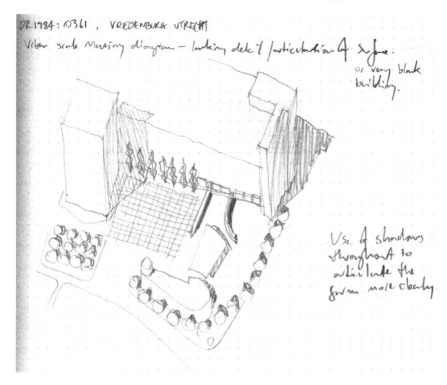

Figure 3.11 Redrawing of DR1984:0361, axonometric drawing of Vredenburg Square Project.

Where Oud's work at smaller scales tends towards careful detailing, there is an almost abstract quality to this drawing, with the only real reference point as to the size of the project being the use of planting across the site. Details are often what gives the viewer a cue as to the scale of a drawing, how to read it, and how to place yourself into it in order to understand how it might work. Similar, more resolved projects such as Hofplein in Rotterdam (Taverne 2001:430[16]) have a common approach of describing the shadows cast by buildings over the site, a consideration absent from the smaller scale drawings. This is of course particularly pertinent at this scale of the design, and wholly appropriate to include. Oud's pragmatism shows that each drawing depicts what it needs to show and no more or less.

The completed project drawings restore some of the detail (Taverne et al. 2001:472), with the square's West entrance marked by a 12-storey tower and a curved building designed for the South-East corner (and subject to some variations as the project was developed). The abstracted versions of the drawings demonstrate the initial stages of the urban design project as

62   Scale and Oud

compositional exercises, the interactions of elements more important than individual details, but Oud's consideration of a range of scales, particularly within the existing city context of Utrecht, mark him out as a different kind of architect to many of his peers, concerned with his architecture working *with* the existing city rather than against it.

Working across a range of scales allowed Oud to consider the human nature of his architecture holistically. By producing fully detailed interiors, the everyday lives of inhabitants could be considered and appreciated. Crossing into larger urban scale drawings, Oud also shows how his works integrate with their urban context, with considerations for flows of people and traffic as well as a response to the existing fabric of the city. This sets Oud apart from many of his contemporaries in addressing some of the failings of modernism and the International Style. He recognised that architecture needed to remain human, and that one of the ways of achieving this was to approach the architectural design project at a full range of scales.

Notes

1. Several examples of which can be found in Stamm, Günther. 1984. *J. J. P. Oud: Bauten und Projekte 1906 bis 1963*. Mainz: Bei Florian Kupferberg.
2. Wiekart, K. 1965. *J. J. P. Oud: Art and Architecture in the Netherlands*. Amsterdam: J. M. Meulenhoff.
   Beckett, Jane, et al. 1978. *The Original Drawings of J. J. P. Oud*. London: The Architectural Association.
3. Loos, Adolf. 1998. *Ornament and Crime*. Riverside, California: Ariadne Press.
4. Giedion, Siegfried. 2008 [1940]. *Space, Time & Architecture: The Growth of a New Tradition*. Cambridge, Massachusetts: Harvard University Press.
5. Giedion going as far as to state that 'his [Corbusier's] houses do not match J.J.P. Oud's infinitely painstaking attention to detail' (2008:541).
6. Taverne, Ed & Broekhuizen, Dolf. 1995. *J. J. P. Oud's Shell Building: Design and Reception*. Rotterdam: NAi Publishers.
7. Hvattum, Mari. 2013. "Crisis and Correspondence: Style in the Nineteenth Century" in *Architectural Histories*, Issue 1(1), Vol. 21, pp. 1–8.
8. Vesely, Dalibor. 2004. *Architecture in the Age of Divided Representation: The Question of Creativity in the Shadow of Production*. Cambridge, Massachusetts: MIT Press, p. 86.
9. Colquhoun, Alan. 2002. *Modern Architecture*. Oxford: Oxford University Press, pp. 112–113.
10. Cohen, Jean-Louis. 2012. *The Future of Architecture Since 1889*. London: Phaidon, pp. 142–148.
11. Van Zijl, Ida. 2010. *Gerrit Rietveld*. London: Phaidon, p. 11.
12. Moore, Charles & Allen, Gerald. 1976. *Dimensions: Space, Shape & Scale in Architecture*. New York: Architectural Record Books.
13. Alberti, Leon Battista. 1988. *On the Art of Building in Ten Books*. Rykwert, J., Leach, N. & Tavernor, R. (Trans.). Cambridge, Massachusetts: MIT Press, p. 425.

14. For more on Oud's collaboration with Metz & Co., including photographs of the chairs depicted in the drawings, see Reinhartz-Tergau, Elisabeth. 1990. *J. J. P. Oud Achitect*. Rotterdam: Uitgeverij De Hef/ Museum Boymans-van Beuningen, pp. 90–110.
15. For more on this, including photographs of the kitchens depicted in the drawings (see Reinhartz-Tergau, 1990: 66–67).
16. Taverne, Ed, Wagenaar, Cor, de Vletter, Martien et al. 2001. *J. J. P. Oud Poëtisch Functionalist: Compleet Werk 1890–1963*. Rotterdam: NAi Uitgevers.

4 Occlusion and deliberately hidden lines: Hejduk's Wall House

4.1 Series of houses

This chapter will draw largely on a series of house designs completed by John Hejduk between 1954 and 1974. These houses are often part of a series, exploring similar issues and developing a range of responses to similar parameters. The chapter proceeds by cutting across this chronology, however, presenting works when they are relevant to the issue under discussion. The first group are known both as the *7 Houses* and *Texas Houses* after the title of a publication featuring them and as the 9 Square Houses after the pedagogical tool he developed from their design, and date from 1954 to 1962. These are followed by the Diamond Series of 1962–1967, where the square plan is set at 45° off the horizontal. During 1964 we see the first Wall House where rooms are distributed across an elongated upright element, a theme he returns to in a range of works. Further projects are described as fractions: 1/4, 1/2 and 3/4 Houses (1967–1970) or as compass points in the North East South West House (1978–1979). Hejduk's early works draw heavily on his interest in early modernism, particularly the Cubist and Constructivist movements.

The Texas Houses are a series which conform to Hejduk's nine-square composition (figure 4.1), which was later developed into a pedagogical tool. This is a problem which was presented to students at the Cooper Union. The arrangement underlines the fundamental positional meaning given to each sector of a subdivided square. Often assumed to render each element of equivalent value, Hejduk's position on the grid is that it immediately gives you perimeter, symmetry, and centrality as qualities. Each of these then has a spatial quality rather than completely equal value. In these projects, Hejduk insists that his work is not fantasy. This could be read as a bold statement given his reputation as a paper architect, building only rarely. It relates specifically to the Texas Houses, but could well inform our reading of the later works.

> I do not deal with fantasies. Architects always have to deal with the problem of gravity. That there is a grade plane. The grade is always there, you always have a problem of grade relative to a cubic configuration. You may want to have a floating cube, but it is very hard to have a floating cube when you have to deal with the problem of gravity. (1985:40)

Hejduk's Wall House   65

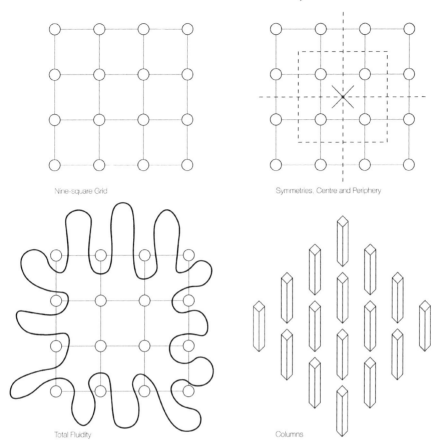

Figure 4.1 Redrawing of some examples of the nine-square grid problem as presented by Hejduk (1971).

Hejduk further explores these houses as 'the result of a search' concerned with form and space. The *nine-square problem* does not predate these works, but was one of the results of this process. The account given of the instructions[1] in the catalogue for the MoMA exhibition of 1971 (their first devoted to architectural pedagogy) explicitly instructs the student to engage with axonometric drawings as part of their investigation, drawing these together with plans in order to understand how two dimensions and three correspond with each other in the design process. The aim is for an indication of the construction to emerge from this exercise.

The problem gave students a grid of 16 columns defining nine squares, 16 feet apart centre to centre. The columns of the grid were set at 1 foot wide, giving overall dimensions of a 49-foot perimeter. The details of the column dimensions are pertinent, as this is one of the options for how the students are to handle the 'problem'—to build inside, in line with, or outside of the

66 Hejduk's Wall House

external grid. The relationship between the abstract grid and the structural grid asks the student questions which are grounded both in geometric understanding and the materiality of building. Writing on the problem, Timothy Love[2] and Alexander Caragonne situate it within a broader historical context, having its origins at the University of Texas School of Architecture[3] and influenced by Rudolf Wittkower's work on Palladio[4] examining the composition of his houses in tripartite bays. Colin Rowe[5] was also influential here, extending the procedures used by Wittkower into the analysis of modernist architecture. The more direct connection with Rowe links Hejduk to both Eisenman and Stirling, and the kit-of-parts approach (presented as something alternative to the nine-square by Love [2003], but I would argue that the problem implies a kit: grid; frame; post; beam; panel; centre; periphery; field; edge; line; plane; volume; extension; compression; shear [Hejduk 1971:7]) has its commonalities with one of the prevailing trends of the period as exemplified by Cedric Price. The frame serves as a datum here, and it could be argued that this conceptual grid is understood to have a presence no matter what form the subsequent architecture takes—either as organisational principles and hidden lines or as a tangible structure.

The exercise operated between the pragmatics of buildings and their construction, and the conceptual procedures essential to design. The aim was to embed planning as a crucial element of the architectural imagination, but more than this, to relate it immediately to the axonometric as a way of conceptualising space.

Hejduk describes the Texas Houses in terms of their fundamental elements, much like Eisenman's search for a nonreferential architectural language, and he pursues the post and lintel, the slab and wall, the ground plane and compressive forces. He continues to discuss these in the terms of the 9-square grid (1985:37–38), writing about the relationships of these elements, their proportions, symmetry, static and dynamic elements. Hejduk argues that these fundamentals were discovered by doing the projects, and did not prefigure them, positioning his architectural work as a form of research inquiry.

Writing on the work of the New York Five, Manfredo Tafuri[6] identifies Hejduk as one of a group of individualistic architects pursuing similar ideas of linguistic analogy and autonomous production of meaning in architecture. He finds in *House 10* a pursuit of Cubist signs, arbitrary and almost wilful in nature. Hejduk's experiments in extending the house along a path seems to Tafuri to be an extension of the project of montage (1976:38)[7], based in a 'neutral' concept of space. Hejduk himself argues that it is through these projects that he arrives at a non-neutral condition: the house projects are a process by which further elaborations of his architecture became possible. Tafuri argues, turning his attention to the Wall House and Bye House that the wall serves the same purpose as a point of montage in cinema, a rupture rather than a continuity.

Hejduk himself, when talking of the Diamond House, discusses the play of shifting from 90° to 45° angles when designing and presenting the work.

He relays a rift between Piet Mondrian and Theo van Doesburg of De Stijl regarding this issue, with van Doesburg experimenting with the angled, 'diamond' composition, Mondrian only experimenting with these angled canvases later in his career. Hejduk's approach to this identifies the significant difference such a small alteration can make, playing with the difference between drawing a square and diamond plan in parallel projection—the kind of drawing which results from this.

> When a diamond form in plan is projected by isometric it becomes a square. This may appear to be a self-evident truth, but such projections, that is, the projections of the diamond forms into isometrics, had not appeared in architectural drawings prior to these explorations. The converse has been in existence and use, that is, the square drawn in isometric which becomes a diamond. (1985:48)

Further experiments show how, when a diamond plan with several floors is drawn in parallel projection, the floors do not read clearly as separate floors, continuing to read as an overlapping two-dimensional form. His argument continues to place the observer into the role of establishing the three-dimensional form, as it is not given by the drawings (or by extension the draughtsperson). This fascination with the angle of the axonometric drawing persists throughout Hejduk's career, with the early house series playing with the ways in which a normally explicit drawing convention known for its clarity of exposition is subverted: hiding elements which would normally be apparent, and misleading the viewer.

4.2 Occluded lines in axonometric and the denial of totality

Axonometric drawings more than most conventions, exploit hidden lines in order to be legible. A simple structure drawn without the concept of hidden lines swiftly becomes a tangle of overlapping forms akin to an x-ray, where interpretation is impossible as the cues lack sufficient clarity. The convention of hiding lines, then, relies on the concept that the drawing is of an object with opacity and thickness.

In Figure 4.2, this is shown clearly. The process of hidden lines is often one of erasure and removal, when drawing using tracing paper and a mechanical drawing board, the drawing practice might involve carefully selecting the lines to be traced for the final, presentation version of a drawing, or in a freehand sketch, the procedure is internalised and the faces which would be present to the viewer are the only ones presented in the drawing. This suggests that there is a complexity to this naturalistic convention, that it might be too obvious a process to warrant much attention in the case of most drawings, but it becomes increasingly important when discussing Hejduk's drawings, as this like the other elements of the convention, is exploited for its fullest creative potential.

68 *Hejduk's Wall House*

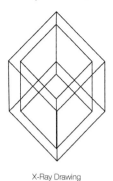 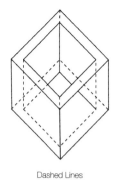 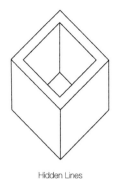

X-Ray DrawingDashed LinesHidden Lines

Figure 4.2 Demonstration of a form drawn first in axonometric projection without hidden lines (x-ray), and the same form drawn using dotted lines and then using hidden lines.

This hiding of information which lies behind an element considered closer to the front by the draughtsperson is often a source of frustration, making the selection of the precise angle of the drawing one of the most important decisions in the early stages of the drawing. Drawing the wrong projection can mean that essential details are missing. All of this gives the parallel projection a subjective quality despite its viewpoint, it has a closer kinship with perspective (and is sometimes grouped with it) than it has with the more objective orthographic drawings, particularly the plan. This is far from being a failing of the convention, but a useful quality: the lack of totality in a representation is an important tool for underlining the experiential nature of the proposed architecture, it is to be appreciated sequentially and as a promenade rather than apprehended in its entirety all at once—a totality.

This is demonstrated through Luscombe's[8] (2013:31) discussion of the importance of axonometric drawing to De Stijl with her analysis of the Schröder House drawings. Two versions of a drawing are discussed, one of which does not use hidden lines and represents both the upper and ground floors of the building together, the resulting tangle allowing the floors to be read across one another. This is consistent with van Doesburg's interest in notions of four-dimensional space, and the privileged totalising viewpoint of this kind of axonometric drawing (referred to as an x-ray drawing here):

> This experimentation supported an art that attempted to portray spatiality where the viewing subject would be aware of all directions of space simultaneously and without being inhibited by the impenetrability of materials. Rietveld, in making his architectural compositions distinctive by introducing transparency, rather than focusing on the surface of the object's foreground, portrayed spatial relationships in architecture beyond what could be seen naturally. For the Schröder house, it is the relationships geometrically derived across the multiple dimensions of space that become important. (2013:31)

Hejduk's Wall House 69

This demonstrates the way in which the conventions of drawing can be opened up for creative potential; that by deliberately subverting the axonometric drawing's rules of which lines are erased and which are given prominence, an alternative reading of the space can be made. The potential is for the axonometric drawing to reveal more than would be possible to someone visiting the space, allowing for deeper relationships to be understood.

The 'axonometric technique became an important signifier of this group's interest in different notions of spatiality' (2013:33) in that the axonometric drawing is both an appropriate, practical solution to the material De Stijl's members sought to communicate, but was also emblematic of their political and aesthetic aims for their work. Luscombe reads this through van Doesburg's manifestoes: that 'architecture is formless and yet determinate' (2013:34), seeing the fulfilment of his aims within the drawings.

Writing on the *Contra-Constructions,* Luscombe describes the way in which van Doesburg uses the drawing as a critique of three-dimensional space, contrasting axonometric drawing with perspective. There is an implied plane of movement between front and back in how the drawing is both constructed and read; an ordering of the surfaces which renders the lines legible. Where perspective can be argued to represent infinity in the distance between the viewer and the vanishing point, the potential for totality in axonometric drawing resides in the relationship between the viewer and picture plane.

> He extends a critique of the constraints of 3-D representation by alluding to the fourth dimension using the axonometric technique's capacity to defy infinity's vanishing point as the dominant resolution of representation in perspective. In van Doesburg's visual experiments, the formlessness of infinity is understood conceptually rather than through its representation. Infinity becomes defined by its permanent deferral and absence from resolution within a picture plane. To reinforce notions of pure abstraction and introduce recognition of the fourth spatial dimension, van Doesburg applies colour in an aim to remove the certainty of the picture's surface (forward and backward) with colour relationships having the capacity to imply depth and reversibility to their location. Each colour implied recession or extension in the visual field not always consistent with its relative location in the image's structured coordinates. (2013:35)

Paul Emmons[9] tackles the line itself in architectural drawing, cataloguing the various weights and patterns of dashed lines—noting the various meanings ascribed to lines such as the outline, indications of texture. More interesting are imaginary lines such as those used to describe symmetry or to depict the cut where a section is taken, referring one drawing to another. Perhaps instead of 'hidden' lines we ought to speak of *erased* or *elided* ones, as the drawing process either removes the marks in question, or a new tracing is produced which elects to draw only the lines which are determined to

70 Hejduk's Wall House

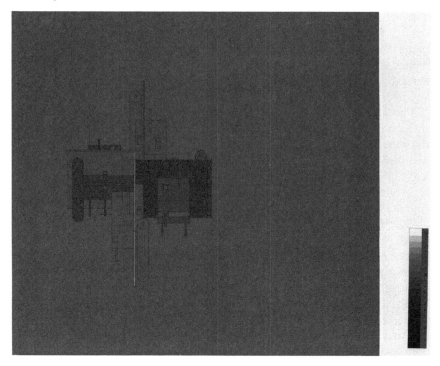

Figure 4.3 John Hejduk, north axonometric for North East South West House, 1978–1979; pen and India ink with coloured pencil over graphite underdrawing on translucent paper, 58.4 × 86.1 cm; DR1984:1517; John Hejduk fonds, Canadian Centre for Architecture, gift of Elliott and Carolyn Mittler.

be visible. These conventions go back as far as Serlio (Emmons 2014:543). In the same special issue, Richard Difford's[10] discussion notes that occlusion of lines is a strategy for depicting depth, establishing a spatial illusion.

Hejduk continues to discuss the stacking of square versus diamond plan forms, with a natural three-dimensional form emerging from the square plan when drawn in this way, whereas the diamond plan causes a 'special phenomenon' to occur: the form appears to be flat and two-dimensional, the floors of the building overlap with one another in such a way as to enhance this sense of two-dimensionality. The drawing convention is a three-dimensional one, but drawing them in this way robs them of that reading. Hejduk writes that 'the forms tip forward … towards the picture plane' (1985:49). This desire for a two-dimensional reading is fully deliberate, and Hejduk makes an interesting observation about axonometric drawing (he calls it *isometric* in his text): that the observer is largely responsible for constructing the space from the data provided by the drawing. There is a process of constructing the space which takes place in looking at the drawing (see figure 4.3).

Hejduk returns to this with greater clarity when discussing the Dag Hammarskjöld Memorial project, a bridge between the Texas and Diamond Houses:

> If you project floor upon floor as in the first isometric drawing you get an overlapping like that which is actually a three dimensional view. Your isometric/axonometric basically, it's once removed from perspective but it's still a three-dimensional view of things. It you take the diamond and you make an isometric of it, it becomes a series of flat screens overlapping each other which then brings on a sense, *a memory condition.* (1985:50)

Hejduk argues that this process of extracting and reconstructing when viewing a drawing allows it to have the same perceptual status as actually being there: The drawing is a proxy for experience in his argument. For this to happen, there needs to be an atmosphere to the drawing which allows viewers to lose themselves in the situation. In this chapter, we focus on the generation of this atmosphere through manipulating and exploiting the conventions of axonometric drawing to enhance the depiction of the architecture, where we shall see a more poetic and loose approach in the next chapter. The house projects are repeatedly discussed as being *discoveries* (1985:59), that Hejduk found things out by designing them. They are not the result of an already coherent and articulated concept; they found form *by being drawn.* This process of discovery includes some unusual sources, and the process is extended by his writing about the work as well as by drawing. He muses, in the manner of an interview, about the interpretations which might be made of his work (1985:61) which he sees as not only including the validated canon of architectural influence such as cubism and De Stijl, but also a *love* for colour and geometry, or the compositions that can be derived from playing with toy soldiers (1985:61).

Writing on Hejduk, Weijing He uses an alternative copying methodology[11], reconstructing the Wall House as a CAD model in order to interrogate the spaces within it. This follows from her redrawing of the plans and elevations accompanied by thumbnail perspectives. It is notable is that this is presented by He as an entirely natural thing to do, rather than a radical way of manipulating the material available on the Wall House: the original drawings, their re-presentation in publications, and the decontextualised building as constructed, at 120 percent of the intended dimensions and in Groningen rather than Connecticut. The redrawing—digital, mechanical, or manual—is an interpretation and analysis through inscriptive practice.

> Hejduk has talked about Wall House designs in terms of occupying the threshold and this is certainly a main characteristic that makes Wall House 2 unusual. The vertical stacking and separation of the living spaces requires that inhabitants frequently cross the major wall thus becoming exposed to the threshold condition and the opposition between the experiential qualities described earlier.

72 *Hejduk's Wall House*

The perspective drawings extracted by He from the three-dimensional model are a radical act of interpreting the design through the practice of redrawing it. The Wall House (figure 4.4) is designed to *defy* perspective (and by extension axonometric) renderings of space. Hejduk's parallel projections are not reproduced in the paper, in favour of the more legible plans.

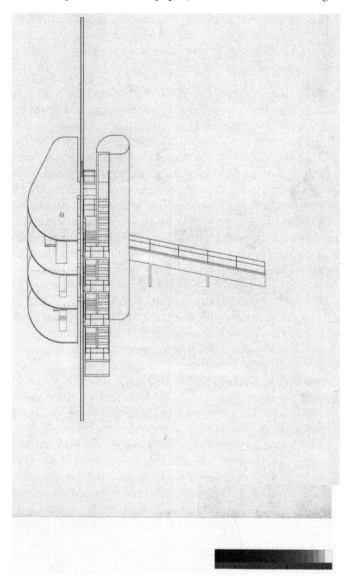

Figure 4.4 John Hejduk, Axonometric for Wall House 1, 1968–1974, ink on translucent paper, 93 × 93 cm; DR1998:0077:026, John Hejduk fonds, Canadian Centre for Architecture.

He's analysis of the building consists of an account of its qualities of detachment, reticence, and denial of anticipation (2005:172). This is discussed in terms of anxiety, an undeniably negative connotation and perhaps one which overstates the case a little. Instead, this explicitly phenomenological strategy undermines the gaze as a totalising perceptual experience and instead proposes a structure which has no possibility of totality[12]. The discreet events resemble pavilions set within a garden, each giving carefully framed views of the next stopping point on a predetermined path, but with points of pause or meditation suggested. Hejduk's living spaces offer views to distant rooms, the route towards them rendered unclear by the large wall which dominates the composition. This is, as He notes, a temporal condition: The denial of totality is an embrace of the passage of time, of allowing the building to unfurl for its inhabitants.

> Rather than merely associating the past with circulation, therefore, we might associate the whole house with a particular structure of memory, one that foregrounds discrete episodes rather than flow, framed images rather than multiple points of view. (2005:173)

He's discussion of Hejduk working with two-dimensional space (2005:175) in this instance is contrary to my reading of the project, as Hejduk frequently worked with indeterminacy between two and three dimensions in his parallel projections when composing these and earlier works.

The logic is one of denial, as He notes for Corbusier in the example of Villa La Roche, denying the architectural promenade so associated with Corbusier. I would argue that flatness is not a two-dimensional condition. Hejduk uses it as a strategy for occlusion, a way of hiding; but more than that, a way of suggesting that something lies beyond. The Wall House is a detective story where the principles of retardation drive the presentation of the narrative. Clues are given, but events are held back and tension constructed, meaning that the following of these clues is the only way to piece the entire story together.

In his introduction to *Mask of Medusa*[13] (Hejduk, 1985), Daniel Libeskind discusses both the Wall House series and its antecedents such as the North South East West house. He brings an interesting perspective to the analysis, suggesting that the projects represent an attempt to critique the very notion of dwelling itself. This is nothing new, of course, and there has been a recent revival in this concept within other disciplines such as anthropology[14]. The resistance of these houses to occupation is addressed by Libeskind here: That, as critical works, they pose a problem of dwelling itself, in the manner of Tschumi's opening of the brief or programme to the creativity of the architect, Hejduk is doing something similar here, but by alternative means, suggesting that 'one doesn't yet know how to dwell' and that inhabiting these spaces might be one way to learn.

74 *Hejduk's Wall House*

It is clear that the aim of these designs is different from the conventional architectural practitioner looking to fulfil the commission of a private home client, with all its attendant desires and luxuries. Similarly to Eisenman, Hejduk is exploring drawing as a theoretical instrument, and posing metaphysical questions through nonverbal means. There is something social about dwelling, and there is a suggestion that part of the project addresses identity and its construction; again as co-construction between environment and people, as well as through the interactions between members of the household.

Libeskind (1985:20) returns to the issue of the convention at hand: axonometric drawing, suggesting that their use is wilful and almost wicked. If axonometrics are abstract and geometrical, Hejduk is not employing them in their usual manner: The inhabitant is the 'coordinating point' in the otherwise subtly discontinuous architecture. Libeskind expresses this as an architecture that does not conform to the distinctions between space and time, and which has an explicitly poetic sensibility (this aspect of Hejduk's practice shall be addressed in more detail in the next chapter). The recourse to modernism's past is not stylistic, but as a result of the questions Hejduk has in common with early modernism before functionalism took hold as the dominant paradigm: the questioning of the status quo, the interest in fundamentals of being and dwelling, both of which implicate temporality in architecture.

4.3 Drawing the 'missing' drawing

In copying the axonometric drawings of Wall House 1, it is notable that the conventional 45° angled plan is not used, and instead a series of axonometric drawings are produced which show the north, south, east, and west views in the manner of a series of elevations (see figures 4.5, 4.6, and 4.7). This challenges some of the descriptions of the distinction between oblique and axonometric conventions in parallel projection (see the discussion of Bryon's differentiation in Chapter 1, for example). The indeterminacy of parallel projection is exploited fully by this, and other projects at the time—frustrating the expectation of the viewer. Axonometric drawings are often held to offer a more holistic view than perspectives, for example: the singular viewpoint being replaced by one which is impossible through optics, and which renders space with a degree of neutral equality between one space and another. Hejduk is well aware of this when he chooses to subvert the convention whilst using it to its greatest advantage.

The wall which dominates this house design is intended to block the view, to offer a plane which separates elements physically and visually. This is therefore a *denial* of the power of axonometric drawing, undermining its privileged position and effectively flattening space. The same strategy is apparent in the sections of this scheme, where an incredibly spare and austere set of drawings demonstrate where we would tell our students *not* to

Hejduk's Wall House 75

place the section line when establishing the drawing. Some sections show only the smallest indentation into the ground plane, others show the thickness of the single wall, before we eventually arrive at the stacked rooms on one side of the wall and the circulation on the other.

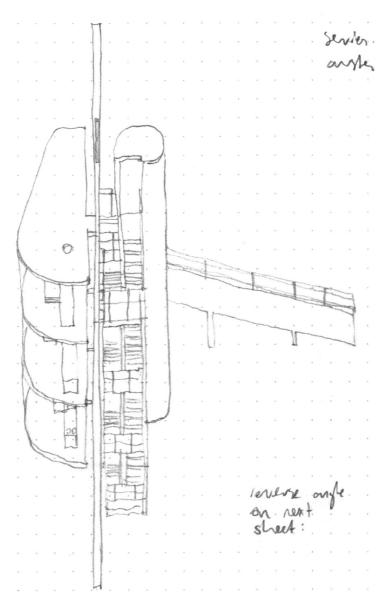

Figure 4.5 Redrawing by Ray Lucas of DR1998:0077:025, axonometric drawing for Wall House by John Hejduk.

76   *Hejduk's Wall House*

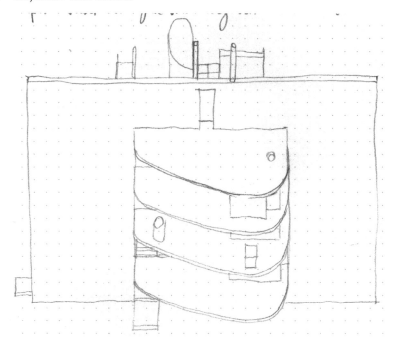

Figure 4.6 Redrawing by Ray Lucas of DR1998:0077:026, axonometric drawing for Wall House by John Hejduk.

If we pursue the differentiation between axonometric projection and oblique discussed by Bryon[15], then we can see that a complication emerges in Hejduk's drawings: They might simultaneously satisfy the criteria for axonometric and oblique drawing. Bryon's distinction lies in the originating profile for the drawings: Starting from a plan and projecting vertical lines downwards gives us the family of axonometric drawings, whilst starting from an elevation and projecting the horizontal lines back gives us obliques. Discussing advances in descriptive geometry in Germany by the Meyer brothers which established a firmer split in approach between oblique and axonometric drawing, but also expanded the scope of axonometric projection to allow for a variety of angles to be shown, such as the reverse-angle or worm's eye view (the full potential of which was to be explored by Auguste Choisy[16]):

> The drawing out of axonometry in the mid-nineteenth century bifurcated the known world of parallel projection. An inherent difference between the axonometric and cavalier or oblique projections became apparent: the axonometric manifests a true spatial representation in and of three-dimensional space and the oblique offers a synthetic picture via shadow, diagram, and two-dimensional extrusion. (Bryon 2008:343)

Hejduk's Wall House   77

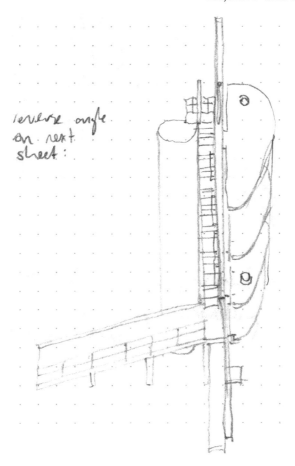

Figure 4.7 Redrawing by Ray Lucas of DR1998:0077:027, axonometric drawing for Wall House by John Hejduk.

Indeterminacy is a feature throughout Hejduk's career, and we shall see the fullness of this approach in the next chapter, where the lines themselves take on a shimmering hesitant multiplicity, scratchy and repetitive whilst possible to read as a single trajectory. Indeed, many of the elements of Hejduk's drawings can be explained with reference to James Elkins's work in opening out the discipline of art history[17]. The certainty of the ruled lines (*orlo* in Elkins' schema) in these drawings is very different to the *contorno*: 'drawing by repetitive approximation' to come in Hejduk's late works.

> A mark might be something that must always be surrounded by a *pale apparition*, hovering undecidably between drawn contour and mere edge. Ideally, the *orlo*, the name of this ghost, would never be securely visible. Alberti's negotiations with *perspectiva* brought him to this idea,

78 *Hejduk's Wall House*

which remains fundamental in concepts of the figure. The *orlo* is often present in figurative work, and it is a reminder of the artificial nature of drawing (that is, that edges are often drawn but not often seen). I like to think of the *orlo* as the ghost not only of visual rays and the geometry of vision, but of written signs, which all have determinate boundaries. The *orlo* is as close as graphic marks get to the rigours of the written sign. (Elkins 1998:44)

Architectural drawings are rather dominated by this *orlo* condition, consisting of a definite mark with a degree of clarity over its meaning; but this is again a process by which the underlying mechanisms of the drawing convention are exposed and exploited by Hejduk in his work. We have marks which are suggested by their absence, lines we know are there, but which are not shown in order to communicate something of the underlying design intention—a space to be experienced a little at a time, experientially, and phenomenologically. This denial strategy is explored by K Michael Hays[18] as one of the key distinctions between Hejduk and Eisenman:

> Here we confront an architecture not, like Eisenman's, indifferent to sensuous experience, but rather decidedly animated and personified even if not quite human. Like the animals in a fable that speak with human voices, Hejduk's objects seem, impossibly, to be aware of us, to address us. (Hays 2015:23)

Hays discusses the Diamond Houses as research, formal experiments into the relationship between perception and form. The idea is that later projects such as the Wall House were discoveries, things waiting to be found rather than inventions of their author. Hays describes the architecture as addressing the viewer, granting an agency to the essential feature in Hejduk's early works: the wall. The blankness of the wall serves as an apparatus of expression, a screen where you might confront the architectural in a heightened form.

> In an early (1963) but oft-repeated explication of the Diamond Houses (the series of carefully calibrated and measured formal transformations, executed between 1963 and 1967, that owe much to Piet Mondrian, Le Corbusier, and Mies van der Rohe), Hejduk constructs a diagram of the history of architectural space, declaring the paradigmatic space of the present to be the compression onto a two-dimensional surface of the space generated by the two legs of a right angle. (Hays 2015:23)

The 'moment of the hypotenuse' is a perceptual event. The flattening of a square to a diamond is used by Hejduk as a diagram to describe the move from plan through parallel projection towards perspective. This diagram essentially explains the move from Diamond to Wall House. The three-dimensionality of the axonometric space is returned to a two-dimensionality as one perceives it: The aim is to undermine three-dimensional space and

Hejduk's Wall House 79

to give the building's visitor an experience of the two-dimensional. The idea is of an architecture that looks at you—it is upright and facing you. It has a gaze to counter the gaze of the people who might look at it—it returns the gaze. Writing on the relationship between flatness and depth, Hejduk himself asserts that there is a notational aspect to his drawings[19]:

> [The architect is]…able to make isometrics, axonometrics and perspectives into the surface, each one giving a different depth connotation ranging from the shallowness of an isometric to the extended deepness of a perspective. All are specifically real (pencil and paper), all are representations of proposed comings, and all are illusions regarding space and depth. Although the perspective is the most heightened illusion—whereas the representation of a plan may be considered the closest to reality—if we consider it as substantively notational, the so-called reality of built architecture can only come into being through a notational system. In any case, drawing on a piece of paper is an architectural reality. (Hejduk 1985:69).

Distinct from other approaches, I sketched an alternative view of Wall House 1, restoring what I felt to be the 'missing drawing' with the aim of making the hidden explicit (figure 4.8), and understanding the

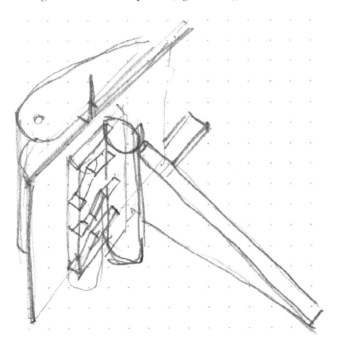

Figure 4.8 My 'missing drawing' of Wall House by John Hejduk. This drawing by the author is set at 45° in order to show the scheme more clearly; noting that this was not Hejduk's intention for the project.

80 Hejduk's Wall House

Figure 4.9 The Sumiyoshi Pine at Katsura Rikyu, a tree planted specifically to deny a view of the complete garden.

three-dimensional implications of the flat, planar forms suggested. This is an analytical drawing, an interpretation of Hejduk's work which defies his intentions by showing too much at once, as though the Sumiyoshi Pine had been removed from Katsura (figure 4.9).

Whilst I maintain a distinction between the early and late phases of Hejduk's career, his research questions remain stable. The space between the axonometric drawing and the building is one such question, answered here in terms of an alternation between three dimensional understandings of space in drawing and an ambition to reduce the lived experience of a building to two dimensions. This is achieved by means of restricting views, hiding and occluding elements to ensure that the moment is held without reference to what has come before or what is coming next. Hejduk continues to examine these fissures between representation and architectural reality in the later projects, but moving from an answer reliant upon temporality to one which deals in spirituality and poetry.

Notes

1. In Hejduk, John (Ed.). 1971. *Education of an Architect: A Point of View*. New York: Cooper Union and Museum of Modern Art, pp. 7–34. This exhibition and book covering 1964 to 1972 was followed by a second volume, covering the period from 1972 to 1985, and shows the persistence of the nine-square problem.
Hejduk, John (Ed.). 1988. *Education of an Architect*. New York: Rizzoli International.

Hejduk's Wall House   81

2. Love, Timothy. 2003. "Kit-of-Parts Conceptualism: Abstracting Architecture in the American Academy" in *Harvard Design Magazine*, No. 19, Fall/Winter 2003, online at http://www.harvarddesignmagazine.org/issues/19/kit-of-parts-conceptualism-abstracting-architecture-in-the-american-academy [accessed 14 August 2008].
3. Caragonne, Alexander. 1995. *Texas Rangers: Notes from an Architectural Underground*. Cambridge, Massachusetts: MIT Press.
4. Wittkower, Rudolf. 1988 [1949]. *Architectural Principles in the Age of Humanism*. London: Academy Editions.
5. Rowe, Colin. 1986. *The Mathematics of the Ideal Villa and Other Essays*. Cambridge, Massachusetts: MIT Press.
6. Tafuri, Manfredo. 1976. "'European Graffiti' Five × Five = Twenty-five", trans. Victor Caliandro, in *Oppositions* 5, pp. 35–73.
7. Notably, Tafuri extends the cinematic metaphor to discuss the work of Hans Richter and Viking Eggeling (1976:43), who sought to make a completely abstract cinema through animated forms famously working with scrolls he had painted, and other experimentations with the technology of film in order to produce self-proclaimed 'abstract' cinema in collaboration with his colleagues in the Dada movement.
8. Luscombe, Desley. 2013. "Illustrating Architecture: The Spatio-Temporal Dimension of Gerrit Rietveld's Representations of the Schröder House" in *The Journal of Architecture*, Vol. 18, No. 1, pp. 22–58.
9. Emmons, Paul. 2014. "Demiurgic Lines: Line-making and the Architectural Imagination" in *The Journal of Architecture*, Vol. 19, No. 4, pp. 536–559.
10. Difford, Richard. 2014. "Conversions of Relief: On the Perception of Depth in Drawings" in *The Journal of Architecture*, Vol. 19, No. 4, pp. 483–510.
11. He, Weiling. 2005. "When Does a Sentiment Become an Architectural Concept? Otherness in Hejduk's Wall House 2" in *The Journal of Architecture*, Vol. 10.
12. I discuss this idea with reference to the design of Katsura Rikyu in Kyoto: Lucas, Ray. 2017. "Threshold and temporality in architecture: Practices of movement in Japanese Architecture" in Bunn, S. (Ed.). *Anthropology and Beauty: From Aesthetics to Creativity*. London: Routledge, pp. 279–291. The argument presents the series of pavilions which make up the palace as presented along a *path of philosophy* arrangement to encourage aesthetic appreciation; and noting the use of devices such as thresholds and paving changes to instruct the individual in how to wayfare around the grounds. Most notable is a denial of the view which would give a prospect of the entire garden, with the planting of a pine tree to frustrate the totalising vision. Hejduk is engaging in an equivalent practice here.
13. Libeskind, D. 1985. "Stars at High Noon: An Introduction to the Work of John Hejduk" in Hejduk, J. (Ed.). 1985. *Mask of Medusa*. New York: Rizzoli, pp. 9–22.
14. In particular, Tim Ingold's *dwelling perspective* (Ingold, T. 2000. "Building Dwelling Living" in *The Perception of the Environment*, London: Routledge, pp. 172–188) is important to cite here (drawing in ideas from both Marx and Heidegger), as it represents dwelling as an ever-evolving process whereby both the individual and their environment are in a state of co-production, each contributing to forming the other. Ingold reminds us that: 'Dwelling is not merely the occupation of structures already built: it does not stand to building as consumption to production. It rather signifies that immersion of being in the currents of the lifeworld without such activities as designing, building and occupation could not take place at all.' (Ingold, T. 2011.

82   *Hejduk's Wall House*

Being Alive: Essays on Movement, Knowledge and Description. London: Routledge, p. 10). See also Lucas, R. 2019. "Home and What It Means to Dwell." in *Anthropology for Architects*. London: Bloomsbury.

15. Bryon, Hilary. 2008. "Revolutions in Space: Parallel Projections in the Early Modern Era" in *Architectural Research Quarterly*, Issue 3–4, Vol. 12, pp. 337–346.

16. Choisy, Auguste. 1899. *Histoire de l'architecture*. Paris: Gauthier-Villars. Available at: Bibliothèque Nationale de France website, https://gallica.bnf.fr/ark:/12148/bpt6k6417116t/f25.image [accessed 6 September 2018].

17. Elkins, J. 1998. *On Pictures and the Words That Fail Them*. Cambridge: University of Cambridge Press, pp. 43–44.

18. Hays, K. Michael. 2015. "Encounters" in Amistadi, L. & Clemente, I. (Eds.). 2015. *Soundings 0/1: John Hejduk*. Florence: Aión Edizioni, pp. 23–43.

19. Hejduk, John. 1985. "The Flatness of Depth: Excerpt from Introduction to *Five Architects*" in *Mask of Medusa: Works 1947–1983*. New York: Rizzoli, pp. 68–70.

5 Indeterminacy and transfiguration: Hejduk's multiple projections

5.1 Haptic space, indeterminacy, and transfiguration

Whilst the early work of John Hejduk sought to extend the cubist ambitions of early modernist architecture, his late work is characterised by a poetic sensitivity, narrative and form-based architecture. In these later works, Hejduk plays transformative games—shifting projections from orthographic to isometric, axonometric, oblique, or perspective. This transfiguration is at its most apparent in the late series noted previously, where the narrative drive suggests such transformations as well as a state of indeterminacy. Some forms drawn in axonometric might be designed or intended to be read as isometric or oblique, giving skewed, distorted versions of familiar forms. The uncertainty introduced gives the drawings a multiplicity of readings which the completed set neither confirms nor denies.

By engaging in a discussion of the temporality and spatiality of the original and copied drawings, this chapter addresses a range of issues surrounding the indeterminate and flexible meaning of Hejduk's deeply coded drawings which shift fluidly within a single inscription from one projection to another. The copying methodology addresses the meaning of retracing as a method of knowledge production, whereby it is not merely a visual reproduction but a haptic replication of the originating work.

The idea of optic space versus haptic space introduced by Gilles Deleuze in his work on Francis Bacon as well as his collaboration with Félix Guattari might have something to contribute to the debate. How might this then be informed by the work of Henri Bergson, who characterised creativity as having a temporal, processual quality?

What effect does copying have on this discussion of haptic and optic, spatial and temporal; to what extent are the paper projects of architects to be treated as works equivalent to discourse; and what knowledge is produced through an informed and directed copy? The idea of optic space versus haptic space introduced by Gilles Deleuze in his work on Francis Bacon as well as his collaboration with Félix Guattari might have something to contribute to the debate. How might this then be informed by the work of Henri Bergson, who characterised creativity as having

84   *Hejduk's multiple projections*

a temporal, processual quality? What effect does copying have on this discussion of haptic and optic, spatial and temporal; to what extent are the paper projects of architects to be treated as works equivalent to discourse; and what knowledge is produced through an informed and directed copy? It is deformation of the square which provides the starting point, implicating isometric and axonometric projection in the process of thinking about architectural space. Discussing the *Sanctuaries* and *Enclosures* series of drawings, K. Michael Hays writes:

> Developing the classicist-modernist axioms of flatness versus depth and opacity versus transparency, Hejduk understands this percept— the image of the flattening or collapsing of deep space onto the square vertical plane—as at once the most basic element of any architecture, the summation of the history of architectural space to date, and a historically specific phenomenon. (2002:69)

Hejduk plays transformative games—shifting projections from orthographic to isometric, axonometric, oblique, or perspective. This transfiguration is at its most apparent in the late works such as *Architectures in Love* (1995); *Pewter Wings, Golden Horns, Stone Veils* (1997); and *Lines no Fire Could Burn* (1999), where the narrative drive suggests such transformations as well as a state of indeterminacy. Some forms drawn in axonometric might be designed or intended to be read as isometric or oblique, giving skewed, distorted versions of familiar forms. The uncertainty introduced gives the drawings a multiplicity of readings which the completed set neither confirms nor denies. This is the game played by Hejduk in the drawings examined, and the detail that might be lost through other means. The transformation is rational, and divides the page along coherent and deliberate lines.

Hays extends his argument to a discussion of the psychoanalyst Jacques Lacan, with the notion of double articulation encompassed by the gaze. The gaze is returned: The phenomena being observed reciprocates at the point of this image-screen, the no-object, the dompte-regard (the object effectively *taming* the gaze). This is the apparatus, the midpoint in the gaze diagram, which allows us to interpret and understand.

> For both Hejduk and Lacan, the image-screen is a representational apparatus necessary for our social and cultural existence—a historically generated repertoire of images through which we as social subjects are constructed. (Hays 2002:71)

In architectural terms, this idea of gaze is explored in much greater depth by Lorens Holm (2010), where the objet a is desired.

> The gaze finds its analogue in the constant but unrequited need people have for recognition, for you to look at me when I look at you, but

Hejduk's multiple projections 85

it would be a mistake to think that it is entirely a social phenomenon. It finds its analogue in the point that vanishes, although it would be a mistake to assume that the gaze is reducible to the vanishing point and that it only obtains in perspective representations or in perceptual circumstances that assimilate to perspective representations. (Holm 2010:15)

In conventional readings of Lacan, there is a strong identification with perspective projections, but Holm notes that the mechanism is not restricted to this. I contend that it can be found within Hejduk's drawings—in a manner which must be sought for and understood, the production of knowledge rather than the presentation of a truth. In describing Hejduk's carnivalesque take on Catholic imagery, Jim Williamson notes that:

> dozens of 'object/subject' constructions travel from place to place like a carnival with its machines, masked actors, and sense of dangerous otherness. There is no sense of permanence, and they offer no temporal or spatial stability… But the drawings of the ensemble of buildings do have a fantastical character, a blending of creature and building and populated by angels and devils, dancers and dogs. They have a surreal, collage-like quality about their composition. There also is a certain medieval quality to them, and they are remarkably similar to the creature/objects in Bosch's Garden of Earthly Delights. (Hejduk & Williamson (Eds.) 2011:64)

This object/subject confusion is present in other works, again with reference to the return of the gaze, and the presence of this narrative architecture. To effectively understand these drawings, a practice of interpretation takes place, where the instability or defiantly rigid adherence to drawing conventions compels the viewer to retrace the gestures which created the work in the first place. This is heightened in the case of speculative, unbuilt projects like many of Hejduk's works discussed here, as noted by Williamson (2011:359). The only way to experience the architectural spaces described is through engagement with the drawings.

> An observer places himself before a painting (standing or sitting— more often standing). The general viewing distance is between four to ten feet. It is a distance. The painting is over there, physically outside of the body of the observer. Whatever the subject or object of the painting, the observer faces a work hung upon a wall surface. The painting is usually framed. The frame defines the physical limits of the canvas. The whole canvas may be seen or a part may be the focus of the vision of the viewer. The space between the canvas and the viewer is geometrized air. It is air of a contained visual volume. (Hejduk, 1988:340)

86   *Hejduk's multiple projections*

Musing on the contrast between the tactile connection with a book as opposed to the visual distancing of a painting, Hejduk characterises our relationship with images as one of a Biblical fall from grace when compared to the immediacy with which thoughts can be imparted by a text. Redrawing challenges this instantaneity, and reinstates the temporality of the event:

> Books take time and give time. In reading, our thought is stretched into the kinetics of the book, and the thread is the actual printed text. (Hejduk 1988:340)

In this sense, redrawing is akin to reading. The temporal dimension of our engagement with the work is restored, as is its status as a practice of knowledge production. The idea of optic space versus haptic space introduced by Gilles Deleuze in his work on Francis Bacon as well as the collaboration with Félix Guattari might have something to contribute to the debate. Simply stated, the painter is close to the canvas whilst engaging with the making of it (however one might characterise their gaze towards a sitter in the case of Bacon's portraiture). By contrast, Deleuze (2003:131) describes the action of the painting's viewer as being optic in character. Conventionally, the bias has been expressed against painting (and indeed architecture) as visual, optic, and totalising acts.

> Haptic is a better word than "tactile" since it does not establish an opposition between two sense organs but rather invites the assumption that the eye itself may fulfil this nonoptical function. (Deleuze & Guattari 1988:492)

As a description of the haptic, Deleuze and Guattari are, here, relating it closely to a variety of creative acts. What might be the architectural equivalent of this close distance, close hearing, or short-term memory? Firstly, this can be understood to explain the difficulties experienced by students and practitioners of any creative discipline, where architectural students can be observed to hit a wall where the plethora of possibilities is paralysing, and arbitrary or consistent choices from these options is problematised to the point of destruction: Progress in the design is halting or absent.

> A painting is done at close range, even if it is seen from a distance. Similarly, it is said that composers do not hear: they have close-range hearing, whereas listeners hear from a distance. Even writers write with short-term memory, whereas readers are assumed to be endowed with long-term memory. The first aspect of the haptic, smooth space of close vision is that its orientations, landmarks, and linkages are in continuous variation; it operates step by step. (Deleuze & Guattari 1988:493)

The invocation of memory with regards to the craft of the writer is also worth noting. In particular, this temporality is not restricted to writing but present in a variety of ways in each creative practice. It is easy to understand architecture through its primary means of production: drawing and model-making, be these analogue and practical or digital. It is, however, to consider the aim of such media—to design spaces and establish places, to understand a context and propose interventions on and in it. As such, is the architect considering a similar scale or temporality of space analogous to the close-range vision of the painting, the close-hearing? Does the practice of producing architecture necessitate a different set of 'orientations, landmarks, and linkages'?

This suggests a consideration of the spatiality and temporality of architectural production practices. Again, we are returned to the issues of form and context in this regard, where issues such as function can be understood as bound up in each of these fundamental generators for design. The improvisational character of design which is overtly formal, where elements are placed on sites as provocations and invitations to users contrasts strongly with the contextual architectures which operate in an analytical mode, seeking to first understand the social and material facets of a site before deciding what is best. The ways in which this is established can be contentious and problematic, to the extent that we must be careful to avoid the preference for the contextual design process simply because it appears to respect the existing fabric, and is sensitive to it. This might act to reinforce reactionary forces, commercial concerns over the social, Imperialist impositions, or other unwanted contexts given cache simply due to historical persistence.

Similarly, the overly formal architectures can by enormously successful structures or, by turns, oversized sculptures which fail to respond to the needs of people, ruin a site, and squander resources. The answer lies, then, not in opposing these two admittedly conventional distinctions, but rather to use them as magnetic poles by which a person might orient a practice's approach. The ideal is to have an architectural approach which finds a balance between the demands of abstract form and the specificity of context. In characterising these two as substantially improvisational on the one hand and analytical on the other, a critique based on the practices involved in design emerges.

The role of such representational techniques is important in discussions of architectural practice, where the prototype process available to product and industrial design is more difficult to achieve due to the scale and contextual nature of architecture. This tension between abstractions and context remains one of the most problematic in the practice of architecture, but it also offers opportunities for creativity. In order to further explore the nature of architecture, it is necessary to consider drawing and inscriptive practices, and understanding the flow of movement and temporality inherent to the practice.

88   *Hejduk's multiple projections*

In many ways, a parallel practice can be found in the practice of improvisational dance described by Maxine Sheets-Johnstone:

> In view of its unique appearance, it is not surprising that a dance improvisation is commonly described as an unrehearsed and spontaneous form of dance. What is not commonly recognised, however, is that that description hinges on the more fundamental characteristic suggested above, namely, that in a dance improvisation, the process of creating is not the means of realising a dance; it is the dance itself. A dance improvisation is the incarnation of creativity as a process. (1999:485)

Despite being founded in the theory of dance, Sheets-Johnstone's concept of thinking in movement has many lessons for the study of drawing, and as a result, the design process itself. The description of improvisational dance given previously could easily talk about the close integration of drawing with the architectural design process[1]. Thus, the process of creating is not the means of realising a design, it is the process of design itself: To draw is to design[2]. In this way, thinking in movement is understood not as the transcription of a preformed mental image, but that 'thinking is itself, by its nature, kinetic' (1999:486). This idea has the potential of being an important reconceptualisation of design practices, and takes Bergson's critique of the homogenisation of time, operationalising it as a means of understanding practices which have become embedded in disciplines without being understood fully.

The potential of such an understanding of creative practice as flows of movement is to understand the nature of thinking through drawing. Essayists such as John Berger (2011) and architectural theorists including Juhani Pallasmaa (2009) and Michael Merrill (2010) agree that there is a knowledge-seeking aspect to the drawing, that there is a desire (and ability) to understand and find things out by engaging in an inscriptive practice. Merrill's account is particularly useful, as it charts the development drawings of Louis Kahn's office (including those by Kahn himself as well as other architects and technicians) for an unbuilt project: the Dominican Motherhouse in Pennsylvania. As such, it is pure design process, revealing the fraught nature of architectural design by engagement with the wealth of archival material. This record or trace of the project is one of the important sites for understanding the architectural project, allowing access not only to the presentation materials designed for the consumption of a client, but also the sequence of drawings which lead to that point. In explaining the appeal of the set of drawings presented, consisting largely of plans, Merrill states that:

> One appeal of the drawings in this book for us as architects must be similar to that of partitas for musicians; for like musical notation,

they are precise without being complete: they slow our vision, engage our imagination, and employ us in the making of the work, which in this case consists of forming spaces in our mind's (trained) eye. In this sense, the drawings presented here are not pictures for consumption, but objects of engagement, invitations to 'collaborate' in the work before us. (2010:12–13)

The preference expressed for the plan and other orthographic drawings by Merrill is, perhaps, overstated, but is used to illustrate a shift in architectural practice with greater reliance on computer models, which serve as images more readily than the abstractions of plan, section, and elevation. This photorealistic representation is often held to be more direct or image-based, but I would argue that the same issues of abstraction and contextualisation remain at the heart of this way of thinking. Thus, the creative tension in terms of temporality and spatiality remains. Discussions of improvisation led to the work of Sudnow (2002) on learning to play jazz piano as well as the strong linkage demonstrated by Ingold and Hallam in their editorial to the collection *Creativity and Cultural Improvisation* (2008:2–24). Fundamentally, each of these issues leads back to flows, movements, intuition, and temporality. The work of Henri Bergson is particularly useful in describing this process, and how such practices occur temporally as heterogeneous and grounded activities. It is with *Time and Free Will* (1913[2001]) that this description relating creative practices to a reappraisal of time that offers an experiential alternative to the homogeneity of scientific time.

But the conception of an empty homogeneous medium is something far more extraordinary, being a kind of relation against that heterogeneity which is the very ground of our experience. (1913[2001]:97)

It is easy to fall into a trap where a preference is expressed for experiential time over mathematical time, but there is much greater potential in understanding and exploiting the differences between these two fundamentally different ways of understanding time or space. The homogeneous space is unique to human activity, an abstraction which offers a clarity that is sometimes dangerous and at other times crucial, to edit out that which is distracting or irrelevant. It is this operational inattention from specific context which allows the architect to act, to provoke through intervention. It is much more useful to realise that there are abstracting and contextualising impulses at play in different aspects of the design process. It is sometimes absolutely necessary to work with measure (1913[2001]:12) and to abstract generalisable principles before working again with the specific context. Measure is used interestingly by Bergson here to indicate not only a quantification, but also an idea of anticipation, and the expectation of future movements.

90   *Hejduk's multiple projections*

We can trace both sides of temporality from an account which Bergson gives of the simple mathematical procedure of counting, which can be understood as a temporalised sequence of numbers, with this very sequentiality being key to the operation. What happens in mathematics, however, is that this sequence is abstracted from reality and experience:

> No doubt we can count the sheep in a flock and say that there are fifty, although they are all different from one another and are easily recognised by the shepherd: but the reason is that we agree in that case to neglect their individual differences and to take into account only what they have in common. (Bergson 1913[2001]:76)

This idea of neglecting the differences[3] is important to the argument, and lies at the root of the abstracting mechanism by which attitudes towards temporality and spatiality alike are evened out into an undifferentiated homogeneous medium[4]. In defining the terms for his query, Bergson works with the categories of extensity and intensity. These two terms are understood to be possible conditions of the same thing:

> we picture to ourselves, for example, a greater intensity of effort as a greater length of thread rolled up, or as a spring which, in unwinding, will occupy a greater space. In the idea of intensity, and even in the word which expresses it, we shall find the image of a present contraction and consequently a future expansion, the image of something virtually extended, and, if we may say so, of a compressed space. (1913[2001]:4)

The conceptual 'space' occupied allows a category difference to be observed, however. More than merely compressing and internalising through the idea of intensity, we have a qualitatively different experience when sensations are so tightly coiled.

> It is only to evade the difficulty to distinguish, as is usually done, between two species of quantity, the first extensive and measurable, the second intensive and not admitting of measure, but it can nevertheless be said that it is greater or less than another intensity. (Bergson 1913 [2001]:3)

It is then much more fruitful to think in terms of a process which flows from extensive to intensive and back again, the precise pattern of this being more descriptive of the creative process than simply understanding the geometry, graphics, and eventual architecture produced. The return to measure in this description is important, as the denial of measure in the intensive phenomenon indicates a perpetual present which looks to memory but does not indicate a future position. There is a parallel to Bergson's concern for the temporal in Bollnow's significant work *On Human Space* (1963[2011]).

Hejduk's multiple projections 91

Bollnow is explicit in his description of this experiential space in drawing the connection to Bergson:

> Just as Bergson explained 'duree', the time actually lived by humans, by opposing it to the more familiar mathematical time, we can also best visualize the singularly of experienced space, at first still difficult to grasp, by contrasting it with the more familiar mathematical space... The decisive quality of mathematical space is its homogeneity. (1963[2011]:18)

The recognition that the concept of experienced space and the intrinsic connection between spatiality and human life is difficult to grasp and must be done in contrast to the homogeneous mathematical space. The necessity of this contrast is interesting in itself, and again reiterates the dichotomy between the abstract and the contextual. What we learn from the practice of architecture, however, is that these two elements in time or space must be united, that there is a flow and coexistence of these two concepts of space[5]. Bollnow details the 'natural' coordinate system (1963[2011]:39–54) as being grounded in direct datum such as things being in front or behind of our body, or related to the horizon in the distance which determines fundamental categories of up and down. This centre is conceptually similar to that expressed within dance theory and notation, particularly Laban notation[6].

Many of the games which Hejduk plays with the viewer were not immediately apparent until I began to redraw them. Starting from a position of sympathy towards the drawings, I initially read many of the most fascinating aspects of the drawings to be mistakes or flaws rather than fundamental to the meaning of each piece.

As explorations of the mystic version of Christianity Hejduk was exploring here, this meaning is not fixed or stable, but rather the introduction of uncertainty instils a desire to know and to understand. These are hidden, disturbing, unsettling spaces between our representations. Hejduk is not explicit about the reasons why he begins to move so fluidly between axonometric, isometric, oblique, and other forms of parallel projection. Hejduk was a knowing draughtsman, however, an able architect and an important theorist. Each act was deliberately made or if the result of a chance procedure, allowed to stand.

There is a continuity with his early work where the hidden line was deliberately exploited and played with in representing his houses. This moves beyond the use of axonometric drawing as a way of showing the building as a three-dimensional, solid structure on the page and moves towards a delicate playfulness regarding what such drawings hide and what they reveal, what we must edit out in order to make a drawing legible, and the contract we make with the drawing conventions in order to be understood.

With the mysticism inherent in his work, Hejduk is insisting that, in order to be poetic in architecture, we need not always be clearly understood,

92 Hejduk's multiple projections

and that the tools we use can introduce uncertainty as well as pragmatic specification.

5.2 The poetic in late Hejduk

In addition to his architectural work, Hejduk also wrote and published poetry[7]. These works are not independent of his architectural works of this time, nor are they directly accompanying text. The texts explore similar themes to the later projects, but by alternative means. These verses can assist us in understanding his later drawn work which has a poetic character to it, hints of narrative, and furtive meanings which are indirect and changeable despite drawing on well-established stories. *Lines No Fire Could Burn* is a book of 73 poems, and is one of the latest pieces completed by Hejduk before his death. It has a clear relationship with his architectural work in the concern with Christian imagery, focusing on angels and crucifixions. The book does not relate the poems to the drawing series, however, and allows the words to stand on their own.

There is no explicit architectural reference in the imagery evoked, but some common concerns arrive through titles common across Hejduk's oeuvre. An argument could be made that the poems are an outlet for elements of Hejduk's thinking which could not be easily represented in drawings: the recurrence of blood as a motif is central to the work—with the mention of flows of blood resulting in movement in *18. The Unearthly Weight* (1999:34), or from *17. The Last Supper* (1999:32–33):

> within his sleeping mother
> her heart filled with blood
> tears flowed
> beneath her closed eyes
> and filled her internal cavities

Similar attention is given to the olfactory: Flowers are the clear motif here, but other scents are used evocatively as well. As an invasive sense where the sensed phenomenon enters the body, smells can overpower, and this is one of the aspects which Hejduk appears to play with here. The implications are that he cannot make architecture with the conventional means, so he has to drift into other modes of making. I argue that these as complementary pursuits which can only be appreciated (but possibly never fully understood) when read in relation to Hejduk's architecture regardless of whether it was built or not.

Bodies are wounded and broken, changed and transformed, immersed in an environment. Again, this serves an alternative purpose to Hejduk's architecture: often mobile in the case of the *Collapse of Time*, or lacking meaningful engagement with context, even built in an entirely different location to the intended one in *Wall House 2*. The materiality of Hejduk's language borrows more from his activities as a painter than an architect: References are to colours more than to structures; transformations are in terms of hues, textures, hardness as in *The Undertow of Thought* (1999:29):

> The albatross turned dark plum
> And bled indigo

Further indications come in *37. The Green Room* and *41. The Wallpaper* where a fictionalised Georges Braque makes an appearance. Here, the use of the word 'pigment' is explicit, with the aim to mix a colour which has not been seen on Earth, a miraculous colour that suggests Hejduk's frustration with his palette (1999:71). Eventually, direct reference to the act of building is made in *46. I Will Build It of Stone*. This intention is framed around primordial geological events, and is more about the will to build than the eventual structure. Another character appears, and interaction with Auguste Rodin has a different character to Braque, in *59. Let Us Return*. Braque (or an angel) addresses the sculptor (1999:99). The dialogue between artists who could never meet provides a brief of sorts for Hejduk: Braque and Rodin are from quite different traditions, but modern in their own ways, and their ways of seeing the world inform his approach to the architectural projects intertwined with his writings.

The book *Pewter Wings Golden Horns Stone Veils*[8] presents a number of Hejduk's later sketchbook projects interspersed with designs for houses from the North South East West series and a cathedral. The contrast between the styles of the earlier ruled drawings and this more expressive work is particularly clear here, but it would be a mistake to separate them too much: There is a nod to convention in the manner of some of these drawings, often an oblique form of parallel projection which may not have the precision of mechanical drawing, but the hesitant lines have other qualities. These drawings are set alongside brief narrative texts and works of poetry by Hejduk, more explicitly allowing the reader to understand the relationship between these pursuits of literature and his works of architecture.

The intention is to read the poems as architecture and the buildings as poetry. The method of juxtaposing these elements allows the reader to access the material immediately, in the sense of *without mediation*. The works are difficult and opaque at times, resisting easy reading, and meaning might be found in the interstitial spaces between the disciplines we are translating between. Translation in this case has a large degree of interpretation: Benjamin's essay on the *Work of the Translator*[9] is called to mind here, where the translated work is in essence a new work which—in a non-pejorative sense—is an *echo* of the originating work.

It might make more sense to write about *transcription* in the case under discussion here. Transferring from one form of inscriptive practice to another rather than from one language to another, translation implies

94   *Hejduk's multiple projections*

language, and this is a source of much debate within architecture. Even the most ardent proponent of the linguistic analogy in architecture will see differences between the nonverbal language of architecture and the written or spoken word; and the fiercest opponent of that.

For the series *Wedding in a Dark Plum Room,* Hejduk proposes a town plan for the distributed programmes: each building serves a role in the narrative, assigned a task and set into a plan (1997:110–111) which presents three distinct zones: the wedding site, the family site, and the town structures. Drawn from his travels in Spain, and specifically noting Seville, the plan is redrawn and fragmented, an abstract figure-ground is produced followed by sequential drawings of silhouettes. Each element is explored through Hejduk's familiar watercolour and ink drawings: bold colours and heavy lines describe the structures in a range of projections. The entry focuses on two chapels: the Family Chapel and Bell Tower (1997:128–129), and the Chapel of the Fallen (1997:130–131). Each has a separate plan, perspective, and parallel drawing in colour, describing in the case of the Family Chapel a turquoise shape, spiky in plan but terminating in a flat edge. This plan is extrapolated upwards to form walls, which are punctuated with openings and projections at irregular points. A campanile tower in warm grey, similarly extruded, shows the logic of parallel projection underpinning the work. A conflict is described by the Chapel of the Fallen, looking somewhat like microbes attacking one another under a microscope, a second turquoise form with the same language as the Family Chapel is penetrated by a dark grey form on one edge; and a crimson one on another. The roof plane is more articulated here, but the formal language of the project is heavily influenced by the logic of parallel projection.

Further blurring of the poetic and architectural are Hejduk's *Masques.* Discussed in detail by James McGregor[10] and Martin Søberg[11]. The *masques* for Berlin, Lancaster, and Hanover were framed as a form of public event[12] not unlike an urban festival:

> Hejduk borrows the term masque from a theatrical genre, extinct since the Enlightenment, which brought nobility and gentry together in a kind of ritual acknowledgment of difference. Its form was spectacle— in which each spectator was simultaneously a participant—and its function was to naturalise class distinction. The demise of the masque as a relevant form of social expression coincided with Enlightenment attacks on a mythologised social hierarchy and with the consequent emergence of Utopian socialisms. (2012:69)

On the division between theory and practice in contemporary architecture, McGregor (2002:59) argues that making and knowledge form a continuum. The projects are made as much by those who encounter them (viewers, observers, readers) as they are by Hejduk and his team. This subverts authority and allows the creative engagement to continue beyond the scope of the construction of each work. This continual state of undergoing making, being made, is consistent with anthropological approaches to contemporary art and architecture from Ingold and others[13]. Whilst it can be argued that Hejduk ignored convention in the later drawings, they instead represent a flexibility towards the coexistence of multiple conventions. Hejduk often experimented, as in the early Diamond Houses, with the impact of misreading a drawing, flattening three dimensions or deliberately misreading an axonometric drawing as an oblique. The later projects and sketchbooks are increasingly flexible with their drawing conventions, often allowing multiple projections to coexist not only on one page, but within one drawing, one object.

Hejduk's narrative consists of characters set into relationships with one another, not explicitly moving but with a suggestion of it; the relationships emerge through encounters between the architectural structures and observers, visitors, who each bring their own interpretations to this open work[14]. The characters exist as implicit biographies, inventories, and suggestions at a life outside of that which is shown; all without being given an actual story to mobilise their interactions.

The status of Hejduk's work is interesting, possibly frustrating any attempt to pin it down as one thing or the other, and belonging to a wider category of speculative works in architecture. Why it cannot constitute architectural theory is something of a mystery. It is to me an architectural theory which uses architecture's means of production to operate, and it is all the more valuable for it.

Stan Allen (Allen in McGregor 2002:61), writing in Hays's *Hejduk's Chronotope*[15], notes that Hejduk is not against theory but rather conducting it by other means, bringing it closer to architecture by using the practices of the discipline in order to theorise. The masque projects mediate between the pragmatics and compromises of built architecture and the distant, loftiness of a purely theoretical construct. The idea that Hejduk, as storyteller, allows or encourages the participants to remain *present* foreshadows my argument which follows, about the drawings themselves: Hejduk remains fully *present* in his work—an extended marginalia, or stepping outside of conventions to call attention to himself. The discussion centres on Hejduk's notion of being in the present with the works, rejecting the nostalgia for either a *golden age* or the forward-facing version of a *utopia*. The idea of the masques is to reject or surpass the traditional role of the architect. They are a 'living portrait' (McGregor 2002:63) which keeps up with events as they unfurl.

5.3 Making present

Figure 5.1 is from John Hejduk's 1991 work *Thoughts Upon an Uccello Painting*[16], part of the *Soundings* series of works. Paolo Uccello (1397–1475) made use of three-point perspective as early as the mid-1440s, laying the groundwork for later developments in this form of representation.

96 *Hejduk's multiple projections*

Figure 5.1 John Hejduk, Soundings: Thoughts Upon an Uccello Painting, 1991; *ink on paper 22 × 28 cm; DR1998:0129:076, John Hejduk fonds, Canadian Centre for Architecture.*

The drawing is notable in that it includes two angles for the presumed upright elements: conventional 90° angles in the upper and lower third of the composition, with the central section setting the vertical lines to 45°; a further constellation of objects on the right of the page maintain their 90° orientation throughout. This combination of different forms of parallel projection in a single drawing is typical of Hejduk in this period, but it would be a mistake to think of these as mistakes or as sloppy draughtsmanship. The shift is deliberate and consistent within the drawing. One option is to understand the drawing as a single convention—a flat, frontally oriented axonometric drawing looking from top down; then the form takes on a curious character, sharply angled in the central section of the form. There are various mental exercises which the viewer can engage in, to extract a form which would conform to a single set of projection rules (see figure 5.2).

The second option is to accept that the form is drawn in more than one convention: Elements which begin in with 90° verticals retain that convention, so the cylinders which originate below the line of the shift maintain their internal consistency. Hejduk is making himself present within this drawing, the hand is clearly autographic, not the clinical coolness of the Texas Houses, but a proposition which relies upon the scratchy hand-drawn lines and frantic cross-hatched shading.

This is consistent with the poetic turn in Hejduk's work; by placing himself at the centre of the works, he is underlining some of the aspects of personal discovery at the heart of his oeuvre. The projects increasingly represent processes of inquiry, ways of finding out about the world, and these

Hejduk's multiple projections

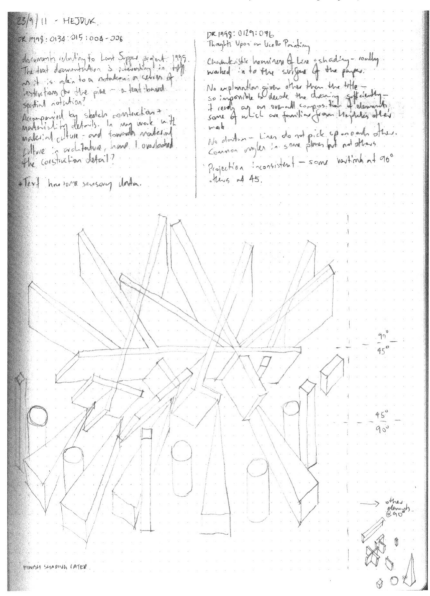

Figure 5.2 Redrawing of DR1998:0129:076, Thoughts Upon an Uccello Painting.

increasingly abandon any attempt at universality. Instead, Hejduk comes to realise that his architecture is always both relational and personal, operating at one level to explore fundamental aspects of being through his own encounters with the world, and making use of common myths and understandings in order to allow others to access a little of his insights. These encounters generate further knowledge, and are not static.

98 *Hejduk's multiple projections*

My encounter with the work is to redraw the works, selecting and editing the moments which I find to be of greatest importance and highlighting the shifts in projection which Hejduk employs. Other approaches would be to examine the process of mark-making, its hesitancy and jaggedness; employing what James Elkins discusses as *contorni* (1998:44); others would focus on the heavy warm colouring, symbolism or form, but my interest lies in the conventions of drawing and how Hejduk knowledgeably, wilfully breaks and manipulates the rules of conventional projection.

Where the other architects discussed in this volume intend to clearly communicate their intended meaning to the viewer by means of their drawings, Hejduk is opening his inscriptions to a multiplicity of possible meanings. He shows us where he is present within the process and allows us to see where decisions could have gone in alternative directions. Meanings are plural, overlapping, coincident, and are produced as much by the viewer as the draughtsman. My process of engagement moves beyond apprehending the work and translating it into my own drawing, but this is not an absolute truth, but instead the meaning produced when this drawing comes into contact with my thinking, my intention, and my baggage.

Notes

1. This connection between drawing and dance is not entirely new, and was poetically explored by Sergei Eisenstein in the essay 'How I Learned to Draw (A Chapter About My Drawing Lessons)' published in support of an exhibition of his expressionist, figurative, and religious works on paper at the Drawing Center, New York. In this essay, Eisenstein asserts that 'Drawing and dancing are branches of the same tree' (2000:26).
2. I do not, of course exclude model making or other means of production, but rather focus on drawing.
3. We see this even in the case of identical or mathematically similar units: 'And yet they must be somehow distinct from one another since otherwise they would merge into a single unit. Let us assume that all the sheep are identical: they differ at least by the position which they occupy space. Otherwise they would not form a flock' (Bergson 1913[2001]:77).
4. A person might begin to understand a number of different practices in this manner, with the idea of the collection standing in contrast to the fuller engagement with objects in use and in context. The conventional model of the museum is a sequential ordering which again neglects individual differences (sometimes through the mechanism of cataloguing them) where an object which is enmeshed in an ongoing practice remains temporal, but as heterogeneous and differentiated time.
5. Bergson is railing against the preeminence of mathematical understandings of time, as this had replaced the intuitive durational time in favour of the physicist's concept—which Bergson contends (Bergson 1913[2001]:109) is rendering time as a fourth dimension of space.
6. See Lucas (2008, 2009) for some more details on Laban movement notation.
7. Hejduk, John. 1995. *Architectures in Love*. New York: Rizzoli.
   Hejduk, John. 1999. *Lines No Fire Could Burn*. New York: Monacelli Press.

8. Hejduk, John. 1997. *Pewter Wings Golden Horns Stone Veils*. New York: Monacelli Press.
9. Benjamin, Walter. 1923. "The Task of the Translator" in Benjamin, W. 1999. *Illuminations*. London: Pimlico.
10. McGregor, James. 2002. "The Architect as Storyteller: Making Places in John Hejduk's Masques" in *Architectural Theory Review*, Vol. 7, No. 2, pp. 59–70.
11. Søberg, Martin. 2012. "John Hejduk's Pursuit of an Architectural Ethos" in *Footprint: Architecture Culture and the Question of Knowledge*, Spring 2012, pp. 113–128.
12. See Browne, J., Frost, C. & Lucas, R. (Eds.). 2018. *Architecture, Festival and the City*. London: Routledge, for more on festivals.
13. See Buchli (2013), Ingold (2013), Pink (2004), and Daniels (2010).
14. See Umberto Eco's *Open Work* (1989) here.
15. Hays, K. Michael (Ed.). 1996. *Hejduk's Chronotopes*. New York: Princeton Architectural Press.
16. A useful discussion of Uccello with a focus on his perspectives can be found in: Roccasecca, Pietro. 2008. "Sebastiano Serlio: Placing Perspective at the Service of Architects" in Carpo, Mario & Lemerle, Frédérique (Eds.). *Perspective, Projections and Design: Technologies of Architectural Representation*. London: Routledge.

6 Axonometry as theoretical instrument: the case of Eisenman

6.1 Form, volume, language, and movement in architectural theory

The early work of Peter Eisenman, another of the New York Five architects, is characterised by his use of axonometric drawing as a practical tool for design and as a theoretical instrument. Eisenman's work explores common postmodernist concerns with the linguistic analogy in architecture, leading him to many novel uses of drawing and tightly argued assertions about the nature of architecture.

Works such as House X by Eisenman explore architecture from fundamental concepts upwards. Informed by his examinations of Guissepi Terragni and other architects, Eisenman puts the axonometric drawing through its paces, designing architecture from a series of reductive 'el/L' shapes, rotating and transforming as a series of operations which prefigure much of today's parametric design.

This archaeology of parametricism demonstrates something about Eisenman's thinking which can be traced into his later work, achieved through computational methods rather than manually. The use of axonometric drawing can be argued to form the foundation of this work, however, despite the apparent distance between these two geometries, it is a difference of degree rather than a difference in kind.

Eisenman uses axonometric projection to explore what architecture can be, and exploits its qualities to produce a graphic philosophy of space. Writing in the introduction to Aldo Rossi's *Architecture of the City*[1], he gives some clear statements regarding his position towards drawing with the production of both architectural design and theory.

> The architectural drawing, formerly though of exclusively as a form of representation, now becomes the locus of another reality. It is not only the site of illusion, as it has been traditionally, but also a real place of the suspended time of both life and death. It's reality is neither forward time—progress—nor past time—nostalgia, for by being an autonomous object it eludes both the progressive and regressive forces of historicism. (1982a:10)

The case of Eisenman   101

This is related both to the notion of locus and that of analogy developed by Eisenman in his response to Rossi here. The function of his drawings surpasses (but includes) representation, they are also critical and analytical. Of Rossi's drawings, he discusses their analogous nature in terms of their temporality, where they arrest time, both processual and atmospheric (1982a:11).

The interplay of memory and history is a recurring concern for Eisenman, finding new ways to interrogate the past is central to his thinking. The notion is of *operative pasts* which remain current, where the inactive past is a kind of baggage, described in the position regarding *propelling* and *pathological* monuments (1982a:6). A deeper engagement with this possibility of an operative past can be seen in Eisenman's analytical engagement with his carefully selected canon.

The production of architectural theory in parallel to building is of great importance in Eisenman's career. Several of these works are devoted to the close formal analysis of other architects' works, crossing over from architectural history to architectural theory. The intent is explicitly theoretical, grounded in Eisenman's belief in *The Formal Basis of Modern Architecture*—the title of his PhD thesis[2]. This pursuit of the formal is important as it is where Eisenman contends that the purely architectural quality of a building resides. Eisenman's project is to understand which qualities are exclusively architecture, rather than reference to other disciplines.

The opening statement of the thesis makes a bold claim about the communicative nature of creative practice,: and it is within this broader linguistic analogy that Eisenman places his architectural theory. Architecture is a language with a grammar: it has the power to communicate using its own means. As such, Eisenman discusses the transmission of ideas[3] through architecture:

> The essence of any creative act is the communication of an original idea from its author, through a means of expression, to a receiver. The means of expression must be such as to transmit the original intention as clearly and fully as possible to the receiving mind. (2006:25)

This undermines the potential for the idea to be developed by way of the 'means of expression' as I would argue. This model embeds all the cognition in the mind, that the process of thinking creatively is a preface to the production of the line. This is problematic given contemporary ideas of embodiment and, a second issue, with comprehension. The model of understanding by the 'receiver' in Eisenman's model is that they decode the information given in order to accurately reconstruct the intended meaning transmitted. This elides the work done by the recipient, who might be in a position, with the weight of their own background and existing knowledge, to produce a meaning entirely unanticipated by the creator. We shall return

102   *The case of Eisenman*

to this discussion of open narrative structures discussed with reference to Cedric Price's work in the next chapter.

Describing the linguistic analogy that runs through his work, basic geometric forms described as elements of a grammar, with some reference to the potential functional implications of these characteristics. As you would expect, the cube is a form given special attention by Eisenman (2006:35). Like Hejduk's fascination for the qualities of the nine-square grid, Eisenman notes the various features of the axes of a cube. The equivalence of each of the surfaces of the cube are a starting point, and allow a differentiation between *generic form* and *specific form* which might be understood as the contrast between Platonic solids and how they actually operate in the world. Whilst the generic cube's surfaces are all exactly alike, as soon as you place a cube into the real world, its faces are differentiated: one or two might have south-facing aspect, one is the bottom of the cube, resting on another surface or support whilst the topmost face can be traversed unlike the vertical faces.

It could be argued that this position towards form is a manifesto for Eisenman at this stage of his career:

> the giving of form is far more than the making of shapes, or the creation of beautiful and aesthetically pleasing objects in themselves, for these only satisfy the perceptual and not the conceptual aspects of the problem... Form, is therefore specific, yet at the same time general. It provides for architecture, the particular means of expressing intent and accommodating function, and the general means for creating an ordered environment. (2006:55)

Volume is essential to Eisenman's thesis, and is discussed as distinctive from concepts of space. Volume is *dynamic* in this definition: it is specific and defined, a contained variety of space, which is understood as having a generic, unbounded condition; 'Architectural form can be thought of as 'volume' that exists in 'space' (2006:59). This understanding of volume is activated by movement. In a reading of Corbusier's villas, Eisenman (2006:71) gives a phenomenological reading of their composition. This is revealed perceptually, primarily visually, but a totality is impossible: the work of reading a building takes time and movement through it. Here, Eisenman is in tension with an experiential understanding, and returns to his preferred *conceptual* understanding of space which we gain from our bodily and sensory engagements. The sedimentation of a piece of architecture in our memory results in a conceptual reading.

The concluding section of the thesis delivers a historical account of the development of architectural theory from Vitruvius through Alberti and towards the diversification of theoretical treatises after Durand and Choisy.

The case of Eisenman   103

This intellectual history of architectural theory itself is interesting, and clearly Eisenman sees his work firmly within this continuum.

> It is the imprecise and metaphorical use of language in architectural theory that has tended to negate its critical validity: and it seems probably that this has come about as a confusion between moral and formal criteria. (2006:351)

This avoidance of metaphor can be seen clearly in Eisenman's design work: the desire to create and work within a discipline of architecture which does not use an external referent. The success of this is another matter, and it suffices to report on this intention here. Eisenman's invocation of *fundamental* principles and qualities (2006:353) is notable, as he appears to be adhering to ideas from the classical, universalist understanding of the world as consisting of underlying truths which can always be understood to be the case. This excludes contextual differentiation, alternative traditions and cultures of building, and seeks to find something inherent to architecture wherever we encounter it. His combination of linguistic and mathematical properties comes from an ambition to find these underlying principles even if, in the position of this author, such universals cannot be held to be true[4].

6.2 Drawing as analysis

Eisenman uses axonometric drawing as part of his work as an architectural theoretician. Two key works on this are his book on Terragni[5] and *Ten Canonical Buildings*[6]. The aim of both books is to inform the *canon* of architecture, to establish an alternative set of exemplars and precedents from which architects can learn more about their profession. Key to this is the use of line drawings, using fine black lines and highlighting some diagrammatic elements with red lines. The code for these drawings is never explicitly discussed, but the aim throughout both volumes is to discuss the underlying diagram of the buildings in question.

Stan Allen, in his introduction, notes that 'Eisenman's canon is definitively not a new orthodoxy' (2008:12); the aim was not to simply extend the list of unquestionably great buildings from the past, celebrating them for their status and persistence, but rather it is intended as a statement of where Eisenman's thinking is at that point in time, and as a suggestion for future directions. Eisenman wishes to open the debate on the buildings in question, to enable further arguments to be made, and suggesting alternative understandings of what architecture can mean. To this end, Eisenman is in opposition to the humanism of writers such as Colin Rowe[7], the autonomy claimed for architecture is of utmost importance: these ten buildings are examples of autonomous, formal architecture, not the continuity of architectural history proposed by Rowe.

104 *The case of Eisenman*

Eisenman writes of his distinction between the *canonical* building and the *great*:

> A canonical building requires study, not in and of itself as an isolated object, but in terms of its capacity to reflect on its particular moment in time and its relation to buildings which both precede it and come after it. (2006:12)

The status of these drawings is worth considering, as they purport to have a diagrammatic quality to them despite making frequent use of the codes of axonometric drawing. This can be understood to open out the idea of what these inscriptions are—both drawings and diagrams simultaneously, both conventional and personal notations. I unpack the idea that a single inscription can contain these multiple qualities in detail elsewhere[8], noting that any piece can be read simultaneously as both/or drawing, map, diagram, notation, sketch, and picture. An inscription might be understood by different audiences in different ways, or even multiple understandings simultaneously. Discussing these as *qualities* of inscriptive practice allows for a finer grained definition of what a diagram is, or a notation. Each has different rules and intentions.

Eisenman notes that the idea of the architect as individual genius emerges in the Renaissance (2003:23), when 'an anthropocentric conception of society displaced a theocentric one', and 'Buildings were viewed as extensions of the creative subject and mirrors of a self-conception.' There have been changes in other disciplines, but architecture clings to this state of affairs to an unhealthy extent, and Eisenman subscribes to this with his assertion that the paper architecture is close to both the conception of the architect, held in the mind, and the building which results from it by a process of transmission.

The analysis is primarily formal, focusing on geometric transformations from simple forms to create more complex ones, so processes and relationships including symmetry, rotation, addition, and subtraction are considered alongside ideas of solid and void, point and plane. Eisenman concludes that:

> building form in this sense is understood as the product of the process of transformation, the modification of some primary configuration. (2003:27)

One of the aims of the diagramming is to allow comparison. By producing these drawings, Eisenman is working with a common language of other architects working at the same time as Terragni, architects such as Le Corbusier and Mies van der Rohe, who figure much more in the existing literature. Drawing suggests equivalence for Eisenman (2003:297–298): the common inscriptive practice allows for direct relationships and distinctions to be made between the works and is crucial to Eisenman's positioning of the architecture as a text to be discussed. It is here that he establishes his theorisation as something more involved than that of Wittkower or Rowe: these are not mere illustrations, but a form of understanding in practice, using the tools of architecture to produce analysis and theory.

Texts can be read in alternative ways, and are much more subject to the reader's agency, and Eisenman's interest is not in aesthetics or the functioning of the architecture (2003:300), but trying to find a way to read the architecture *as* architecture. His formal analysis takes account of basic architectural forms: windows, doors, walls, floors, ceilings, roofs. This means taking the object itself seriously—not as a sign of some other interest, but as a phenomenon with its own qualities.

Verbal language is limited when discussing architecture and requires a great deal of technical jargon to convey what a drawing is capable of showing almost immediately. Geometric relations, when explained in writing, involve a complex language of coordinates and relationships that obscure the aims of the exercise. Drawings are clearly more efficient tools for over-drawing, annotating, and explaining other drawings.

Writing on his choice of *Ten Canonical Buildings*, it is important to note the alternative understanding Eisenman develops of schemes such as Stirling's Leicester University Engineering Building, proposing an analysis which does not indulge the usual art historical process of tracing influences (which are important, of course), or even his wilful use of materials. The building is, to Eisenman, self-referential, developing Stirling's architecture through reflection on his own past works.

Writing elsewhere about diagrams, Eisenman makes some comments about his approach which are useful here:

> while the diagrams which attempt to describe these relationships are analytic, nevertheless they are potentially an integral part of the design process. In addition the diagrams act as a set of instructions; they attempt to make legible the relationships which an individual may not see. They provide what can be called a conceptual framework for this understanding. (2004:39)

As part of *Canonical Buildings*, Eisenman discusses the drawings of others as well as producing his own reinterpretations. Axonometric drawings are used extensively here, and as noted in Chapter 2, they separate elements of the composition in order to explore their relationships with one another as well as their discreet identities. Sequences of drawings[9] allow an argument to be followed closely, relying on the ability of the reader, assumed to be a trained architect, to read these visually presented arguments. Sequential drawings are heavy with the paths left untaken, and the order in which decisions and moves are depicted becomes an element for critique and understanding.

6.3 Entanglements

In his essay, *Cardboard Architecture*[10], Eisenman develops an alternative to the term *paper architecture*, which is often used to describe speculative, unbuilt projects. Many of Eisenman's projects, however speculative they might seem, are also competed and constructed pieces of architecture. Eisenman is suggesting that his built architecture be understood similarly to models: if we are to think of them as 1:1 scale models built out of cardboard from his drawings, they are easier to consider as possessing theoretically engaging intentions.

Responding to a page of 24 axonometric drawings, described tellingly as *diagrams* and showing the process of House II, Eisenman describes them as abstract, formal propositions. This is generated by an underlying process, allowing it to respond to a given context. Again, his formal interest emerges, 'The coordinates of a cubic space are described by its edge or its centre; the edge composed of lines or planes, the centre by a line or a volume' (2004:35).

Axonometric diagrams are often presented as sequences by Eisenman; there is a linear progression and a reference to the nine-square problem posed by Hejduk to his students. The development is not fully described as the paths experimented with and not taken are edited, elided from the account. Elements of *line, plane,* and *volume* are described as being *deployed*—placed as if according to military strategy. We see here that the *grid* element is supposed to be neutral; akin to *datum* in nature—something for the deliberately designed elements to react off and make reference to. This status division shows that these formal experimentations require a structure, despite the lack of context in the drawings, and there needs to be some rule or measure, an interval with which to describe the relations.

The possibility of fluctuating conditions for these elements is discussed here under the *bi-valent* (2004:37) condition of elements: any element of a design can have more than one role assigner to it, fluctuating between column and wall, and offering the possibility that the viewer is held within this flux when apprehending the structure. Perhaps more importantly is the idea that the architecture is to be appreciated as an *assemblage* or *entanglement*, and that the combinations of elements is more important than the discreet qualities of each part.

This intersection with archaeologist Ian Hodder's work on *entanglements* is useful to explore further, as it suggests a material culture reading of Eisenman's axonometric drawings and architecture. Writing on the various schools of material culture which frame his work, Hodder discusses Ingold's critique that the thing itself is left out when the discussion is so centred on the various social, economic, and cultural interactions of objects. Hodder's entanglements are categorised through a series of possible connections: production and reproduction; exchange; use; consumption; discard; and post-deposition (further material interactions after humans have formally disposed of an item)[11].

Eisenman's architecture, whether drawn, modelled, or built, takes the form of an encounter between a person and the thing. To borrow from Hodder, *humans depend on things*, and *things depend on other things*. The autonomy of Eisenman's architecture still relies upon a human encounter in order to make sense, and it is also the entire compositions which form his architecture and not constellations of elements. Eisenman's House projects still fail as architecture if they neglect to include stairs, for example, which would allow people to move from one floor to another: much in the same way as one small metal part holds the 26-foot Columbia boat together as described by Hodder (2012:51).

Returning to bivalency, Mario Gandelsonas's account of Eisenman's axonometric model of House X[12] demonstrates some of this thinking: the model which uses a drawing convention, and denies the usual benefit of the model over drawing; the model which has only a singular viewing position. Gandelsonas discusses this as part of Eisenman's wider critique of both humanist and functionalist approaches to architecture. By being both a model and a drawing, the axonometric model defies our expectations, and is not proposed as a useful, pragmatic solution but rather a critique and a thinking tool.

> But the axonometric model of House X is a three-dimensional draw-ing. It does not provide knowledge of the object in a dimensional sense; it is not about reality, but about fiction; it provides phantasmagoric images—a sequence of anamorphisms—among which the 'right' image is very difficult to discover. It makes the 'normal' image appear to be an anomaly: we perceive it only at the instant where we see this false image—the model as a two-dimensional drawing—while the 'abnormal' images are in fact the only ones that describe the true nature of the three-dimensional object, the model. (1982b:28)

Eisenman's own account of this model (1982b:158) highlights that it was produced after it became clear that House X would not be built. The model, therefore, became the final expression of the design, playing with viewpoints and the fixed nature of our normal viewing of a model. There is a reversal with the nature of the axonometric drawing, which has a fixed frontal view; the model alters radically when a person alters their position, with the true angles and lengths of the axonometric drawing subverted by a model which deforms in order to produce one apparently true viewing position. The relationship with the photograph of the model further complicates the matter (1982b:159), the photograph conforms to the conventions of axonometric drawing, but it is itself a representation of a model.

Whilst this is the most obvious bi-valency in Eisenman's representations, there is a more subtle one, perhaps born of necessity: his use of collage (see for example House VI[13]) in constructing the coloured axonometric

108 *The case of Eisenman*

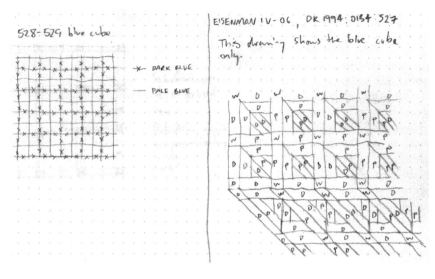

Figure 6.1 Redrawing of DR1994:0134:527, showing collage drawing of overlapping gridded cubes. Note the projection here is down at 45° from a 90° set plan drawing.

drawings. These are collages designed to operate as drawings. They, again, have an axonometric logic to them, and appear, once the layers are carefully aligned, to conform to the conventions of parallel projection. Layering is a common part of architectural drawing, so this is not what sets them apart, yet they do have a different quality to them, a physicality that most drawings erase or deny, a two-dimensionality that these can only achieve once photographed (figure 6.1).

6.4 The el-form, wallness, and planeness

As part of his proposed internal logic for architecture, Eisenman puts forward a number of elements and attitutes which can have fluctuating qualities. Indeterminacy is explored through the 'el' form used as components of the House projects (figure 6.2). This is described in *Diagram Diaries*[14] as a form of interiority, a device developed to overcome materiality when considering his formal experiments. Further development of form comes with a distinction between the qualities of 'wallness' and 'planeness' coined by Eisenman. Planeness is used to describe a condition found in the fine arts, where the plane is a prominent condition. You could argue, as De Stijl did, that a planar architecture was possible, but Eisenman wishes to return to the *wall*. Wallness, then, is a vertical structure which carries the sign and function of 'wall', one of the fundamental architectural forms which Eisenman identifies.

The case of Eisenman 109

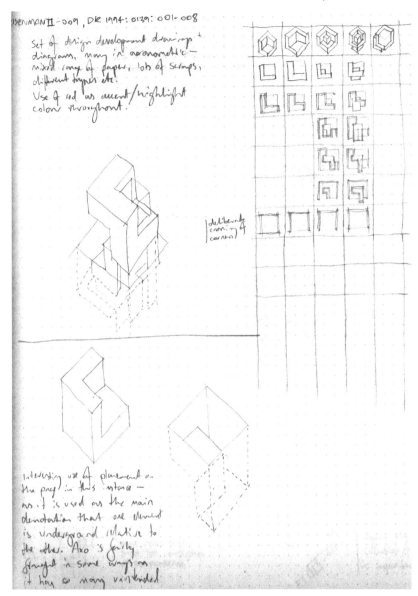

Figure 6.2 Redrawing of DR1994:0139:001-008 showing the el-form and its deformations, combinations, and collisions.

The aim of this element is to overcome the linguistic message it carries and its functional necessity. Once that has been achieved, the remainder, Eisenman argues, is *architectural*. Eisenman's *el-form* is a strategy for finding this condition of pure architecture by using a repeating form which sits between the condition of wall and column, its status is relational and

110 *The case of Eisenman*

contextual, possibly fluctuating or being two elements simultaneously. The el-form in question is simply a truncated 'L' shape, extruded into three dimensions, it becomes a cube eroded by a second cube. These elements are then arranged, rotated, and eventually transformed. The el-form creates a potential interior, having excavated part of the original form, it is suggestive without being prescriptive (figures 6.3 and 6.4).

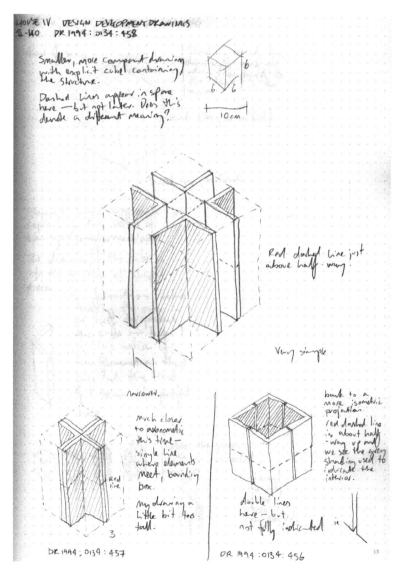

Figure 6.3 Redrawing of DR1994:0134:458 showing initial simple experiment with el-form.

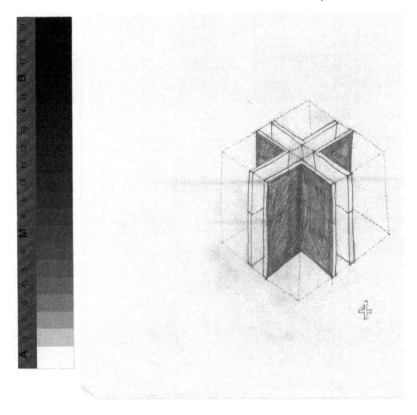

Figure 6.4 Peter Eisenman, axonometric sketch for House VI, Cornwall, Connecticut, 1973; graphite with coloured pencil on translucent paper 23 × 26 cm; DR1994:0134:458, Peter Eisenman fonds, Canadian Centre for Architecture.

Several of Eisenman's early House projects make use of the el-form, with House VI (1971), House 11a (1978) and the Guardiola House (1988) providing some of the clearest examples.

Writing on his House X (1975) project[15], Eisenman arranges the piece as a dialogue between two characters: the *Architect* and the *Voice*. The *Architect* in this case represents the architect of House X, and the *Voice* switches between being the voice of a critic, or the architect of all the preceding houses in the series before House X.

The process for House X, as the conclusion to the series, is a little different from those which preceded it. A series of formal operations, flexible enough to allow for intervention by the architect, are set into motion. These include ways for patterns to interact, how to handle sequences and relationships, with the aim being a process which reveals itself as it progresses. The protocols are not explicit as they would be in a contemporary parametric

112 *The case of Eisenman*

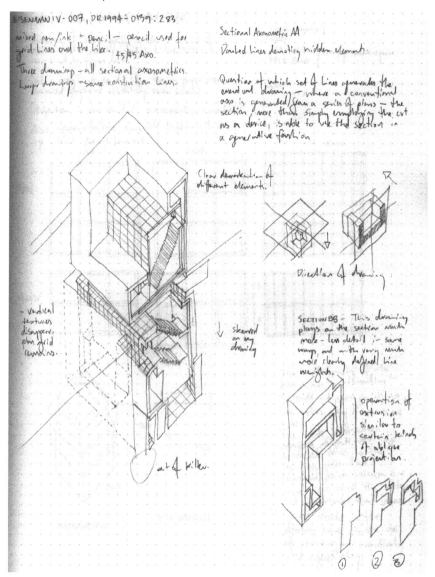

Figure 6.5 Redrawing of DR1994:0139:283; sectional axonometric of House 11a.

design process: the algorithms are not given in detail, but are felt out by Eisenman as he develops them by hand (figure 6.5).

Given the aim of the project is to expose the limits which created it, producing a rather flattering analogy of himself as an archaeologist or geologist who is discovering or uncovering the houses a process of revelation rather than design. He is quick to step back from the archaeologist as role model, however, as he wishes to rid himself of the social, political, and historical context. He similarly steps back from the geological, as 'His methods may be rigorous but not scientific' (1982b:38).

Whilst Eisenman has long developed the idea that he is looking to free architecture of its external referent, the idea of meaning is contested. Eisenman disentangles significance from meaning as a way out of this conundrum, as the content he wants to convey is different from the kinds of meaning ascribed to historical examples. This is still by way of an age-old process of the architecture revealing its significance to the viewer in the manner of modernist architecture exposing the interior workings of a building by its external form[16]. For Eisenman, the significance pre-dates the architecture, and it is the role of the building to demonstrate its significance. The significance is essentially the form, and the process by which it is arrived:

> The development of these notions is continued in House X, where the *strategies and forms*—as opposed to the meanings—are thought of as pre-existent, as belonging to the larger, still unarticulated universe of form which remains to be excavated. Thus, the decompositional design 'process' in House X is used as a probe to uncover hidden, unavailable, or latent means of conceptualising. In a sense, the process is used to uncover pre-existent processes and the forms are used to uncover pre-existent forms. (1982b:40)

Critiquing others including Massimo Scolari, Eisenman discusses the drive towards meaning in their architecture, which has a selection of pre-ferred forms, arranged in careful compositions, meaning that architecture has a finite set of possibilities. This leads to a discussion of *icons* and the position of the earlier House projects (I–VIII) regarding this: these early houses are purely architectural icons as opposed to the broadly cultural icons of other architects' works. His contention is that House X surpasses this by being an object cleansed of architectural 'pieties'.

The process itself is distinct from randomness and arbitrariness, recog-nising that it might be possible to produce similar results without the strat-egy of decomposition, or reversal of conventional ideas of composition. The design, and the axonometric drawings, is a process of uncovering and discovery, the results of which cannot be known in advance. The result-ing house reveals its processes and origins, shows the trace of its defor-mations over time, the actual process, further described, begins with an 'act of approximation' and each subsequent decision is either pursuing *con-sistency* or *correspondence*. This *garden of forking paths*[17] allows a kind of archaeology into the process which could reveal alternative outcomes where the option chosen might be different in one or more position. In this sense, the house is a matrix of all the possible outcomes of the formal evo-lution initiated by Eisenman.

114   *The case of Eisenman*

The process uses square and el-shapes, with the asymmetric hollowed out cube being the three-dimensional form of Eisenman's el-shape. The el-shape has 'no particular aesthetic value' and no other significance according to Eisenman: it is absent of associations and conventional ideas of meaning.

The prose employed by Eisenman demonstrates the limitations of verbal language when discussing drawing in any kind of detail: the aim becomes precision, which actually begins to obscure the intended meaning as precise mathematical terms are required to discuss the operations which might more easily be given in a gesture, or indeed a trace on the surface of the paper. An in-depth discussion of various ratios used by Eisenman (1982b:56) is one example of using verbal and numerical language to describe things which are much easier to grasp in a drawing.

Eisenman states an aim here to be that the process contains the possibility of infinite extension: that it can produce endless variation unlike those postmodernists whose work he critiques. This could be argued to have a similar aim of infinity to the analysis of perspective by Pelletier and Perez-Gomez[18], and the potentially infinite picture plane of orthographic projection.

The volumetric version of the el-form, Eisenman argues, can only be read as an erosion from one of the corners: it is not an extension or extrusion. It is also not a pre-existing form, but represents a process applied to a regular cube form, providing us with a new set of similar forms, giving an overall unity to any composition that uses them, but also a directional aspect: the erosion is not a reversible process, and is an image of the passage of time. This can be understood with reference to the notion of reversibility of processes within Bergson[19]: as this remains a *creative* rather than *speculative* (mathematical or scientific) issue is underlined here; whilst the house shows the traces of the process by which it was created and suggests the potential other ways in which it might have developed, had alternative choices been chosen, the process is *irreversible* once it has been undertaken.

6.5 Seriality and montage in House III

House III is a weekend house in Lakeville, Connecticut, for a family designed and built between 1969 and 1971 (figure 6.6). The main feature of the design is the intersection of two cubes constructed as open frames. This collision gives a degree of complexity to the structure as the two forms interact with one another in unexpected ways.

The design is set on a podium, a device which manages the context by establishing a neutral ground for the house to sit on: context is an issue which Eisenman's work, particularly from this period, is accused of ignoring: an accusation which he might agree with to an extent, given his interest in the development of his autonomous architectural language. The datum is an external referent which gives form, and it is important to Eisenman's aims here (for right or wrong) that his formal explorations are not interfered with.

The case of Eisenman 115

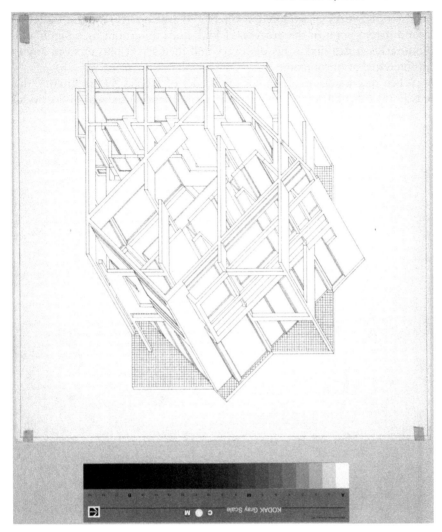

Figure 6.6 Peter Eisenman, axonometric for House III, Lakeville, Connecticut, between 1969 and 1975; black ink on vellum mounted on wove paper 55.9 × 55.9 cm; DR1994:0131:212, Peter Eisenman fonds, Canadian Centre for Architecture.

The drawings are sequential; differently temporal to those of Stirling, as they are intended to display the processes of the deformation (figure 6.7). The end result is relatively static, not designed as a promenade: temporality exists in the prefigurative period of Eisenman's design, the acts of rotating, intersecting, interpenetrating, offsetting, and colliding. A relatively small set of acts create a complex set of forms once they are set into motion, and Eisenman's design is the end result or output of this design process. Contrasting this with Hejduk,

116 The case of Eisenman

whose early works (as explored in Chapter 4) are opportunities for discovery at a different point in the process. Hejduk finds things out by designing his houses; Eisenman makes his discovery and then sets it into motion, almost disinterested at the outcome.

When discussing his axonometric model of House X, Eisenman[20] discusses the role of discovery in his work. He argues that the work is a critique

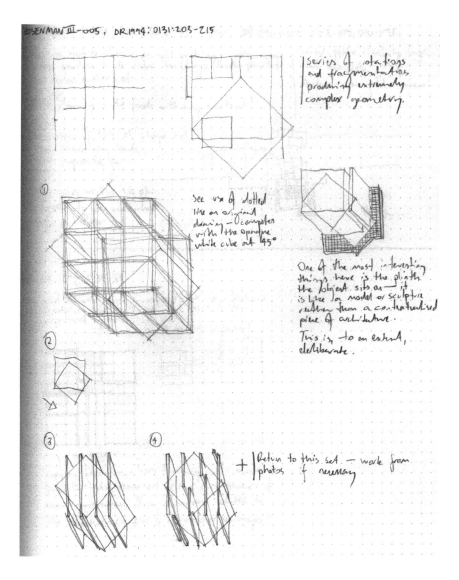

Figure 6.7 Redrawing of DR1994:0131:203-215, studies for House III showing developments in the geometry of the design.

The case of Eisenman   117

of modes of representation themselves, aware of the baggage carried by orthographic and parallel projections as well as the craft of model making:

> In traditional terms, the axonometric is an abstract two-dimensional drawing that allows us to 'see' the three-dimensional object in two. It does not pretend to provide a naturalistic image of the building but simply to depict the more objective presence of every element or aspect in the building and their relationships. These relations are measurable, since there are no dimensional distortions as a product of the artificial vanishing point of perspective. That is, the axonometric truthfully provides knowledge about a certain reality of the object; through scale reductions it represents the additional dimensions of space to the knowledge provided by plan and section. (Eisenman, 1982:28)

The aim of his axonometric model is to produce a physical object which replicates the view of the building in parallel projection. This can only be seen from one angle, and the viewer must move around the object until the appropriate view is revealed. The model is a puzzle which allows the viewer to understand more about the deformations necessary to every form of representation, even axonometric which purports to maintain the plan proportions and angles at the expense of the vertical angles which are badly distorted.

Desley Luscombe[21] has investigated the importance of the relationship between Eisenman's drawings and the resulting buildings with reference to a later entry into the House series. With regards to House III, this importance lies in the working drawings depicting the process of developing the design. Similar to, but distinctive from the conventional iterative process of making an initial design which responds to a brief, then revising and refining through iterations, some of which can involve radical revisions, Eisenman presents us instead with purely formal investigations: the assignment of purposes to rooms such as kitchen, bedroom, or living room are somewhat incidental: the development of the form is the primary concern, and the building the outcome of that process. That process is itself the theoretical intent behind the work of radically re-envisaging architecture as an autonomous and abstract process of finding form, argued by Eisenman to be a continuation of the modernist project as interrupted by functionalism.

The process drawings show the development of an argument which attempts to use space and form as its constituent parts; the spaces between the drawings in the series[22] are important parts of their communication; points of interruption, intervals, or montage[23]. Seriality is crucial in understanding the works, rendering a reading of the single drawing as somewhat unhelpful as so much of the information is contained in the spaces between the drawings. The drawing of the entire scheme in Figure 6.6 is, then, a collapse of the process into a single point, almost like exposing every frame of a film simultaneously. This is an alternative to the experientially unfurling

118 *The case of Eisenman*

temporality of Stirling's promenades; the unfurling is a conceptual one rather than embodied, a process of cognition through drawn architectural theory. A useful analogy when assessing the role of seriality in Eisenman's critically informed architecture is to consider how convincing a written theory would be if it were to only show its outcome, rather than the argumentation which validates the conclusion. The serial axonometric drawings in Eisenman are a form of argumentation over time, to be understood as a process of thinking open to further extension, alternative paths untaken, and not as a singular result.

Notes

1. Eisenman, Peter. 1982a. "Editor's Preface" in Rossi, Aldo. *The Architecture of the City*. Cambridge, Massachusetts: MIT Press.
2. Published as: Eisenman, Peter. 2006 [1963]. *The Formal Basis of Modern Architecture*. Zurich: Lars Müller Publishers. R.E. Somol notes that this was intended as a critique of Christopher Alexander's work, Somol, R. E. 2001. "Dummy Text, or the Diagrammatic Basis of Contemporary Architecture" in Eisenman, Peter. *Diagram Diaries*. London: Thames & Hudson, p. 7.
3. The means of expression in this case including such architectural features as 'scale, harmony and pattern' (2006:25); formal order is not the overall aim of the project, but is instead an underlying structure which renders the meaning of a building legible. Eisenman is most clearly influenced by the work of Charles Sanders Pierce here, and also cites Roland Barthes and Ferdinand de Saussure.
4. See Lucas (2019) for more on the basis of this in a broader anthropological understanding of architecture.
5. Eisenman, Peter. 2003. *Giuseppe Terragni: Transformations Decompositions Critiques*. New York: Monacelli Press.
6. Eisenman, Peter. 2008. *Ten Canonical Buildings 1950–2000*. New York: Rizzoli, which includes his discussion of Stirling's Leicester Engineering Building.
7. Rowe was a huge influence on Eisenman's thinking, having been his PhD supervisor; but fundamental differences in their thinking emerge on issues such as this one.
8. See Lucas (2006) for more on this.
9. See Eisenman, 2001:75–76, for an account of a sequence of drawings made into an animated film for the Milan Triennale in 1973; Eisenman reports that the result was unsatisfactory as the gaps were at times too large between one frame and the next, so the eye could not keep up with the transformations.
10. Eisenman, Peter. 2004. "Cardboard Architecture" in *Eisenman Inside Out: Selected Writings 1963–1988*. New Haven: Yale University Press, pp. 28–39
11. Hodder, Ian. 2012. *Entanglements: an Archaeology of the Relationships Between Humans and Things*. Chichester: Wiley-Blackwell, pp. 42–44.
12. Gandelsonas, Mario. 1982b. "Introduction. From Structure to Subject: The Formation of an architectural language", in Eisenman, Peter. *House X*. New York: Rizzoli International, p. 28.

    The model itself is DR1987:0858, part of the Eisenman fonds at the Canadian Centre for Architecture.
13. The following references from the CCA collection are good examples of the collages: DR1994:0134:522, DR1994:0134:529.

The case of Eisenman 119

14. Eisenman, Peter. 2001. "Interiority: El-Forms" in *Diagram Diaries*. London: Thames & Hudson, pp. 72–83.
15. Eisenman, Peter. 1982. *House X*. New York: Rizzoli International, pp. 34–168.
16. Eisenman's approach is somewhat different from this, however: *'Beginning with an el as a base form does away with the very simplistic concept which pervaded much of the twenties and thirties design, namely the concern with making architecture look as though one could read the inside and the outside simultaneously, or the inside through the outside. The el provides an element which inherently contains the desired approximation of a disjunctive and potentially decompositional artefact. Moreover, its volumetric character signals a conceptual break with the earlier houses.'* (1982b:54)
17. See Borges (1964) here.
18. Pelletier, Louise & Perez-Gomez, Alberto. 1997. *Architectural Representation and the Perspective Hinge*. Cambridge, Massachusetts: MIT Press, p. 243.
19. Eisenman is in an interesting tension with Bergson here. Bergson presents us with the idea that 'the truth is that in philosophy and even elsewhere it is a question of finding the problem and consequently of positing it, even more than of solving it. For a speculative problem is solved as soon as it is properly stated. By this I mean that its solution exists then, although it may remain hidden and, so to speak, covered up—the only thing left to do is to uncover it (Bergson, 1992:51). If, as Eisenman is suggesting, his process is partly one of uncovering, perhaps it is a speculative problem and a process can be engineered to return each of the architectural elements to an original state.
20. Eisenman, Peter. 1982. *House X*. New York: Rizzoli International.
21. Luscombe, Desley. 2014. "Architectural Concepts in Peter Eisenman's Axonometric Drawings of House VI" in *The Journal of Architecture*, Vol. 19, No. 4, pp. 560–611.
22. The idea of the series is, in itself, important to Eisenman's early development. Sandra Kaji-O'Grady notes the influence of Sol LeWitt and Rosalind Krauss on this aspect of his thinking: 'all the planning and decisions are made beforehand and the execution is a perfunctory affair' (LeWitt, in: Kaji-O'Grady, Sandra. 2012. "Formalism and Forms of Practice" in Crysler, C. Greig; Cairns, Stephen; Heynen, Hilde [Eds.]. *The Sage Handbook of Architectural Theory*. London: Sage Publications).
23. For more on the qualities of intervals within inscriptive practices, see: Lucas, R. 2009. "Gestural Artefacts: Notations of a Daruma Doll." in Gunn, W (Ed.). 2009. *Fieldnotes and Sketchbooks: Challenging the Boundaries Between Descriptions and Processes of Describing*. Peter Lang Publishers.

7 Cedric Price's 'In Action' drawings

7.1 Too much architecture

Absent from the drawings of many architects are people. This might seem at first to be a rather trite observation, but it is notable when people do appear in axonometric drawings, and they are present in abundance in the drawings of Cedric Price.

Cedric Price (1934–2003) was a fixture of the British architectural scene as a practitioner, educator, and provocateur, frequently asking awkward questions of the profession and encouraging a more free-thinking and experimental way of being an architect[1]. He saw each of these things as part of his role as an architect: expanding the scope away solely from designing polite buildings solely according to the specifications of clients. Price remains influential on subsequent architects, his social conscience and broad idea of what it is to be an architect informing recent debates on scarcity and agency in architecture[2].

Price is best known for the London Zoo Aviary (1961), for his unbuilt Fun Palace and Potteries Thinkbelt projects and similar utopian re-imaginings of how we live and work. His architecture was often utilitarian, prefabricated, and formally simple. Despite this, his work is acknowledged to have a sense of mischief and a socially progressive edge. Much of his work remains unbuilt, propositional, and speculative—reimagining social structures as well as architectural ones, and as such, most exist as paper projects.

People are present in these drawings. Occupying space rather than presenting it as sculptural and perfect, Price gives groups of people their place and shows us that these spaces must be inhabited to make sense.

Conventional wisdom denies this in parallel projection: orthographic drawings are often cluttered with cut-and-paste figures from drawing catalogues. This gives us a clue as to the regard for axonometric and isometric as technical drawings: explorations of structure and detail. Price acknowledges this and uses the drawings in this way, having an exposed-structure aesthetic in his work. What is most notable, then, is that Price is in agreement with this utility for technical details, but he still cannot conceptualise this without people in it. As such, his drawings demonstrate a belief that there should be no separation between technological and engineering solutions and the social conscience of architecture.

In her comprehensive work detailing Price's practice[3], Samantha Hardingham discusses the various roles drawing played within the practice. Four categories are given, of which the most famous are the 'In Action' drawings, externally facing works which are designed to convey information as clearly as possible—either to a public audience or to other actors in the building process. Within the practice, many more drawings were produced as part of the internal process of design, communicating between different members of the practice and not designed for general consumption. These 'In House' drawings are refinements of earlier sketches and notes—designated as 'In Head'. Hardingham describes these as 'a form of personal visual literacy developed as a design tool, most frequently referred to as "cartoons"' (2017:15).

One further category speaks volumes of Price's ambition to communicate, and provides Hardingham with the vast collection's title: *In Forward-Minded Retrospect*. These drawings are post-rationalisations of projects, a means of summarising the key points of a scheme in order to communicate it, once complete, to a broader audience.

Parallel projection proves particularly useful for Price, as his architecture is often presented as a series of parts, a kit which can be assembled in a variety of ways. The underlying politics of this approach was elaborated in a piece for *New Society* magazine in 1969, where along with Reyner Banham, Peter Hall, and Paul Barker, he pinned his colours to the mast of "Non-Plan: an Experiment in Freedom". Writing in retrospect, Paul Barker notes:

> Non-plan was essentially a very humble idea: that it is very difficult to decide what is best for *other* people.' (in Hughes & Sadler 2000:6)

It is tempting to read the title of the article as set against the drawing convention of the plan, and whilst these are rarely the important drawings in Price's schemes, the aim of the article is rather more wide-ranging and explores a possibility of reconsidering town planning (and architecture) as a discipline. This position against the planning authorities is what gives rise to Price's preference for pods, moving parts, scaffolds, and frameworks. The logic follows that if the architect is not going to decide what is best for other people, then how can an architecture allow people to make their own decisions?

7.2 The presence of people in architectural drawing

Price's drawings are notable in that they depict movement and construction processes, including people in them. These figures are not the decorative indicators of scale used so frequently by architects, but they are engaged in pertinent activities: actually making the building, assembling components

122   Cedric Price's 'In Action' drawings

and directing them, engaged in performances, and animating the scene. People are tricky to draw in this projection which is best suited to regular geometric forms of cylinders, prisms, and cubes; the distortions introduced can make figures look rather alien when depicted in this way. There is no single style within Price's office for this representation. Sometimes the figures are fully rendered in a loose, cartoony style, complete with hairstyles and facial features. Other times, silhouettes are used, conveying postural information alongside indications of what people are wearing. The third variation is a stamp, where a few alternatives are blocked in, providing swift crowding of an otherwise empty space.

The presence of people throughout the office's output speaks a little of the ambitions Price had for the drawings, that they aspired to the communicative quality of the *cartoon*[4]. The qualities[5] of the drawings is an interesting issue—the idea of the throwaway drawing created by Price and his office is both consistent with their general approach to redundancy and obsolescence, whilst maintaining a strong house style. The architect is present but not precious, accurate but not meticulous. That said, there is a great deal of quality to his penmanship; it simply conforms to a paradigm of the expressive gestural mark more than that of the ruled tyranny of the Rotring pen.

The Donmar Warehouse project (1963) (figures 7.1 and 7.2) is a case in point. A 30/60° axonometric (Price Fonds, Canadian Centre for Architecture, DR1995: 0212: 014) drawing of his experimental workshop theatre is accompanied by separate drawings of components (DR1995: 0212: 016).

The space here is heavily populated, almost crowded when compared to similar interiors drawn by other architects. The figures are stamped on: a set of characters are repeated—seated, jumping up with arms raised in the air, and standing in conversation. Price wants us to understand that the social function of the space is important to the scheme: it is not enough to provide spaces. The aim of the design was to engender an atmosphere of spontaneity, described as *soirees*[6] in Price's correspondence with his long-term client/collaborator in the Fun Palace project, Joan Littlewood. This space was designed to allow for impromptu performances and gatherings with no fixed programme—an approach common to the Fun Palaces.

Whilst the project was never realised, some of the components made it as far as detailed specifications for the furniture to be fabricated. Imagined as more than isolated pieces, the drawings depict these modules in situ, occupying the design's proposed mezzanine space and clustered together in a range of useful configurations. The descriptions given to the furniture components are typical of Price—*conversation box, small stage, chair-table, platforms* all have a naive quality to them. Oversized castors render the platforms slightly out of scale at first glance; the fanning out of the rippled small-stage elements are shown combined; conversation boxes are shown with two occupants (loosely hand-drawn in this case rather than stamped)

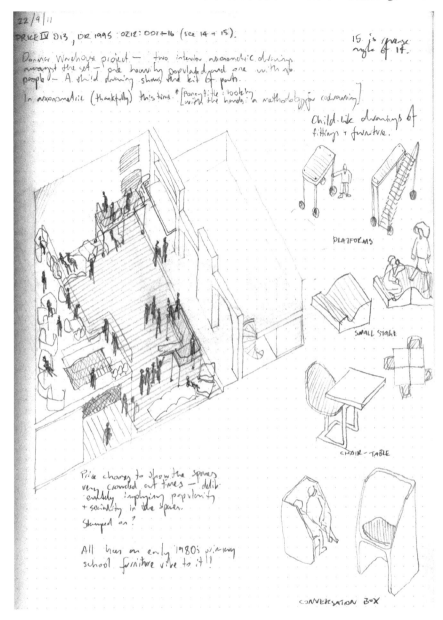

Figure 7.1 Redrawing of DR1995:0212:014 and DR1995:0212:016, Donmar Warehouse axonometric drawing.

in very close quarters; and pinwheel arrangements are suggested for the combined chair-table elements. The projection is loosely adhered to in this sheet, with some shading used to indicate materiality. The same pieces of furniture are used in the axonometric drawing of the interior.

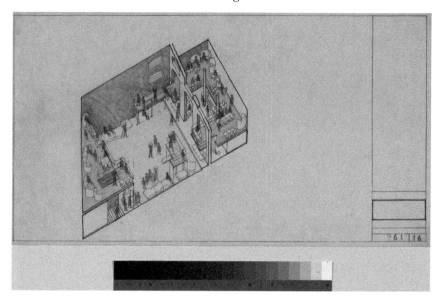

Figure 7.2 Cedric Price, axonometric interior view with figures and furniture for the Donmar Theatre, London, England, 1963; black ink, graphite and black pencil on wove paper 38 × 71.6 cm; DR1995:0212:014, Cedric Price fonds, Canadian Centre for Architecture.

Further arrangements are therefore suggested by these drawings. This idea of suggestion runs through Price's drawings, where there is often a deliberate simplicity in the presentation: a minimum number of lines and indications of form rather than a full description.

This *indication* process consists of an extension of the principle of the hidden lines so often used in parallel projection. Where a conventional axonometric drawing would show each of the vertical elements, Price chooses to omit these where another element gives adequate description (figure 7.3).

This is particularly apparent in units designed to be manufactured from plastic or tubular steel, allowing the quality of the line to describe the plastic forms against the planar ones. Looking again at Figure 7.1, the *chair-table* unit shows this contrast in the treatment of materials most clearly with the steel frame and moulded plastic seat using one set of lines, and the hard-edged table another.

7.3 Assembling and dismantling

Parallel projection is ideal for describing discreet elements as discussed previously. Whilst the fixed viewpoint hides some elements of each unit (easily overcome by drawing a second view: allowing most faces of the project to be shown with two drawings rather than the four elevations and plan

Cedric Price's 'In Action' drawings 125

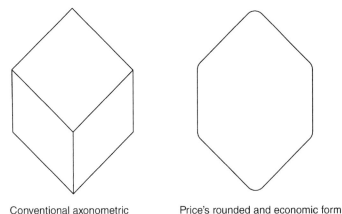

Conventional axonometric   Price's rounded and economic form

Figure 7.3 Comparison of two cubes in parallel projection. The first is a conventional drawing showing all of the vertical elements. The second shows how Price tends to draw, allowing the upper surface to carry the description of the form and omitting the vertical edge nearest the front. This economy of line extends further to unfinished vertical elements and sometimes also horizontal lines. The determining factor is whether another plane can do the work of describing the work. If so, then lines can be suggested or indicated rather than actually described and drawn.

required by orthographic projection), a more complete view of each component is possible.

The description of the broader context gives further clues about how each drawing is to be used. Drawings showing individual parts without any context are intended to describe each element with clarity: showing the form in terms of volumes, surfaces, and materials. The focus is on the construction of the piece. This is supplemented by more schematic drawings which show potential arrangements. These can be read as one composition of many when they are taken as a set of drawings with the components. Without that additional information, it is possible to misread the example layout as a definitive one.

Drawings often interact with one another, and it is a mistake to think of them as in isolation whether drawn as part of a set with the conventional plan, section and elevation including site and roof plans, detail sections, or considering a stack of iteratively redesigned projects on sheets of tracing paper. Here, the drawings rely upon one another in order to make sense.

Projects such as the Fun Palace (1960–1966), Potteries Thinkbelt (1964–1967), and the Generator (1976–1980) further exploit Price's strategy of designing a kit of parts, but on a substantially more ambitious scale.

By far the most influential of Price's unbuilt projects is the Fun Palace. Price was one part of a greater organisation in this case, and the project was under the oversight of avant-garde theatre director Joan Littlewood. The idea for the Fun Palace was to fundamentally challenge what was meant by theatre, performance, education, and leisure time. In a period of great optimism about the technologies of the future and how they might free people from the need to work regular hours. The scheme is explicitly utopian, and is Price's answer to Littlewood's question (rather than brief) for the project: what could architecture bring to the Fun Palace?[7]

The proposal by Price was a large piece of infrastructure. Steel space frames from which a variety of stackable prefabricated pods and elements could by supported, the approach belongs to the genre of capsule architecture pursued by a range of groups including Archigram in the UK and the Metabolists in Japan. Inspired by space race technology, the science-fiction imagery of these groups produced a positivist technological utopia in contrast to Price's aim, which was driven by social needs first and foremost.

One frequent analogy used for the scheme is a port (Hardingham 2017:55), and the project does echo the engineering of a large container dock. The heroic scale of moving elements and efficient pieces of machinery forms a continuity with Corbusier's use of analogy in *Towards a New Architecture* with its celebration of factories, silos, cruise liners, aeroplanes and automobiles.

The project is about the facilitation and enabling of whatever takes peoples' fancy. There is a frivolous aspect to this as well as social justice and democratic implications, with the importance of play as a human activity

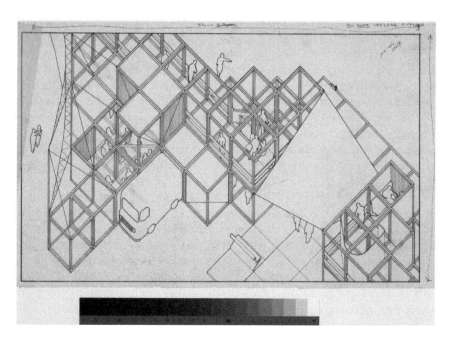

Figure 7.4 Cedric Price, axonometric drawing for Fun Palace, ca. 1964; ink, coloured pencil, and adhesive film on translucent paper 38 × 69.1 cm; DR1995:0188:128, Cedric Price fonds, Canadian Centre for Architecture.

Cedric Price's 'In Action' drawings   127

which is not reserved for childhood[8]. Littlewood was increasingly concerned with the retrenchment of postwar culture towards the bourgeoise establishment, reasserting its power after a brief period of possibility.

The project noted that there was a need for some organisational principles to be applied, otherwise there was no way to balance the desires of one Fun Palace user over those of another. Conflict was possible as some activities would not overlap happily, however intellectually stimulating such occurrences might be. The movement established a *cybernetics committee* which included Gordon Pask, and drew inspiration from the car manufacturing industry. These industrial processes were intended to become invisible over time, and allow for a customisable experience for each visitor or group of visitors.

The drawings for the Fun Palace were largely promotional images[9], designed for an external audience as part of a lobbying process to enable the structure to be built. Figure 7.4 shows the interior of the proposal in use, giving an example of where various elements might be positioned. The drawing is unusually free from annotation, leaving the viewer to fill in the blanks of the various elements: immediately recognisable elements such as escalators (for which proposals are drawn with them pivoting from their base to allow the circulation to adapt), raked seating in front of some sort of screen, canopies, and partitions. Otherwise, the drawing leaves much to the imagination, perhaps realising that including too much detail might lead viewers to invest too greatly in that particular layout.

Drawings of the Fun Palace depict it either as a large scale totality, omitting many features such as the superstructure, or closer in, with the dominance of the underlying grid shown in detail. The relationship between the superstructure and substructure is unclear, with a straightforward stacking organisation shown (figure 7.5). The potential occupation of the site and the versatility of the module is communicated clearly here, with familiar silhouette figures engaged in seated discussions, peering over balconies, and directing the elements still under construction, and even climbing up the back wall. The inclusion of a van shows the interest in the logistics of the project which, despite the utopian ambitions, had to be pragmatic and achievable. The line quality is even throughout this sheet: some of the lower floors and texturing of panels has a lighter quality, but otherwise a medium weight pen is used throughout: there is a homogeneity and equal value given to each of the cube units: prioritising some would undermine the intention of the drawing fundamentally, and indicate to the viewer that one part of the example is more important than the others.

Figure 7.4, at 1:48 scale, shows 11 variants for the Fun Palace cubes. Whilst sequentiality is discussed later, this sheet represents another genre in Price's work: *serial drawings*. The overall effect is to show variation, placing as many versions of what can happen in one cube on the same sheet. Using the same language throughout, the aim is—not exhaustively— to show the versatility of the proposed system. Starting with basics such as floor and wall variations (some of which are tricky to use in isolation,

128 *Cedric Price's 'In Action' drawings*

such as the diagonal wall), more elaborate structures are included such as moulded benches and complete stairwells. The line weight, often underused in Price's drawings, indicates the dimensions of the cube module with a faint line, the various instances drawn in bolder lines and including silhouette figures using some of the units. It is clear that some elements of the scheme are not resolved in the drawing, and details not pertinent to the target audience are omitted. Whilst some elements are drawn with material textures and thicknesses, the walls and floors are not. Also, the depth of the structural frame is not depicted, such that elements of the transition from one cube to another and the manner of their fixing to one another are not fully clear.

Price continues reconsidering cultural institutions with his subsequent Potteries Thinkbelt project for his home-town of Stafford, a post-industrial part of England known for its large-scale ceramic production. A long period of decline had left large swathes of industrial land unused, creating an opportunity for Price. The project is essentially a speculative critique and reimagining of the university sector, utilising transport infrastructure and large volumes of prefabrication.

The project was published in *New Society* and *Architectural Design* in 1966, and was proposed on a very large scale, with several types of housing alongside the facilities needed for the alternative university of 20,000 students. Working without a client, his aim was to lobby for the production of the Thinkbelt. Price did not limit himself to the directly spatial implications of the project, and proposed that students be paid a wage as their intellectual labour was valuable to the economy in the longer term. Price's proposal was unbuilt, however, and the government of the time went ahead with the Open University, based in the new town of Milton Keynes.

The housing units are designed to accommodate different needs, and named using neutral terminology:

> Types of housing
>
> There will be four main types of housing: **crate, sprawl, battery** and **capsule**. These will put little strain on the local building industry because much of the construction work will be undertaken by other national industries such as light engineering or motor manufacture. (Price in Hardingham 2003:18)

Price's secondary aim was to decouple the university from the city: to subvert the idea of civic design, and to propose an alternative to the campus or 'town and gown' distinction found in many British university cities. The whole scheme was envisaged as a vast railway network, with stations and exchanges for carriages housing seminar rooms, self-study areas, and audiovisual facilities.

Rather than the reconfigurable Fun Palace, the Thinkbelt was designed around units which could be moved and redeployed as needed, upgraded and replaced—similar to other capsule schemes. The drawings here are

Cedric Price's 'In Action' drawings 129

machine-like, a heavily engineered aesthetic. They are unconvincing in places due to this, arbitrary connections indicate how things *might* work, and how the linear arrangement would be utilised, but the spaces for interpretation are often very large, covered by the lightweight technical detailing of the familiar territory of the housing drawings.

The Thinkbelt has an interesting quality, however: one necessitated by the 100-square=mile territory of the project rendering adequate representation difficult. Here, the drawing suggests that the modules repeat by drawing the units all the way up to the edges. The grids, frames, and units all repeat endlessly from this example.

The Generator project drawings are presented in 30/30° isometric projection on portrait-oriented A4 paper with holes punched for compilation in a ring binder[10], the line weights are maintained throughout, ensuring that there is no subtle information being lost to the inexperienced reader. The project itself was for a reconfigurable multifunctional space, commissioned by Howard Gilman for the staff at his paper manufacturing plant in Florida[11], the site being described as 'jungle' in the correspondence for the work. The project developed many themes of Price's work, with innovations in cybernetic theory drawn from Price's work with Gordon Pask[12].

The drawings for the Generator are sequential, showing how the project would go together in a step-by-step manner. This is not presented in an abstract fashion, describing what each stage looks like, but includes vehicles, lifting machinery, and, most crucially, people.

Again, *indication* is used to lessen the number of lines shown on the page. This gives the drawings a clean and straightforward character, showing form as much as is required, but focusing more on the arrangements of elements according to an overall system, and the means of constructing it.

Figure 7.6 describes this most clearly: the drawing shows two construction workers lifting a panel into place. This is against a background of the grid of foundation pads and part-completed and finished units of the repeated module. Other drawings in the series show how parts are delivered to the site and assembled with the assistance of a crane.

Sequentiality is an important theme in this project, as the architecture precludes the possibility of a total image that reveals the entire project at once. It is consistently presented in a fragmentary fashion, largely decontextualised and focusing on the system. Instances of use are given as examples rather than a definitive form. Such performative and responsive architecture requires some improvisation in terms of its representational strategies. Much like drawing in front of a student or client allows an understanding to emerge line by line, the sequential drawing parses information into manageable chunks. If the steps are too small, the distinctions are difficult to see; if the steps are too large, it becomes impossible to see with any precision, how the change is made[13].

By including the swing of the opening doors, Figure 7.7 shows the degree of consideration given to the operation of the complex system. The possibility of openings on both the horizontal and vertical plane renders the

130 *Cedric Price's 'In Action' drawings*

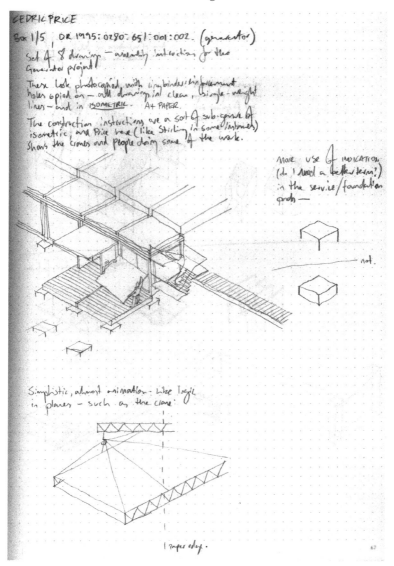

Figure 7.5 Redrawing of DR1995:0280:651:001-2. These drawings show the way in which construction was considered as a practical reality of architecture, not abstracted out from the work of the designers.

underlying organisation of the grid as rather more complex than it seemed at first. The kit of parts is explored thoroughly, with the cube elements opening and closing in various ways to provide an external walkway or overhead canopy, with options of two-door and single-door openings offering significantly different geometries.

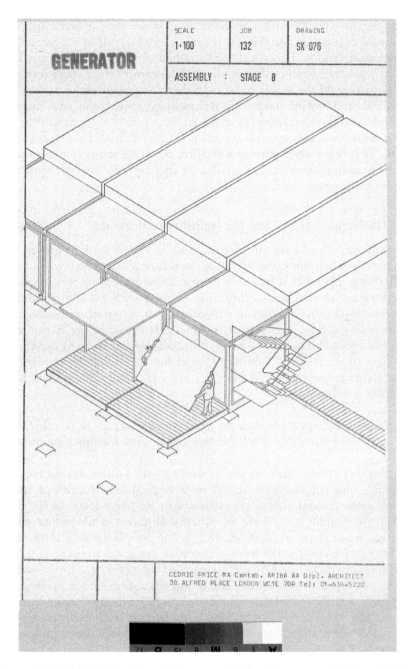

Figure 7.6 Cedric Price, Assembly, stage 8 for Generator, Yulee, Florida, 1967–1979; electrostatic print on paper with red ink stamp, 29.7×21 cm; DR1995:0280:651:001:008, Cedric Price fonds, Canadian Centre for Architecture.

132 Cedric Price's 'In Action' drawings

Implicating people in his architecture is more than a decorative indication of occupation for Price: it is often crowded, full of life rather than demonstrative of it. This speaks to his ambition for the architecture to be socially produced rather than a physical container. He is more interested in the nature of the soiree to be held there, the possibilities afforded by platforms and moving stages. The technical expertise deployed is therefore secondary to the social purpose of the architecture, even though the technical detailing and honesty of materials provides much of the aesthetic of his work. This is not decorative architecture, but architecture that allows you to make something of it. Essentially, the architecture does not exist until the people turn up.

7.4 Deliberate naivety and the legibility of drawing

In many ways Price's architecture responds to earlier work by groups such as De Stijl, where the condition of architecture was represented as a constellation of planes as if frozen in a vortex. The stated aim was to provide free-flowing internal space, confusing internal with external conditions: Price envisages this as a literal movement, not a sign of past movement, albeit one which requires infrastructure, control, and heavy machinery in order to enact it. The results may not initially appear to be as dynamic as the likes of the Rietveld Schröder House, but they fulfil the manifesto or brief rather more completely. Price describes his planar fascination in *The Invisible Sandwich*[14]:

> *Design is about more than the juxtaposition of planes, whether vertical, inclined or horizontal, whether audio, visual, thermal or material.*

He goes on to assign each floor of a building with a different role, recalling Hejduk's nine-square problem, but on a vertical axis. According to this formula, the ground floor is characterised by its direct access to the wider world; the middle floors have an equality of access, a ubiquitous nature which can be expanded endlessly; and the top floor has potential for access and to provide cover in the form of canopies. Price uses the sandwich analogy in his characteristic manner, asking the reader of *Re:CP* to 'devour this book, as if a pig'. What is important to our discussion here, however, is his assertion that the material is open ended, both intellectual and accessible. Whilst the office was acutely aware of how to present itself, controlling when and where their ideas were circulated, Price was keen to be a public intellectual as well as an architect[15]. The drawings are one part of this. The drawings which sometimes appear as naive or simplistic are in fact carefully tuned to communicate complex ideas without the need for expertise in architecture. One description of Price's drawings might, therefore, be *democratic:* they invite debate and discussion, respond to social conditions and encourage an architecture firmly rooted in the needs of its time.

Cedric Price's 'In Action' drawings 133

Writing of the similarities between his non-membership of the Metabolist group and Price's to Archigram, Arata Isozaki[16] finds there to be a fundamental distinction between the approaches of Archigram and Price:

> But while certain of Price's ideas and technical proposals did exert a powerful influence on Archigram, his basic working style and thinking, especially his methods in raising issues and his approach to them, prove decisively different. In Plug-In Capsule or Instant City, Archigram turned the upbeat-named architectural illustration into a means of conveying an ideology as well as a technical solution, with particular emphasis on figurative breakdowns and diagrammatic exposition. All his effort goes into raising issues and describing solution processes. As a result, he utterly ignores formative aspects, neutralising his expression into the realm of the instantly forgettable. (in Price 2003:26–27)

The distinction between illustration and the techno-futurist ideology for Archigram and the process-based work produced by Price demonstrates a depth, a focus not on an ideal image but communication via *diagrammatic exposition*. This raises a question of the status of the drawings as diagrams, but in a different manner to that proposed by Eisenman. Price uses a deliberately straightforward, even deadpan language for his projects, without the pop art exuberance of Archigram. That is not to say that they lack humour, but the aim is not to produce an image of joy, but to provide the circumstances where something truly unexpected and fun can happen.

This very diagrammatic nature sometimes has the opposite effect on expert viewers, however. Writing in *Cedric Price Opera*, Robin Middleton (in Hardingham 2003:29) expresses some difficulty with the 'extreme' diagrammatic nature of Price's drawings. This extends to the prevailing opinion that Price preferred not to build, based both on his large number of unbuilt schemes and occasional questioning of whether a building was required at all[17]. This sells Price's pragmatism short, however, and he saw an expanded role for the architect as a consultant on spatial matters: he did not limit himself to building.

The larger issue to contend with for our purposes here, however, is this professional distaste for drawings designed to communicate widely. This exposes a preference for complicated and exclusive practices which fail to communicate outside of the profession, something which Robertson Ward Jr discusses elsewhere in the same volume: the quality of the communication embedded in Price's deceptively simple drawings.

One theoretical framework through which this can be discussed is that of audience and spectatorship studies. Throughout his career, Price sought publication in general audience periodicals such as *New Scientist* and *New Society*, later to be incorporated into the *New Statesman*. This shows the

134 Cedric Price's 'In Action' drawings

ambition for his speculative projects—that public opinion was the theatre for the work, and that it needed to be accessible to a broad audience. The aim was often to influence policy on a grand scale, rethinking many of the institutions which had been inherited, such as the theatre, the university, or even the city itself. This was Price's 'anticipatory design'[18]:

> More than anything, the term [anticipatory design] draws attention to the central role that people play in Price's work: for the architect to be an enabler there needs to be a continual involvement of all the parties engaged in the life of the building, from its initial conception to its eventual demolition. (Hardingham 2017:14).

This alternative role for drawing means that the inscriptions themselves will have a different character, an alternative nature. Much like the polemical *Price Cuts* collages published in the *Architects Journal* in the late 1990s and a number of the *73 Snacks*[19], he used alternative methods to get his message across, and the form of drawing or representation was chosen carefully.

Simple is not simplistic, of course, and the clarity of Price's work is carefully constructed and the result of editing to ensure the intended meanings are present in as efficient a form as possible. Several qualities emerge in Price's drawing practice as noted by Ward (in Hardingham 2003:30–31), present in the parallel projections in particular: clarity and economy. Every drawing is subjected to a radical editing process whereby every line has to work as hard as possible. There is very little slack in each drawing (although this might occur when reading *across* drawings in a set).

One issue raised by this is the degree to which the drawings leave some room for interpretation on the part of the viewer. By not saying much, the reader fills in some of the blanks. This is alluded to by John Frazer[20] when discussing Banham's critique of the Fun Palace, musing that Price himself did not know what the building would look like. Not showing and not saying is an interesting strategy in and of itself, and an initial refusal to show any images of the scheme leaves space for possibilities as one would expect both of that project, and of Price's architecture more broadly given his questioning of whether we ought to build at all sometimes[21], or if 'technology is the answer—what was the question?'[22]

All drawings require a degree of editing, and the process leaves a trace of the decisions made during the drafting process. This quality of efficiency determines the degree to which a total image is desired, and this is something which runs counter to the design philosophy of Price. The total image is denied, as Price's architecture is performative and unfixed. It denies the possibility of completeness as it is always in flux, contingent upon the people who are there at any given time.

Editing is theorised in a range of other disciplines, most notably in film, where the relationship with montage provides a theoretical underpinning

Cedric Price's 'In Action' drawings   135

dating back to Eisenstein's pioneering cinema and theory in the 1920s[23]. Further elaborations include those by Tarkovsky[24] in the 1980s towards a more open model rejecting Eisenstein's didactic montage. Later, Gilles Deleuze[25] turns his attention to cinema, which provides an opportunity to discuss both temporality and image, presenting multiple different forms of montage based on different movements and national cinematic trends. This regard for juxtaposition and selection has a great deal to offer architecture, a field which has long offered much to architectural theory[26].

Deleuze's theory in particular illuminates two key elements of Price's drawing practice. Deleuze develops a theory of image based on cinema: the two volumes use cinema as a lens through which to consider ideas of image production, and the complexity of the image presented on the screen. Through cinema theory, the theory of montage develops beyond the simple practicalities of shooting reels of film, where a limited amount of the physical stock is required and even more limited attention span of the audience. Eisenstein notes that cutting, selecting, and assembling are all essential to making sense out of the material gathered, even the key creative act in filmmaking.

Tarkovsky's view echoes others writing about narrative at the time[27], and invites the audience back into this meaning-making process. Opposing Eisenstein's view that meaning is transmitted directly to the viewer, Tarkovsky instead considers the way an audience brings their own memories to bear on what they are viewing: they are not passive. Tarkovsky's films are of course designed with just such a space for the audience to inhabit and dwell within. By refusing to over-specify, the viewer gains purchase on the events, bringing their own interpretation and reactions based on their perceptual and emotional memory. This is similar to Price's drawing strategy which leaves space for the audience.

In the *Movement Image*, Deleuze discusses a number of strategies for movement in film. The manner of various schools of movement is described, be that kinetic (early French), dualistic (German expressionism), dialectic (Russian avant-garde). The movement image, then, is an additional quality which exploits the fissures in the 24 frames per second unfurling of still images: the nature of the movement and the underlying intent behind representing it that way. We have a regard for movement in Price's drawings. Beyond the indication of door swings and sliding partitions, there are various indications of sequentiality which undermine the myth of permanence which architecture so often perpetuates.

The storyboarding of key frames is one aspect of this: by presenting drawings as part of a longer story, we can see progression from one step to another. Movement and the passage of time are suggested by these, recalling Deleuze's discussion of the cut in film as an indirect image of time. Time passes when film cuts from one scene to another, patches of broader context and establishing information are used to reconstruct how much time has passed (as well as in which direction). The steps in Price's drawings use a similar structure, and in some cases show the building's construction, changes over use, and finally being dismantled.

Our focus in editing has to return to the simple act of selection and how it relates to the process of drawing: there is an impossibility, however hyper-realistic the representation, of showing everything. As such, every drawing is a series of choices of what to show and what to leave out. Axonometric projection exposes this mechanism immediately, as the

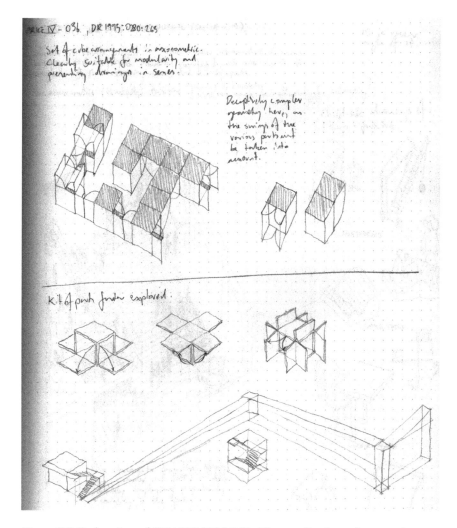

Figure 7.7 Redrawing of DR1995:0280:263. The application of conventions to describe the swing of doors demonstrates both the complex geometry possible with the Generator (necessitating the programmed instructions to ensure access), but also adds an unusual layer of notation to parallel projections.

construction of a simple form such as a cube involves the selecting of some lines, prioritising certain planes over others, and allowing elements to hide others, which are relegated to being 'construction lines'.

Eliding information focuses the act of viewing, allowing the lines to appear as a solid mass by occluding the lines which are drawn as behind one another. The editing process allows an axonometric drawing to make sense, ordering what is closest to the eye. This might seem like an obvious thing to point out, but it is crucial when it comes to comparing the drawings made by different architects. At one extreme, the confusing mass of lines presented by Daniel Libeskind in his *Micromegas* drawings: accumulations of suggestive details which must be navigated by the viewer without a reference point. Here, we have a drift towards efficiency, suggestion and indication of where lines would be, taking the place of the act of drawing the line.

As noted before, this strategy of sparseness is both deliberate and useful, theoretically consistent with Price's ambitions for his open architecture. Former editor of *Architectural Design* Peter Murray (in Hardingham 2003:87) writes that the 'aesthetic of the drawings which were both cryptic and clear' suggesting that his vagueness was a deliberate strategy which gave him some room for interpretation.

The process of copying Price's axonometric drawings is one of precision and care: there is little tolerance for elements to be drawn incorrectly, as a small miscalculation in one of the repeated parts would multiply its errors and get increasingly out of sequence with the infrastructure designed to service it. Measure is, therefore, important: returning momentarily to the description Isozaki gives of his similar capsule architecture—that he made use of the concept of *ma,* or interval when writing of 'erasing architecture into the system.'[28] Interval can be related to Eisenstein's theory of montage[29] in several places: the spaces between things can be more important than the things themselves.

This care and precision is a little at odds with the qualities of Price's more cartoon-like drawings and diagrams as these are quick and gestural at times, using coloured crayon for annotations as well as whatever else is to hand, be that graph paper or tracing paper. In a sense, these have a strong sense of the autographic mark noted by Nelson Goodman in his categorisation of artworks. The cartoons exhibit the author's hand clearly, and are not notational as the personality of the maker is embedded into the traces and lines. Price's work shows another set of possibilities for parallel projection, that efficiency in mark-making can be deliberately indirect, allowing the viewer to interpret the spaces left blank and the unspoken phrases. A variety of methods are used to retain this imprecise precision, different to Hejduk's manipulations of the convention: Price holds some things back in order to focus our attention on what he'd like us to see and, more importantly, how he would like us to engage with the project.

Notes

1. The underlying politics of this are examined in detail in Aureli, Pier Vittorio. 2011. "Revisiting Cedric Price's Potteries Thinkbelt" in *Log*, No. 23, pp. 97–118.
2. Awan, Nishat, Schneider, Tatjana & Till, Jeremy. 2011. *Spatial Agency: Other Ways of Doing Architecture*. London: Routledge.
3. Hardingham, Samantha (Ed.). 2017. *Cedric Price Works 1952–2003: A Forward Minded Retrospective*. London & Montreal: Architectural Association & Canadian Centre for Architecture.
4. For further commentary on this cartoony nature of Price's house style, see Hardingham, S. 2005. "A Memory of Possibilities" in *Architectural Design*, Issue 1, Vol. 75, p. 16. Here, Hardingham takes issue with commentators who describe Price's work as 'anti-style' and instead refers to Price's appreciation of the economy of line in cartoons, such as those which appear in newspapers.
5. One might talk of the grain of the drawings here in a manner similar to Barthes's notion of the *grain* of the voice (1977:181): the qualities of the drawings here are all of the aspects of the marks which do not contribute directly to their meaning, such as the coordinates and directions of lines. Qualities of lines would include their weight, the manner of indicating corners and vertices, the hesitancy or directness of the line.
6. See Hardingham (2017:160–161) for more details of the intended events; the proposal was almost a soft launch for the theatre envisaged by Littlewood: a more egalitarian theatre which blurred the line between performer and audience, which could happen anywhere—preferably well away from the proscenium arch. Tanja Herdt places the project as a prototype for the Fun Palace rather than a proof of concept: 'For this location he had conceived a stage construction that could be moved in all dimensions, allowing a broad spectrum of presentations to co-exist. The architecture simply provided the functional infrastructure with which visitors could pursue their different interests' (Herdt, 2017:27).
7. This question continues to be asked today, as the Fun Palaces movement revived the idea in 2013 in the form of an annual event or festival. The community-based democracy, art, and education events are self-organised within an overall framework developed by the codirectors Stella Duffy, Sarah-Jane Rawlings, Hannah Lambert, and Kirsty Lothian, and occur in late October each year. The challenge to the dominant modes of cultural production is retained by the current movement which seeks to reflect the communities within which the events are run. See www.funpalaces.co.uk for more details.
8. Herdt (2017:49) notes the influence of Johan Huizinga here as well as connecting elements such as the Identity Bar, where visitors could borrow costumes in order to try out alternative personas, to the work of Erving Goffman. See more in Goffman's application to architecture in Lucas (2019).

    Huizinga, Johan. 1950. *Homo Ludens: A Study of the Play Element in Culture*. Boston: Beacon Press.

    Goffman, Erving. 1959. *The Presentation of Self in Everyday Life*. London: Penguin Books.
9. See Rufford (2011) for more on this.
10. As described in Hardingham (2017:38), the habit of using A4 paper was a deliberate introduction by Price with William Coburn to make drawings easier to handle on site. These were given the name 'in-action' drawings. This interest in site-handling is most fully articulated in the McAppy project

(Hardingham 2017:xx), where the firm developed prototypical health and safety reforms for the large construction company McAlpine. Whilst much of the literature on Price focuses on anecdotes around his persona, the work of Cedric Price Architects had a serious social agenda. Taking on this project for his good friend and political opponent showed a pragmatic sense of care towards the construction industry and the people who worked there. This included designing facilities for workers to change and eat breakfast at the start of the shift to protective gear appropriate to the construction workers in question.

11. Described by Hardingham, the intention was for a new, responsive architecture without precedent. The brief from Gilman reads as follows:

    'An architectural complex with no previous title and no preferred use, only a desired end effect.
    a. A building which will not contradict but enhance the feeling of being in the middle of nowhere.
    b. Has to be of private and public access.
    c. Has to create a feeling of intimacy conducive to creative impulses—has to accommodate audiences.
    d. Respect environment (jungle)—accommodate a grand piano.
    e. Respect history (with theatrical licence)—be innovative.' (2017:447)

12. Herdt (2017:44) describes how this early cybernetic theory influenced the practice, manifested most clearly in this project. A home computer was programmed with the various possibilities for configuring the Generator, so that the building users could enter their requirements and receive printed instructions for the building's staff. This interest originates with the Fun Palace, with Pask as a member of the Cybernetics Committee drawing on experience of contemporary industrial manufacturing to measure flows of people through the building, and allow for customisable experiences of space. Stanley Matthews notes that this takes a sinister turn, however, with a parallel intention to *control* the building visitors and to nudge them into approved behaviours (2006:46), describing visitors as entering *unmodified* and leaving as *modified* by the experience.

13. See Lucas (2009) on a similar problem with the stepping of sequential information.

14. Price, Cedric. 2003. "The Invisible Sandwich" in *Re: CP*. Basel: Birkhauser. pp. 11–13.

15. Hardingham (2017:16) and Hardingham (2007:16).

16. Isozaki's Osaka Expo Plaza (1970) bears strong similarity to the Fun Palace; with a space frame roof structure and hanging pods, this was the result of similar programmatic requirements.

17. Some of which are discussed in: Rufford, Juliet. 2011. "'What Have We Got to Do with Fun?': Littlewood, Price, and the Policy Makers" in *New Theater Quarterly*, Vol. 27, No. 4, pp. 313–328. Notably, the government of the time went with alternative models for both postwar theatre with the National Theatre, and for education with the Open University. Rufford asserts that a significant hurdle for the Fun Palace was that despite its presentation, it represented a fundamentally radical re-imagining of performance, theatre, education, and leisure. Implicated in this were ideas about what it meant to work and play, and opened questions around both identity and selfhood.

18. Hardingham (2017:14–15).

19. A selection of which are reproduced in *Re:CP* (Price 2003:14–24).

20. In Hardingham (2003:46–48).

140 *Cedric Price's 'In Action' drawings*

21. For example, the Lung for Midtown Manhattan (1999) project where he suggested the competition site be left alone, prefiguring the upsurge in the contemporary interest in rewilding. See *Re:CP* for more on this (Price 2003:47–49).
22. This oft quoted phrase originates in Price's slide presentation for the Generator project found here in Hardingham (2003:47).
23. Eisenstein, Sergei M. 1991. *Writings Volume 2: Towards a Theory of Montage*. London: BFI Books.
24. Tarkovsky, Andrey. 1987. *Sculpting in Time*. Hunter-Blair, K. (Trans.). Austin: University of Texas Press.
25. Deleuze, Gilles. 1992. *Cinema 1: The Movement Image*. London: Athlone Press.
    Deleuze, Gilles. 1994. *Cinema 2: The Time Image*. London: Athlone Press.
26. See Lucas (2002, Chapter 2; 2006:254–285) for more on this.
27. See for example, Eco, Umberto. 1989. *The Open Work*. A Cancogni. (Trans.). Cambridge, Massachusetts: Harvard University Press.
28. Isozaki in Price (2003:46).
29. See Eisenstein, S M. 1949. *Film Form*. London: Faber and Faber.

8 Cognition, image, and embodiment

8.1 Cognition and drawing

The central contention of this book is that drawing is a form of knowledge production. This idea comes from anthropological debates, and reframes the idea of knowledge as a process of how we come to know things rather than discussing it as a fixed, final, and completed process. How we come to know things is inextricably linked with what we know and architectural knowledge, as produced in design processes, is made through drawings and models as well as other activities such as client and user based discussions, site visits, and a range of other practices.

Drawing constitutes a thinking tool, a form of knowledge production equivalent to the written word. This is not a controversial statement within the field of architecture. It is well understood that drawing is the way in which ideas are developed and refined, a process of making rather than of describing our preconceived ideas about a scheme. This is, like much architectural knowledge, a tacit understanding, one which is often seen as so obvious as to require no further exploration and rarely challenged.

This means that it is certainly worth challenging and developing a deeper understanding of precisely what we mean by thinking in drawing, and how we can use this understanding to further develop our methods. Key to understanding this mode of cognition is to pay attention to our hands, and how we think not only in our minds but as a wholly embodied experience. A useful account to begin with is the physician John Napier[1], a specialist in the physiology of the hand who wrote an account which crosses disciplines in underlining their importance. Whether we draw directly with a pencil, use instruments such as compasses and parallel motion, or use a trackpad and mouse, drawing engages the hand by way of a tool. Napier discusses the use of tools under the umbrella of the *social and cultural aspects of the hand*, differentiating it from the structures found in the hand's bones, muscles, joints, and tendons, or the evolutionary development of the human hand as distinctive to those of primates. Indeed, tool use is often (and increasingly incorrectly) held up as one of the things which makes humans distinctive in the animal kingdom. The extension of the

142 *Cognition, image, and embodiment*

body and its capabilities through the use of tools is, despite such ongoing enquiries, pertinent to the discussion of drawing as external supports and instruments are required in order to give persistence to the traces we make.

The neurologist Frank R. Wilson[2] takes this line of thought further, making a direct causal relationship between the use of our hands and human culture in all its variety. Wilson expands his account to discuss the role of the entire arm in drawing briefly, noting the whole movement of a trained draughtsperson allowing for a transferable set of skills to develop (1999:140–141) when required. Both authors cite the grips which are unique to the human hand, the *opposition* of the thumb relative to the other fingers. Napier gives two forms of this grip (1993:55–66): the precision grip and the power grip. These simple movements can be used in combination, switching from the accuracy of one grip to the security of the second. Wilson's ambition for his book is to consider how education might be reconstituted in the face of evidence of the hand's importance. His question: "How does, or should, the education system accommodate the fact that the hand is not merely a metaphor or an icon for humanness, but often the real-life focal point—the lever or the launching pad—of a successful and genuinely fulfilling life?" (1999:277). This is all the more evident in architectural education where the drawing maintains an important position, but one which is at risk of erosion as curricula become ever more crowded. We shall cover the connection between Wilson and Ingold in the next section, where there is agreement in the dissatisfaction both have for a cephalocentric model of intelligence (1999:295), and that Ingold proposes instead an idea which resides in the whole integrated animal rather than a single organ.

The connection between drawing and cognition is made much more clearly by psychologist Peter van Sommers[3], whose study of simple drawing practices offers some insights into the process of drawing. The work describes a series of experiments which establish the accuracy and error rate in copying drawings, differences in preference for stroke direction in left- and right-handed participants, and the degree of contact between drawing implement and paper. This builds a catalogue of strokes and factors involved in very simple drawing exercises, a catalogue which can be of great use when describing more involved practices of professionals such as architects. Of particular relevance here is the discussion of forward planning in drawing:

> Drawing as a skill represents a unity in our minds because of its special communicative and expressive significance in culture. But many of the principles that govern its execution do not enjoy any unique status on account of this they are often simply general features that apply to any controlled movement where a degree of accuracy is required. *Anchoring*, or more generally *end control* of lines, provides an example of such a general aspect of skill. It reflects a balance between control effort and the obtrusiveness of miscalculation. Its significance is broader

Cognition, image, and embodiment 143

than this, however, since it provides the background for important aspects of graphic planning as well as controlling immediate action. (van Sommers 1984:37–38).

We have, in the microcosm of the single line, a model for how drawing allows a person to both plan ahead and to manage the termination of a line, a balance between maintaining the consistency of the current action: the line as it is being drawn as well as planning the position and manner of its completion. Through such forensic examination of the order in which lines are completed in a simple drawing, van Sommers is able to distill some fundamentals about how drawing is a temporally oriented practice, as we shall discuss in greater detail in Chapter 9 with reference to Henri Bergson. It is with reference to failures that we find a great deal of substance in van Sommers's account. Grouping the errors together in broad categories of *defects* and *anomalies,* the drawings' shortcomings are assessed according to a model being copied, notably a more complex model than in his other experiments. The quality of *defect* describes drawings which are unsuccessful, with angles drawn incorrectly or lengths exaggerated. *Anomalous* drawings have a different order of error, however: where a figure has three spurs coming from a centre, the participant might have drawn four, for example. Van Sommers uses these different forms of mistake to situate drawing as evidence of our perceptual analysis: is so-called poor drawing skill an error in this ability to process our sensory stimuli?

8.2 All drawings are failures

In my own creative practice, I have found a sense of dissatisfaction to lie at the root of my architectural and anthropological projects. These projects shed light on how a deeply felt unease with the status quo can be a key driver for new projects and new ideas. In this instance, however, I would like to speak of the status of a small number of drawings, drawings which for various reasons are disappointments and frustrations to me.

> Honour thy error as a hidden intention (Peter Schmidt & Brian Eno, *Oblique Strategies*, 1975)

These are not 'bad' or 'terrible' drawings per se: I am much too egotistical to allow certain of my failures to see the light of day so publicly, but these are drawings which have something to tell us about the nature of drawing as a material practice.

The first drawing is relatively competent, and represents a conversation between myself, anthropologist Jen Clarke, designer Neil McGuire, and illustrator Mitch Miller[4]. The conversation was held in Miller's studio space in Glasgow, and afterwards by way of response, I produced this drawing of the room in axonometric projection (figure 8.1). A key exchange between myself and Miller gives me my heading here: that all drawings are failures. This is a

144 *Cognition, image, and embodiment*

Figure 8.1 Mitch Miller's studio in axonometric projection, Ray Lucas, 2017.

phrase which might appear attention-seeking, looking for validation from the reader that the drawings are 'good', but this is not my intention here. I would rather investigate some of the various ways in which a drawing can fail.

In our discussion, we spoke about how a drawing only very rarely satisfies the draughtsperson. In a conversation around some of the assumptions made by people who do not draw about how it must be rewarding, relaxing, fulfilling, and other positive terms; we spoke about the role of drawing in communication: representing ideas we have and allowing our perceptions of the world to be shared. Drawing is frustrating, exhausting, time-consuming, and ultimately leaves you fraught and mourning the marks which did not turn out how you had hoped. That is not to say that it doesn't go right sometimes, or that it is ultimately a damaging pursuit to engage in, or indeed that some people do not find it to be a joy all the time.

Failure needs to be rehabilitated in our discussion of drawing, which is increasingly practice and process based: all drawings are failures because failure is essential to creative practice. I present here some abandoned attempts at one drawing (see figures 8.2a to 8.2d). The drawing is from a series called *A Graphic Anthropology of Namdaemun Market*. The series consists of architectural drawings of market carts from this general market in the centre of Seoul, and the specific instance is of a money-changing booth which shows traces of iterative construction and adaptation.

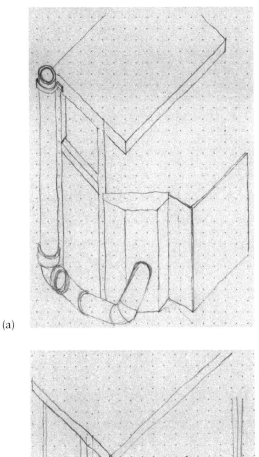

(a)

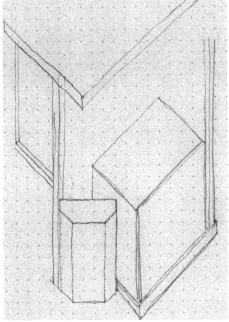

(b)

Figure 8.2 Failed drawings of Namdaemun market stall (a-c) followed by the 'final' version (d). Ray Lucas, 2016.

(c)

Figure 8.2 (continued)

Cognition, image, and embodiment 147

(d)

Figure 8.2 (continued)

This presented me with an interesting set of problems when drawing it. The geometry of the structure is deceptively complex. On first glance it looks rectilinear, and is composed of flat panel materials, but closer examination of the type required to translate my photographic record into the geometry of an axonometric projection reveals that the stall has a logic of overlapping and compression perhaps akin to the planar compositions of De Stijl architects such as Cornelis van Eesteren and Theo van Doesburg.

The elements presented me with challenges resulting in abandoned attempts, multiple erasures, corrections, sketched composition, poor placement on the page, and eventually a satisfactory drawing at A5. If we are to

148 *Cognition, image, and embodiment*

consider drawing as a practice, should I always show this working when using these drawings to explain my approach to the architecture of this market? Is the drawing the final attempt alone, or all of my scratched-out and erased versions which enabled me to gradually understand the geometry of the unit.

Another space for failure is to ask: why did I make these drawings?

Sometimes the failure is one of intent: these drawings appear to serve no purpose in and of themselves, and may represent threads which lead nowhere. Sometimes this eventually establishes a future practice with relevance to a research project, but for the time being I wonder about these depictions of ephemera from a Japanese street festival (figure 8.3) including not only the pertinent examples of portable shrines and temporary stages, but also apparently peripheral objects such as bento boxes, traffic cones, and trestles.

The focus on drawing in architecture ebbs and flows significantly, with the most recent period of paper architecture occurring from the late 1960s through the 1970s and recurring in the 1990s. During this time, commissions for firms were very hard to come by, so many practices would develop sophisticated theoretical positions through developments in architectural theory and propositions for buildings which would rarely be constructed. Leading the charge would be figures such as Peter Eisenman, Daniel Libeskind, Zara Hadid, Stephen Holl, Bernard Tschumi, and other leading lights of the postmodernist and deconstructivist movements. Additionally, consolidated movements would include Archigram (UK), the Metabolists (Japan), and Superstudio (Italy). Is the speculative architecture which is never built to be considered as a failure, or can the musings be argued to lead our thinking somewhere in time?

The sketchbook in Figure 8.4 is part of an ongoing investigation into a *Taxonomy of Lines*, a categorisation of mark-making practices, and has resulted in live drawing exercises as part of the ERC research group Knowing from the Inside in a range of locations including Japan and Scotland. Grids are inherently interesting, and have a long history in architectural drawing, often ignored or erased, they form a basis for further action.

This notebook attempts to interrogate the line and put it through its paces, to think through lines and to categorise them: to take some of the threads and traces which form the discourse around lines as literal, material things. A drawing is a thing, not an image. What allows us to read this set of lines as a grid? It is hand-drawn, on a long-haul flight whilst unable to sleep. How far from the horizontal and vertical can a line go before we stop reading it as part of a grid?

Architectural drawing practices speak of tolerances, as a reflection of the materials being specified in a detail drawing. Some materials can be specified with millimetre or even finer accuracy (sometimes costing money, or causing problems when it heats up and cools down with the daily solar cycle) whilst others can only be measured with a range of +/–10 mm or similar. This flexibility, this give, is a fact of life. A rough sketch can be

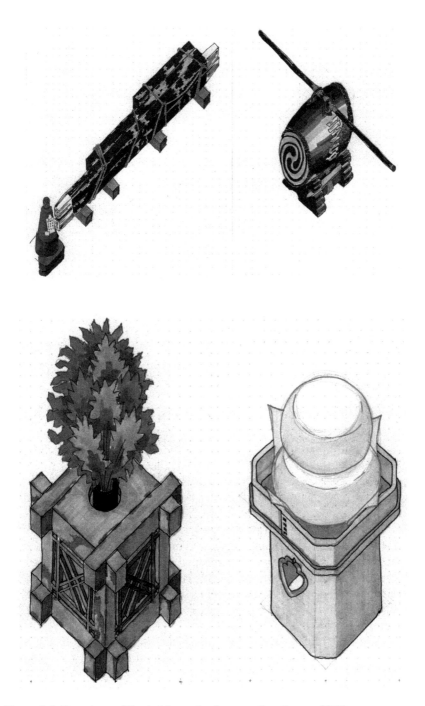

Figure 8.3 Drawings of Sanja Matsuri ephemera. Ray Lucas, 2017.

150 *Cognition, image, and embodiment*

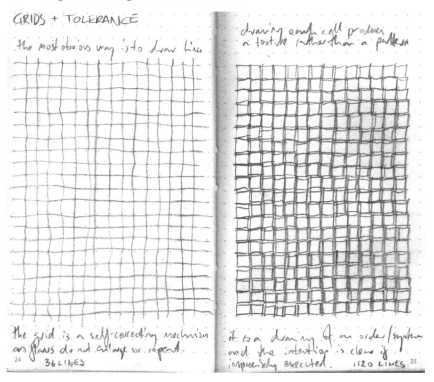

Figure 8.4 Extracts from *A Taxonomy of Lines* sketchbook.

made accurate by adding annotations of dimensions: even if the lines are slightly out of proportion with one another, the annotation acts to correct the drawing. The closer a person gets to this grid, the less convincing it is, but the lines correct one another. Together they form a grid that is just about good enough.

As material practices, drawings deal with media and supports: drawing instruments and drawing surfaces. The interactions of certain types of paper, board, and canvas with specific pencils, pens, and brushes is a subject for much enthusiasm amongst people who draw. Personal preferences for how one type of instrument handles compared to another are commonplace, and some take it to the extremes of collecting and hoarding art materials.

This drawing of a mikoshi (portable shrine) (figure 8.5) from the Sanja Matsuri (festival) in Tokyo makes use of mechanical pencils first, 0.5 mm 2B graphite, which is later to be overdrawn with Copic fine-liners in a range of line weights from 0.3 to 0.7 mm and a range of colours for differentiating outlines in black, brown, grey, and green. Finally, Copic markers with a brush nib and heavily pigmented ink are used to apply colour. These markers are most often used by Manga comic illustrators and enthusiasts, and come in a wide

Cognition, image, and embodiment 151

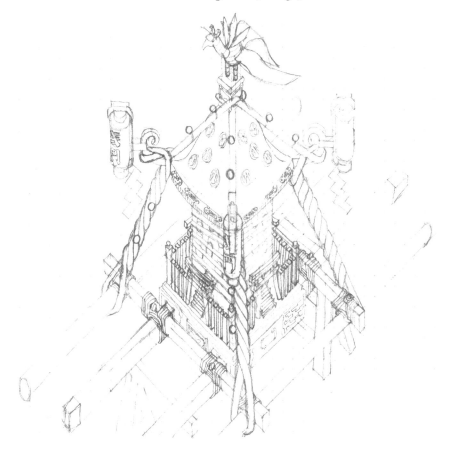

Figure 8.5 Axonometric drawing of a mikoshi, Ray Lucas, 2017.

range of colours. This is all on the support of a sheet of A4 Bristol Board, a form of thick, smooth, illustration paper which I have prepared with a grid of pale grey dots from an inkjet printer.

Halfway through the colouring stage of the drawing, one of the markers became unruly and misbehaved, dropping a large dollop of purple ink on the page. A decision has to be made at this stage regarding the drawing: several stages are completed. The underlying pencil drawing reproduced here is least risky, and can be corrected and adapted as I go along. These lines are destined to be erased in time, effaced once the ink is applied over the top, giving an illusion of crispness to the hesitant line. The inking and colouring phases are risky, however, as errors cannot be corrected. The quality of an ink line is therefore different to the pencil, which can afford a confidence and fluidity where constraint and control is demonstrated even by a freehand ink line. I decide not to abandon the drawing, despite the obvious imperfection (on top of the ones less clear to others).

152 *Cognition, image, and embodiment*

Happenstance and serendipity are part of drawing: unintended marks can become important to the overall composition, and flaws might be said to give character to the work. This is fine when a deliberately uncontrolled form of drawing is used: graphite powder applied directly to paper; brush and ink allowed to drip and spatter; applications of texture in watercolour through the use of inclusions and masking; surfaces which interact with the media to create unexpected moments of chance.

The examples here, however, are largely from attempts to use drawing to communicate architectural structures and urban events. The errors and failures are not deliberate, but do speak a little to the drawing as a site of experimentation. Failures are essential to working in this way, and fear of failure is paralysing to creative practice. Overinvesting in the outcome stultifies the process of making, where failures can be accepted and left as they are, corrected, covered up and hidden, or used as a lesson for the next iteration, the next attempt.

Drawings are material things with the interactions of body with instruments and surfaces, they are multiple objects, either in series with similar drawings, or the cumulative result of many attempts. All drawings are failures—and failures in multiple ways simultaneously—but this does not devalue them so much as expose the humanity underlying their production. The authorship is made present by these idiosyncrasies, traces of a performance with moments of faltering amongst moments of virtuosity. In the end, the drawing which the draughtsperson releases to the world is often *good enough*, a perfected drawing sometimes being rather too clean and clinical and lacking the energy and verve of an earlier iteration.

8.3 Why a drawing is not an image
(and why that might not be a problem)

When I draw observationally, I am selecting and editing, focusing on some qualities over others. Sometimes innovating and sometimes following a path, I move from Bergson's speculative problems to creative ones and back again throughout the course of a drawing. When I am not drawing, I am often thinking about drawing, constructing ideas for drawings I would like to do: dreaming them ahead of time without producing a fixed image or plan of work.

Image is a notoriously slippery concept to define, and a number of theorists from a wide range of disciplines have used the term to denote a variety of more or less esoteric aspects of pictures, representations, and depictions. As such, it is a discomfort that is difficult to express, but which relies on a clearer definition of precisely what is being opposed.

Some uses of image would include Kevin Lynch's *Image of the City*[5] which in 1960 brings the mental map to urban design and architecture, describing our navigation of the city through an attractive abstraction of urban elements into five key elements: *paths, nodes, edges, neighbourhoods,* and *landmarks*. His presumption is that city residents hold an image in the form of a map in their minds, and that by asking respondents to draw these maps, aggregating results from a large number, problems with the city's image can be diagnosed and solved.

Gilles Deleuze develops an alternative model of images in his oft overlooked work on cinema: *Cinema 1: The Movement Image* and *Cinema 2: The Time Image*[6]. He associates the interstices of film, the points of montage as being *images* which are superior to simple representations as they take place over time. By contrast, Jacques Rancière associates the image with the gaze in *The Emancipated Spectator*[7], describing the image constructed by a spectator as an active creative engagement with the work, essentially 'compos[ing] their own poem, as, in their way do actors or playwrights, directors, dancers or performers' (2009:13). This conceptualises image construction as a performance by the spectator, with the drawing itself as a score. As already discussed in Chapter 7, this recalls directly the presentation of cinema by Tarkovsky as subject to the mental apparatus of the viewer: something he deliberately exploited by creating an expansive cinema where meaning was not pinned down.

In *Being Alive*[8], Ingold gives us a sense of this discomfort through a related distaste for the fashion for academic '-scapes' of many kinds:

> The landscape is of course visible, but it only becomes visual when it has been rendered by some technique, such as painting or photography, which then allows it to be viewed indirectly, by way of the resulting image, which, as it were, returns the landscape back to the viewer in an artificially purified form, shorn of all other sensory dimensions. (2011:136)

This requires some further unpacking for my purposes here, and might at first glance appear to be counter to my purpose of not only understanding but also celebrating drawing. What is clear to me, however, is that this trend to consider the visual in this way not only misunderstands the landscape but also the painting (and by extension drawing) made from that experience. A further trend focuses on the spectatorship of images, interrogations of paintings and drawings through the act of looking, ignoring the *making* of the drawings (Ingold 2011:137).

I would paraphrase Ingold to say that we should not be fooled by academics who write about the consumption of drawings and paintings only as images. Such inscriptive practices are much more than that, and to reduce not only drawings, but also paintings, photographs, and films to images is to do them a great disservice. The image often implicates the mind, either the image held by the draughtsperson before putting pencil to paper, or the image extracted from a work by the viewer. Interestingly, a connection is drawn by Ingold in this same volume between images and production, images and capital. This is an analogy I would like to extend by appropriating the notion of candidacy from the study of the commodity status of things.

154   *Cognition, image, and embodiment*

Can drawings be said to have image phase, candidacy, and context as a set of qualities, a range of possibilities representing the temporality, conceptual and contextual nature of its intention and reception, a fluid state which says sometimes the drawing may be understood as an image, but in a range of ways, and sometimes not at all. The temporality is a case in point. When we presume that a drawing is made with an image in mind, transmitted by hand to the paper, we then feel that our task as viewers is to decode and return to the image as an original state. Writing in *Making*[9] and with reference to the work of artist and researcher Patricia Cain, Ingold writes:

> This observation, which tallies with what many graphic artists have to say about their work, flies in the face of the common belief among non-practitioners, not least historians and anthropologists of art, that the essence of drawing lies in the projection onto the page of interior mental pictures. They would have us suppose that in drawing an object, the draughtsman would first obtain an image in his mind, by way of the intromission of light through the eye, fix it in visual memory, and then, in a reverse movement of extromission, would shine the image onto the page, going on to draw around its outline. (2013:127)

In my experience, this is one of the greatest blockages experienced by students of architecture: the expectation that an image can be fully formed in the mind before being transmitted onto the surface of the paper resulting in a delay to practice. Drawing to find out, drawing as exploration, testing, and the process by which results are manifest.

This train of thought takes us to the later section, where Ingold states:

> To correspond with the world through drawing, therefore, is to practise not ethnography but graphic anthropology or, to coin a term, anthropography. (2013:129)

I prefer *Graphic Anthropology,* and indeed have run an undergraduate course with this title since 2010, encouraging architecture students to approach a context free from their usual assumptions, learning about it by drawing, diagramming, and notating it in a variety of ways. It is this blockage that is established early in *Making*: that images are blockages in the flow of life, of consciousness; their counterpart of objects representing the same problematic halting in the flow of materials.

We should not seek to arrest the drawing as an image, to resist the steadiness of this mental picture and focus instead on the parameters and intentions behind a practice, allowing that activity to flow at its range of temporal registers, sometimes easy following of an established path, other times forging a fraught but exciting and unexpected adventure. A drawing will move across a range of such conditions during its making and, hopefully, its reception. Images are like memorials to what was once a drawing: a way of fixing them and halting them, holding them in place.

Defining what drawing *is* or *can be* is a more fruitful way to proceed. Institutions from London's Victoria and Albert Museum to the Drawing Center in New York struggle with pinning this down, veering from the vagueness of 'works on paper' to a wide-ranging discussion of the various intentions which lie behind an assemblage of lines.

My earlier work addresses one possible approach[10]. Dealing with a range of inscriptive practices, the idea of what qualities these possess is discussed at length. The work of Nelson Goodman[11] is increasingly important as I continue to work in this area: his clear-minded descriptions of *scripts* and *scores*, *allographic* and *autographic* marks serves as a model for how to describe rather than stable categories which I would subscribe to unswervingly. The conclusion was that any given inscription can simultaneously possess a range of qualities, speaking to different audiences according to their knowledge and ability to understand each quality. Thus, an architectural drawing can have an aesthetically pleasing pictorial quality at the same time as it is a set of instructions—a notation for the construction of a building.

Most of the attention in architectural drawing literature is spent on the emergence of perspective, or the dominant modes of orthographic projection of plan, section, and elevation. Axonometric, isometric, and other forms of oblique or parallel projections are the poor relations, however. My mode of inquiry has been to copy and to redraw. Through careful copying, redrawing, retracing the steps, I found that my understanding was enhanced enormously through this act of retracing, re-enacting. That is not to say that I could place myself entirely into the context in which each drawing was made, but a deeper understanding is possible through practicing the relevant form of knowledge production: drawing.

I also produce drawings as descriptions and theoretical instruments (figure 8.6). Recent visits to Tokyo have been arranged to coincide with the Sanja Matsuri, a three-day festival in May which involves a vast disturbance to the everyday life of the Asakusa district of the city. The festival involves a constellation of temporary and mobile structures, the most celebrated being the mikoshi—portable shrines which are boisterously carried through the streets. The effort and weight involved giving a real practical presence to this radical and traditional architecture. Drawing is an important way of understanding the spatial implications of this event and its various stages, and the project includes a series of axonometric drawings; a set of long cross-sections showing the volumetric implications of the festival; and most ambitiously a series of Laban movement/dance notations again drawing upon earlier work. A similar set of drawings is also underway, describing Namdaemun Market in central Seoul, another socially produced space with a great many lessons for architects. A selection are also in the exhibition.

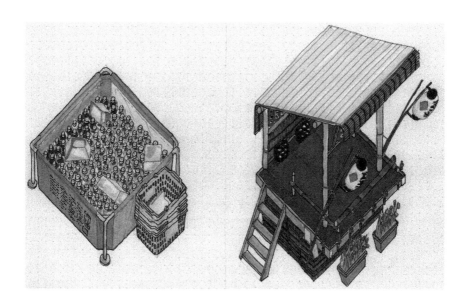

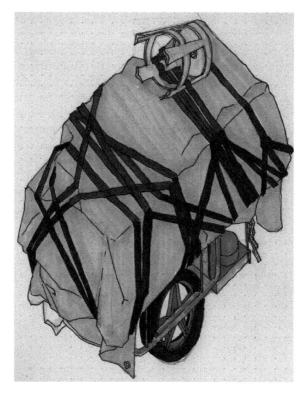

Figure 8.6 Examples from the graphic anthropology of Sanja Matsuri, 2017, and the graphic anthropology of Namdaemun Market. Ray Lucas, 2016.

Cognition, image, and embodiment   157

A drawing is trust. In this book, I show my sketchbook interpretations of far more accomplished draughtsmen. This chapter shows other uses of axonometric drawing from my own recent projects and opens up about their relative success and failure. This is an expression of trust. There is something very exposing about showing drawings, an associated fear of judgement, an anxiety about what people will think about the work: are the marks childish, boring, inscrutable, just bad? You can overcome such difficulties to an extent, but they lurk at the back of the mind whenever you chose to display a drawing to someone. Why does it expose a person so much to show their drawing? What is so personal about it? Many of us will have similar concerns about writing, not wanting to share a draft until it is ready, honed, tightened. Drawings have a heightened version of this.

An exception is when drawing with someone, sharing the burden. Often, in the architectural design studio, students and tutors draw with one another. Most often in turn, communicating what they mean by graphic means; more rarely by making marks on the same drawing. Completion is the problem here: the finishing of things that causes us so much trouble. A drawing is never finished as every fresh viewer makes it anew, and this is disconcerting to the one who drew it, as they relinquish control to someone else.

If drawings are not images, then what are they? One answer is to understand the drawing as a record of a gesture. Not all gestures have the same aim, and it falls to media theorist Vilém Flusser[12] to describe a great many human movements in his collection on gestures.

Flusser on *The Gesture of Painting* (2014:65):

> One analyses problems to be able to see through them, and so to get them out of the way. Problems solved are no longer problems. One analyses enigmas to enter into them. Enigmas solved remain enigmas. The goal of an analysis of the gesture of painting is not to clear painting out of the way. Rather, it so sits of entering into the enigma of painting more deeply so as to be able to draw a richer experience from it.

Contrast with his account of *photographing*—notably not *photography*— (2014:72):

> A photograph is a kind of 'fingerprint' that the subject leaves on a surface, and not a depiction, as in painting. The subject is the cause of the photograph and the meaning of painting. The photographic revolution reverses the traditional relationship between a concrete phenomenon and our idea of the phenomenon . . . In fact, the invention of photography is a delayed technical resolution of the theoretical conflict between the rationalist and empirical idealism.

The gesture of *drawing* is different again, offering greater precision at times than the enigmatic painterly gesture—whilst some of the best architectural

158 *Cognition, image, and embodiment*

drawing maintains this uncertainty and lack of prescription; offering a palimpsest of lines drawn, undrawn, and suggested: dividing surfaces into those to be perceived as figure and those that are ground.

If a drawing is a record of a gesture, then that set of gestures can be understood as a performance. Whether in public, for an audience, or architects drawing in front of their clients as a way of communicating and describing an intention, the sequence of acts which constitute a drawing are performed. Where a score is present (and performance suggests a script of some sort), this can give instructions which govern the performance, allowing variations within a set of parameters. This could be Ruskin's exercises for drawing, my own notations describing a drawing, or any number of fine art practices.

Architectural drawings in particular use common conventions. These are the rules which allow for precise meaning to be conveyed by a line, determining its role as a surface, a material, an outline, or a dimension. The grander scale governs how a drawing such as a cross section works, a conceptual slicing through of an object to reveal its volumes, or the construction of Renaissance perspective, also a geometric system as described by Perez-Gomez and Pelletier[13], and Robin Evans[14].

There is a great deal of resistance to convention in drawing, particularly as much of the literature has its origins in fine art practices. It has a bad reputation, representing a kind of limitation or constraint which is unwelcome and unhelpful to creative practice. Conventions exist for a purpose, particularly within the discipline of architecture. There are two distinct modes of operation for convention: the precise communication of ideas and purposeful investigation of particular qualities.

The precision with which drawings can communicate is important in design disciplines, where the manufacture of buildings or products is divorced from their specification. The conventionally produced drawing conforms to a stable set of rules which allow an observer to decode them.

The second quality of investigation is more interesting, however, as it is one of the unexplored norms of architectural education: that the building is designed best as part of a set of drawings, and no single projection gives all the required information, and attempts at a totality become too complex too quickly, tying design decisions down unhelpfully early. Often, however, the massing of a group of objects is described through axonometric drawing whilst circulation requires a plan; sections are our best tool for volumetric information whilst context and proportion are handled by the similar projection of an elevation.

Convention is a social system, an agreed set of rules allowing disparate temporal and physical contexts to produce drawings which can be understood with precision. This social system is not overwhelmingly positive, as it afforded the march of the universal dreams of classicist and modernist architects alike.

Jean Luc Nancy, in the *Pleasure of Drawing*[15], describes the act of drawing (2013:62) as informed by a desire to own or possess a thing. I have also discussed this, describing the sketchbook as a form of museum, a collection which does many of those things critiqued in studies of these institutions: divesting the thing of its context and function, with Jean Baudrillard[16] critiquing this system of objects as a docile pet, domesticating the world around us. The copies in my sketchbook run many of these same risks, but without altering the conditions of the original drawing in a material fashion: the access of others to an item I have drawn, for example, is unaffected by my collection of it.

This all sounds dangerous conceptually, and is rebutted by Ingold's[17] recent defence of observation:

> it is important to refute, once and for all, the commonplace fallacy that observation is a practice exclusively dedicated to the objectification of the beings and things that command our attention and their removal from the sphere of our sentient involvement with consociates. As should be clear from the foregoing, to observe is not to objectify; it is to attend to persons and things, to learn from them, and to follow in precept and practice. (2015:157)

The tension between these positions is fascinating and useful, however. Whilst notations can be understood as a distinct inscriptive practice, the instructional qualities which define notation can be found in all manner of drawings and other inscriptive practices. Sometimes that instruction is simply to look, to look in a particular way, to see this rather than that, to understand this piece of paper as figure and another as ground. More sophisticated instructions follow from this: you cannot see behind this, we are looking up from an impossible viewpoint underneath the floor, or this line indicates a celestial being.

The drawing can be a score, then. A score for action manifests in a variety of ways: the instructions for how to construct a building or a model for the student to understand. This suggests that the quality is one which might not be present for every observer, or might not be the same instruction to all who see it. In drawing Korean market carts (figure 8.7) in a highly coded form of architectural drawing, I am instructing the viewer to understand these as one of the set of things which are drawn in this way: to include them in the canon of architecture by describing them in that same language[18].

There is an aesthetic enthusiasm in beautiful materials. The handling of drawing materials gives consideration to the specifics of the support, the paper; as well as the medium, the scribing tools. The textures and tactile qualities of these materials and their handling within a drawing context are fascinating.

This enthusiasm runs the risk of overinvesting in the beauty of an Italian leather-bound sketchbook, to the extent that it paralyses action: it is too beautiful to ruin with a bad drawing, and we are hesitant to make a mark. One might ration rare sheets of paper, knowing my supply of Etchu Washi

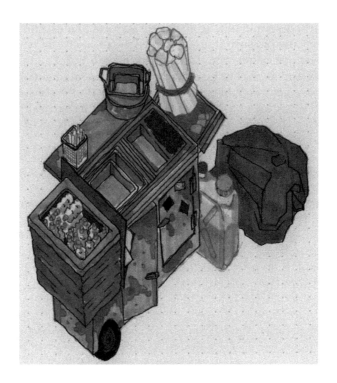

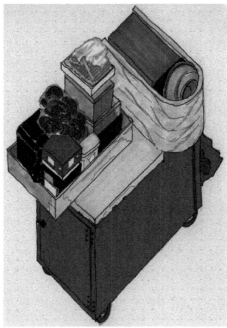

Figure 8.7 Examples of market carts drawn in axonometric. Ray Lucas, 2016.

Cognition, image, and embodiment 161

Figure 8.8 Material enthusiasm: collaborative live drawing exercise with Jen Clarke and Sekimoto Kinya in Gallery Turnaround, Sendai, Japan, Ray Lucas, 2015.

is impossibly limited and difficult to replenish; or I might adapt sheets of Bristol Board, printing a grid on the sheets and cutting them down to a suitable size. There is a simple pleasure in unexpected materials. The waxy crayons used in the *Taxonomy of Lines* live drawing project with Jen Clarke are an example here (figure 8.8), the surprise of the springy plastic tape we used, the delight and glee in tipping graphite powder onto a surface. Working with materials is crucial to the act of drawing.

Drawings are not only made up of lines. Shading is more than some awkward offshoot or tightly packed set of lines, but one of the fundamental strategies of drawing that is about territory. Simply drawing a box as in one of Ruskin's famous exercises describes an exterior and an interior. More than this, filling that box in makes a statement about the nature of that territory: a colour, a texture, a weight. Some definitions of drawing describe them as works on paper and hence including watercolour painting. It is clearly possible to draw with a brush as well as a pen or pencil, and watercolours often include an aspect of delineation either in another medium or with the paint itself. Drawing with inks also allows for fields of colour, and many of my own works use field conditions to describe the geometry of observed structures and objects.

162 *Cognition, image, and embodiment*

The architectural theorist Dalibor Vesely, writing *Architecture in the Age of Divided Representation*[19] has some interesting things to say, regarding the drawing not as an interaction with the environment but understood as the creation or provision of an environment in itself:

> When we are involved in the process of drawing, the table in front of us is no doubt part of our environment. The drawing, not as a sign on a piece of paper but as an event leaving traces behind, is also an environment. (2004:59)

Bergson tells us that there is 'No perception that is not full of memories' (2002:33)[20]. My contention, that brings us to the brpader theme of this book, is that drawing is a mode of perception. Whilst I discuss my own practice of observational drawing in this chapter, this argument can and does extend to speculative and projective design drawings, gestural drawings which are observations of your own body, abstract drawings which are spare and edited tightly, but still a mode of perception. Drawing is perception and drawing as a practice informs my perception even when I am not drawing.

Notes

1. Napier, John. 1993 [1980]. *Hands*. Revised by Tuttle, Russel H. New Jersey: Princeton University Press.
2. Wilson, Frank R.. 1999. *The Hand: How Its Use Shapes the Brain, Language, and Human Culture*. New York: Vintage Books.
3. van Sommers, Peter. 1984. *Drawing and Cognition: Descriptive and Experimental Studies of Graphic Production Processes*. Cambridge: University of Cambridge Press.
4. The transcript of this conversation is published as: Lucas, R. Miller, M. Clarke, J. & McGuire, N. 2017. "All Drawings Are Failures" Illustrated interview transcript in Clarke, J. (Ed.), *Koryu*. Aberdeen: Knowing from the Inside. Open access PDF available at: https://knowingfromtheinside.org/files/#about
5. Lynch, K. 1960. *The Image of the City*. Cambridge, Massachusetts: MIT Press.
6. Deleuze, G. 1992. *Cinema 1: The Movement Image*. London: Athlone Press. Deleuze, G. 1989. *Cinema 2: The Time Image*. London: Athlone Press.
7. Rancière, J. 2009. *The Emancipated Spectator*. London: Verso.
8. Ingold, T. 2011. *Being Alive*. London: Routledge.
9. Ingold, T. 2013. *Making*. London: Routledge.
10. Lucas, R. 2006. *Towards a Theory of Notation as a Thinking Tool*. Unpublished PhD Thesis. Aberdeen: University of Aberdeen.
11. Goodman, N. 1976. *Languages of Art*. Indianapolis, Indiana: Hackett Publishing Ltd.
12. Flusser, V. 2014. *Gestures*. Minneapolis: University of Minnesota Press.
13. Perez-Gomez, A. & Pelletier, L. 2000. *Architectural Representation and the Perspective Hinge*. Cambridge, Massachusetts: MIT Press.
14. Evans, R. 1995. *The Projective Cast: Architecture and Its Three Geometries*. Cambridge, Massachusetts: MIT Press.

15. Nancy, Jean-Luc. 2013. *The Pleasure of Drawing*. New York: Fordham University Press.
16. Baudrillard, Jean. "The System of Collecting" in Elsner, J. & Cardinal, R. (Eds.). *The Cultures of Collecting*. London: Reaktion Books.
17. Ingold, T. 2015. *The Life of Lines*. London: Routledge.
18. For more on these drawings, see: Lucas, R. 2018. "Threshold as a Social Surface: the Architecture of South Korean Urban Marketplaces" in Simonetti, C. & Anusas, M. (Eds.). 2018. *On Surfaces: Contributions from Anthropology, Archaeology, Art and Architecture*. London: Routledge.
19. Vesely, D. 2004. *Architecture in the Age of Divided Representation*. Cambridge, Massachusetts: MIT Press.
20. Bergson, H. 2002. *Key Writings*. London: Continuum.

9 Conclusion: The purpose of axonometric drawing

9.1 The liveliness of drawing

This chapter discusses the reasons why axonometric drawings retain their relevance. This persistence lies in the convention's role in the production of architectural propositions and knowledge.

Architectural practice has shifted fully from mechanical drawing to digital models, resulting in a substantially different practice of drawing whilst the end products might be said to be almost identical. Architects still use axonometric drawings, but the crucial point is that they often make them differently, by extracting a rendering or set view from an already existing digital model. In this manner, the axonometric drawing is not generative, but demonstrative: its role is to communicate rather than contribute to the design process.

Some forms of inscriptive practice have more in common with musical performance, where the trace is the result of a set of gestures. Ingold (2007:72–75) contends that in many cases, the trace can be regarded as incidental, and that the gesture and movement which generates it is more significant.

The practice of axonometric drawing gives designers the benefits of exploring components through cutaway and exploded drawings as well as a wide variety of scales from interior and furniture studies up to urban projects, all of which are difficult to replicate by other means. Massing, spatial relationships, and form are given in conjunction with surface detail and textures; the possibilities of the hidden line or reverse-angle projection all combine to give an architecture which has a regard for orderliness (even where that regard is subverted as in the case of Hejduk).

This chapter reinforces the central theme of this entire book: that drawing is not merely a manner for communicating a preformed idea held in the mind, but is rather a way of thinking through and developing that idea. As such, the conclusion is a defence of the process of making and thinking through axonometric drawings, something at risk should we not be mindful of the substantial changes being made in architectural practice.

Whilst I do not subscribe to the dominant narrative of a 'death'[1] or other end to practices of hand and mechanical drawing in the face of

Conclusion: The purpose of axonometric drawing   165

CAD and other forms of computerised drawings, there remains a need to argue for the continued relevance of producing axonometric drawings. A great many parallel projection drawings are still *produced*, but this is subtly distinct from the actual activity of drawing them. For example, many CAD packages will now produce a full three-dimensional model of a piece of architecture from which orthographic, parallel, and perspective projections can be generated. Axonometric drawings, in common with other conventions, have inherent affordances: well-resolved designs are often produced by balancing plans, sections, elevations, and parallel projections.

The question is then to define what it is that actually drawing an axonometric brings to the design process, which can be presented in the manner of a manifesto of sorts:

Volume. Volumetric information is conveyed succinctly by axonometric drawings, with a shorthand often based on the extrusion of plan forms upwards to define heights. Parallel projections are widely understood by stakeholders such as clients and building users. This is due in part to their use outside of architectural practice, commonplace in illustration and graphic design as well as computer and video games.

Precision. Precision is a feature of axonometric drawing (isometric less so), as the deformation of angles is restricted to one plane, and measurements of length retain proportions across the piece. The same cannot be said of perspective drawings, where an expert eye is required to discern the relative sizes of elements as they recede towards the vanishing point.

Hybridity. Parallel projection allows for hybrid drawings, using the logic of plan drawing or cross sections, allowing for detailed information to be given. Extreme examples such as Hejduk's late drawings push at the boundaries of this, and are produced for their own purposes, but the capacity of parallel projection to work with other forms of projection is important. They can be drawn with the aid of plans and elevations, and represent a compilation of information from other sources.

Clarity & occlusion. Much of this paints a picture of a representational strategy which is open and transparent. There is a feature of axonometric which contradicts this: occlusion. The erasure of hidden or construction lines is an essential aspect of transforming a process drawing into a finished work. During the construction of a parallel projection drawing, a mass of lines are produced, resembling an x-ray of the proposed structure. The designer needs to select and edit these lines carefully in order to produce a legible drawing. Surfaces which would be hidden need to be removed and

166   *Conclusion: The purpose of axonometric drawing*

hidden, to give the appearance of solidity to those uppermost elements. As we have seen in Chapter 4's discussion of John Hejduk's Wall House, this can be used deliberately as a device; and in the description of Eisenman's early House projects in Chapter 6, suggestions are made as to the possibility of the tangle of unrealised lines for an architecture without external referent.

Enchantment. It is clear from the work of Stirling and Eisenman that the beauty of the drawing as a thing in itself was hugely important. Referring to Gell's ideas of *artworks as traps*[2] and the demonstration of virtuosity as a process of validation which guarantees the expertise of the architect.

Scale. One feature of axonometric projection and similar conventions is its ability to work at a range of scales. This is of course a feature of many forms of drawing, with floor plans transforming into urban plans or figure/ground diagrams, long topographical sections using the conventions of the cross section. The other dominant three-dimensional projection, perspective, becomes problematic when scale is discussed. A number of parallel projections were developed specifically to tackle the needs of furniture design, and axonometric and isometric drawings have been used to describe buildings in a multitude of scales from furniture and fixture designs up to urban context. The clarity of the convention is maintained throughout, and offers a uniquely unifying form of representation when used.

Malleability. It can be argued that axonometrics and their ilk are amongst the most model-like drawings produced by architects, and share many of the benefits of building a physical model. Cognitively, the drawing's parts and components can be understood as malleable, subject to modulation of their surfaces, alterations in their dimensions, and open to perpetual repositioning.

Composition. Parallel projections are compositional in nature, and allow for arrangements of elements to be experimented with and tested. This in turn encourages an architecture which consists of separate elements, blocks which can be reconfigured and rearranged during the design process, sometimes halting the development of the individual blocks prematurely or resulting in a fragmentary outcome. The possibility of using parallel projections as part of an iterative design process allows the designer to test—often swiftly— various solutions to the same issue, in order to select the one most consistent with the project in hand.

The above manifesto is by no means exhaustive, but does show some of the elements of a design process that are under consideration when making an axonometric or other parallel projection drawing. The terms are not

Conclusion: *The purpose of axonometric drawing*   167

exclusive to parallel projection, and are not offered to give this convention priority over orthographic projection or perspective, but instead to remind us of what this form of drawing offers.

9.2 Temporality and creativity[3]

Making is rarely addressed in discussions of architectural drawing. Even where it is discussed as a practice, there is an abstraction away from the pragmatics of making marks on a surface in an intelligible order. In defending the production of axonometric and other parallel projections, then, it is crucial to be clear what we are talking about. In this section, I detail the production of axonometric drawings from an earlier project, connecting these with Henri Bergson's discussion of temporality and creativity. All of this is closely aligned to Tim Ingold's focus on making. Parallel projections are more than images to be consumed and received; they are important methods by which certain forms of architectural knowledge are made possible.

Invoking the name of the philosopher Henri Bergson carries certain implications. Bergson's theory allows us to reposition our object of study away from the spatial and into the temporal. Rather than being some pseudo-mystical move—as might be suggested by Bergson's concerns for reinstating the study of metaphysics—the focus on time is rather more pragmatic in nature and intention. On its simplest level, this repositioning allows the consideration of processes more fully, and also allows us to challenge the very notion of a completed and fixed object of study. This ingrained notion of a completed object sits uneasily with the entire project of anthropology, and is also one of the factors holding the discipline back from a fuller analysis and understanding of creative practices.

What might begin as a simple move away from the spatial to the temporal swiftly brings with it significant implications. These implications are rather fundamental to our approach, and it is here that Bergson's philosophy is of the greatest aid to the study of creative practices in general, and inscription in particular.

Discussion of Bergson opens up a discussion of *virtuality*. Rather than the fashionable notion of virtuality borrowed from mainstream science fiction novels and films, Bergson's separation of the *virtual* and the *possible* is a crucial categorical difference with implications for what we regard as real (as opposed to actual). Memory is also high on our list of key concepts in Bergson. This ties in to the definition of *speculative* versus *creative* problems in Bergson. This is where the temporality of creativity lies, and is an important starting point for the description of making a drawing: defining creativity as essentially durational in character. The next section considers the drawing as the relationship between a line and the surface that supports it. The line in drawing forms territories on the paper,

168   Conclusion: The purpose of axonometric drawing

bounding areas with edges and defining them with textures. The empty space of the page is understood as a reserve, which may or may not be used, and which has its status altered during the drawing process, from reserve to surface, object, field.

Bergson's overall project considered the nature of *durational* time as intrinsic to the life histories of individual organisms. This aspect of time contrasts with measured or scientific time in that it is entirely subjective. This comes in a context of the emergence of sociology on the one hand and psychology on the other. Bergson stands aside from both of these debates—not in a simplistic way as a bridge between them, but with an alternative form of understanding, an intuition and metaphysics that lays claim to none of the scientific jargon of social science or psychology. Bergson's work is particularly interesting given how radical a break from conventional architectural attitudes it is to deny space as a category altogether. By rejecting space, and placing time as the primary concern for architecture, the object of architectural discourse becomes what Bernard Tschumi[4] might term *events*—such that the architect's role is to manipulate events by means of physical form. These forms, however, might be regarded as similar to the lines of an architectural plan—a set of instructions or notations within which we can choose a course of action either in compliance with, or rejection and reaction against, the built structure. In practical terms, this has resulted in some architects regarding the very brief of the project to be of primary importance, having the potential for manipulation—and as an aspect of creative choice rather than a simple fulfilment of the client's wishes (while hopefully avoiding the obvious pitfalls for the too-arrogant architect of cliché).

The central themes from Bergson that I wish to pick up are as follows. First is a notion of *intuition* which, rather than a wooly process relying on imprecise gut feelings and tacit knowledge, is a fully formed approach to philosophical problems. This approach is one which, typically of Bergson, is rather hard-nosed and dismissive at times, and which finds itself concerned only with real *differences in kind*. Their corollary, *differences in degree,* are a category Bergson rarely has truck with, save to identify them as false problems unworthy of investigation. This analysis of problems is fascinating, however, and can lead to some useful and interesting observations[5].

Bergson's work on matter and memory has some interesting implications when brought to bear upon the architectonic notions of space and place as augmented by the studies of Michel de Certeau. In equating matter and memory with space and place, I am using Bergson's temporocentrism to understand spatial phenomena. Given architectural interest in both place and space, the specific locality that has already been perceived and interpreted, that perception being full of memories where space is an operable reserve, potentiality for use in the design process. Memories are important in Bergson, and he reminds us that pure perception is a theoretical

Conclusion: The purpose of axonometric drawing   169

construct that can never really happen. By extension, all inscription, all drawing, is full of memory.

9.3 Bergson and problem solving

Bergson offers us many insights on the nature of problem solving. In stating a problem correctly, Bergson holds that a scientific or speculative problem may be solved, as the solution to such problems is possible, or inherent in its correct statement. We are reminded that 'the possible is only the real with the addition of an act of mind which throws its image back into the past, once it has been enacted.' (Bergson 1992:100)

> We imagine that everything which occurs could have been foreseen by any sufficiently informed mind, and that, in the form of an idea, it was then pre-existent to its realisation; an absurd conception in the case of a work of art, for from the moment that the musician has the precise and complete idea of the symphony he means to compose, his symphony is done.' (Bergson 1992:21)

It is in this respect that Bergson finds more interest: the creative problem, which resists such possibility forces us into a solution that relies upon duration. A process must be engaged with over a period of time. This definition of the *possible*, as supported by Elizabeth Grosz (2001:11) uses the term to denote an action which is prefigured, where a series of causal events lead to a knowable outcome lacking surprise or accident. The *virtual* is the opposite to this, as there is the potential for things to take another path. Events themselves as they unfold are categorised as the *actual*. In axonometric drawing, I argue that there are elements of both the *possible* and the *virtual* and that by tracking a drawing process, we can begin to identify the points at which decisions are made (the virtual) as well as the times when we follow process to its logical conclusion (the possible). Grosz outlines the very definition of creative practice for Bergson—that we might regard creativity as virtuality in this sense, rather than merely possibility. A creative act might not happen or have the unexpected outcome—its results are to a greater or lesser degree (and the degree is relatively unimportant to the analysis at this point) unknown, or rather unknowable.

This unknowable quality presents a rather obvious problem for any study of creative practice, and this is why alternative approaches became so essential, including temporalising a debate that has long been solely spatial, and engaging with practices as an alternative way to know something.

All of this calls for an engagement with *process*, which informs this research in a variety of ways. The creative drawing, for example, is a process which must be engaged with from start to finish in order for the creative 'problem' to be solved. It is an image of that problem, or rather a trace of the entire problem-solving process, rather than having a single

170　*Conclusion: The purpose of axonometric drawing*

answer possible within it. As Bergson points out, the duration of solving speculative problems can potentially be reduced to zero, whereas the duration of dealing with a creative problem is fully contingent on its solution.

I aim to show the potential of understanding the tension between speculative and creative problems. In order to do so, I shall refer to a part of my own *Getting Lost in Tokyo* project which consisted of a series of drawings, notations and diagrams describing my experiences of navigating the Tokyo Metro[6]. This part of the work was presented at an exhibition at Dundee Contemporary Arts' Centrespace Gallery in June 2005 as a hand-bound book of original drawings. What I am looking to expose are the complexities within a practice—a practice that is never entirely creative or entirely speculative. The interactions of such virtual and possible outcomes comprise a rich field of analysis.

This is to suggest that a *possible* event is *always real,* before and after that instant during which it was *actually there.* Understood in this way, the predestined event is perpetual, always real, and simply 'waiting to happen.' The virtual might or might not become actual—it is not real until it becomes actual, and is less predictable.

> In short, time thus considered is no more than a space in idea where one imagines to be set out in line all past, present and future events, and in addition, something which prevents them from appearing in a single perception: the unrolling in duration would be this very incompletion, the addition of a negative quantity. Such, consciously or unconsciously, is the thought of most philosophers, in accordance with the demands of the understanding, the necessities of language and the symbolism of science. Not one of them has sought positive attributes in time. They treat succession as a coexistence which has failed to be achieved, and duration as non-eternity. (Bergson 1992:18)

Our categories of the possible and the virtual can, then, be experienced in terms of the real and the actual—and noting the absurdity of treating an artwork in the same way as a fact of science. The example suggested by Bergson of sugared water is instructive here. The fact that sugar dissolves in water is real before it is actual in each case, whilst Picasso's *Guernica* was not real prior to its execution.

> As we have said, when one wishes to prepare a glass of sugared water one is obliged to wait until the sugar melts. This necessity for waiting is the significant fact. It shows that if one can cut out from the universe the systems for which time is only an abstraction, a relation, a number, the universe itself becomes entirely different. (Bergson 1992:20)

This passage speaks a little of that virtuosity by which an idea might appear to be held complete and crystalline by the mind before its commission to paper.

Conclusion: The purpose of axonometric drawing 171

I have argued fundamentally against this notion, for it exists, like Bergson's pure perception, as an ideal only. The actual practice of inscribing the work is often a struggle to realise the idea held; to make it actual still requires an act of gesture, of will.

> We can imagine that everything which occurs could have been foreseen by any sufficiently informed mind, and that, in the form of an idea, it was thus pre-existent to its realisation; an absurd conception in the case of the work of art, for from the moment that the musician has the precise and complete idea of the symphony he means to compose, his symphony is done. (Bergson 1992:21)

In this, the play of the possible is understood as that which is already constituted: a proposition awaiting only the due process of speculative problem solving. The virtual is a projected form of the present, relocating it to the future, and to alterity. The openness represented by the virtual is what characterises the creative act, and shows us the central quality of Bergson's philosophy—of duration as a quality of time rather than a spatialised measurement of the quantity of time spent.

The possible and the virtual are real categories of difference, that is to say differences in kind as Bergson understands them. These, rather than mere differences in degree, are the true differences on which we should focus our attention and theoretical effort. This relates again to the alterity at the heart of anthropological discourse: different ways of engaging with the world remain equally valid, as opposed to the singular and totalising truths of philosophy. In this way, it becomes possible to hold differing and even mutually exclusive concepts in order to act creatively, despite the Orwellian overtones and implications of such 'doublethink.'

This brings us to question which problems can be solved by drawing in axonometric projection? The range of architectural issues regarding programme, form, and construction are all relevant to the convention: but our focus here needs to be on what constitutes essentially axonometric knowledge? Axonometric drawing describes elements of architectural compositions as discreet parts; the kit of parts suggested by Price, or repeated, rotated, and deformed elements found in Eisenman. These are represented with clearly defined deformation, allowing three faces of an object to be clearly shown. The relationships of these parts to one another are shown, and they can also be separated out to reveal each element's qualities in isolation. This generates a kind of architecture based not only on an extruded geometry, but also one which has a constructional logic: according to the logic of parallel projection, buildings are made up of parts.

Alternative logics overlap with this, or present alternative understandings: cross sections often render buildings as a cavernous mass from which spaces have been excavated; only special conditions such as fenestration are rendered with their construction intact. The particulate logic

172 *Conclusion: The purpose of axonometric drawing*

of axonometric drawing makes it suitable for design processes: as parts responding to the brief, placed into relationship with one another through a series of iterations and experiments.

9.4 The surface and the mark

It is important to return to fundamentals at this point, reflecting upon the case for the primacy of process in drawing, it is therefore crucial to question the surface and the inscribed mark. The term 'drawing' covers a great many different activities, and can be understood as a component of many if not all inscriptive practices, even writing by hand. One way might be to look at other inscriptive practices and to distill these from drawing, so that the essential quality we name 'drawing' is excised of its notational and diagrammatic properties. A drawing is not, however, simply the condition left over, the remainder when all the other aspects of inscriptive practice are removed. It is a thing in itself, a way of describing and understanding which, like those other qualities, might be found elsewhere, even in relatively unlikely places.

   In my study of drawing more broadly, the notional description of 'any mark made onto or into a surface', with additional qualifications suggesting the deliberateness, communication, and description, has held a great deal of influence. The work thus far has considered the mark itself, the trace left by a gesture; but the other side of the practice—the surface itself—has been left rather untouched, like the blank sheet of paper that a person faces when beginning a written composition or, indeed, a drawing.

> If painting presents Being, the drawn line presents Becoming. Line gives you the image together with the whole history of its becoming-image. However definite, perfect, unalterable the drawn line may be, each of its lines—even the last line that was drawn—is permanently open to the present that bars the act of closure. (Bryson in de Zegher 2003:150)

The relationship between the line and the surface is crucially important in drawing, and also reveals difference in the regard that the various other inscriptive practices have for the surface. This approach contrasts with that enshrined in codes of Western oil painting. Whilst such codes were largely deconstructed over the course of the twentieth century, they still form the basis for painters and artists to respond to; rebelliously or respectfully as appropriate. The painter sees their task as being to cover the entire surface of the canvas with paint—marks and colours that are entirely the choice and responsibility of the artist[7]. The surface in painting is something to be obliterated or covered over so that it does not reveal its existence—the illusion of painting relies upon this effect, even where the 'painterly' applications of paint command attention, as in the thick brush marks of Vincent van Gogh.

Conclusion: *The purpose of axonometric drawing* 173

Similarly, we might begin to look at the role of the surface in the notation or the diagram. The space here is deemed to be neutral, as background, or white space which, like Bergsonian time, prevents everything from being given at once. This attitude towards the white space is deceptively complex—the relationships between surface and line being the very stuff of inscription, the core of what it is we are seeking to understand.

The drawing, be it a sketch made in situ or an architectural facade completed in the studio, has a particular flexibility regarding the surface. This flexibility might in itself seem like a fairly weak defining feature, but the capacity for the surface to be read in many different ways in a drawing is one of the crucial components of the practice. Indeed, this same flexibility is apparent in the line in drawing which might, within the same work, represent an edge, a texture, or a thread. The line in drawing can form territories on the paper, areas which, once they are defined, are read differently to the rest of the paper. By establishing a series of such territories, forms can begin to emerge, be the lines fluid or ruled, the territories open or bounded. The simple act of drawing a line on the page gives us one side and the other—a way to orient the territory with a single mark for reference.

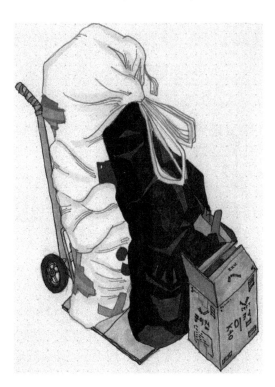

Figure 9.1 Examples from *Graphic Anthropology of Namdaemun Market* (2014–2017) by the author depicting a variety of found pieces of architecture from around the general market site.

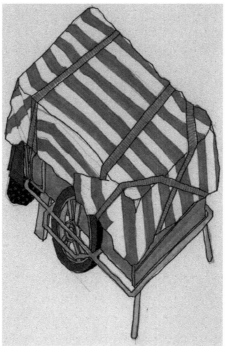

Figure 9.1 (continued)

Conclusion: The purpose of axonometric drawing   175

This interplay of surface and line is apparent from these sketches of Namdaemun Market in Seoul (figure 9.1). The drawing does not respect the surface as a frame, instead occupying sections of the page, and allowing a section of paper bounded by lines to read as platters and the remnants of a meal whilst another section of the page denotes the interior of a bin. Similar smaller subdivisions show the way in which the lines have different purposes related to their contexts, operating interchangeably as edges, textures, and threads, such as in the case of a striped tarpaulin or shrink-wrapped goods on a trolley. Indeed, blank spaces in the textures can also be understood as edges—the play of a positive and negative being understood pictorially by a trained eye. The reserve of blank paper is seen in the spaces between the steel members making up a market stall, the blank white between these reads differently to the white space of a stripe.

> A key consequence of the reserve is that the drawn line can be released from painting's imperative to bind each and every area into the totality—or tyranny—of the image as overall design. Instead in the moment that it is drawn, the line can determine its nature and shape with reference only to the local area to which it immediately belongs: a 'vignette' that exists as a single cell of design, sequestered from its surroundings, cordoned off by the neutralising effect of the reserve's protective coccoon. (Bryson 2003:151)

Norman Bryson's essay in *The Stage of Drawing—Gesture and Act* (1993) places the empty white surface in the position of a 'reserve' which lies empty. In the case of painting, this must be filled, but in the case of drawing decisions must be made about how much of this reserve to use, how to define areas, and so on—there is no imperative completely to cover the surface.

Bryson continues to define drawing in terms of its comparison to painting—stressing the immediacy caught by drawing a line:

> An immediate art, then: the present of viewing and the present of the drawn line hook on to each other, mesh together like interlocking temporal gears; they co-habit an irreversible, permanently open and exposed field of becoming whose moment of closure will never arrive. (1993:150)

In comparing the drawings of Francis Bacon with his paintings, Bryson finds all the qualities of ecstatic, tortured flesh from the paintings to be found in the more economically executed drawings. Whilst this is true, and Bryson's point regarding immediacy is well made, it remains that the diagram found in the paintings is absent from the drawings—only the figure is shown[8]. It is worth noting here that Bacon held his drawings in low regard, as simple working documents that he regularly destroyed, never exhibited or sold, and of which he repeatedly denied the existence throughout his career.

176 *Conclusion: The purpose of axonometric drawing*

This relationship between drawing and painting according to which the former is preparatory to the latter, is interesting and often assumed without foundation—Bacon, for example, did also produce painted studies for his paintings. It might be that the very immediacy of the line drawings is part of the reason why he held them in such low regard, when compared to his goal—the totality represented by painting.

The codes or schemata of drawing are important to consider here, as they, more or less strictly, define how it is that a line on a surface is to be understood—or to put it another way, these schemata determine the way in which the artist responds to a phenomenon:

> Drawing is a machine to which the hand and brain of the artist become adjunct. Who operates the machine? The artist, of course. But once set in motion, the machine goes by itself. (Bryson 1993:153)

We return here to the gesture and the notion of the drawn mark as the trace of a gesture. This is important, and is key to the rupture between what is drawn by hand and computer. This rupture is a potential site for the creative act, and the computer drawing can still be understood as the trace of the gesture it resembles, even though the actual generative gesture was a series of wrist and finger actions rather than a bodily engagement with the equipment of parallel motion, set-square, straight-edge, and pen, ink, and paper.

> Perhaps no other medium possesses the quality of instant interplay that the drawn line involves, between active and repetitive states: Active, the line drives the image forward under the artist's guiding will, but the moment it launches forth, it exists in the outer world, no longer transparent but opaque, dense, obdurate. (Bryson 1993:158)

The artist William Kentridge exploits this fascinating ground between surface and mark with his publication *Cyclopedia of Drawing* (Kentridge 2004). In this artist's book, Kentridge draws over a reference work on drawing issued by the 'American Technical Society' in 1924. Kentridge's intervention introduces a red pencil grid into which a figure is drawn in heavy charcoal or graphite. The figure of a young man transforms into a bird in flight before rolling to a landing as an old man. The book plays out like an animated flip book to this effect. The drawings are aligned off-centre, towards the right-hand side of the page, all the time drawn directly over the pages of another book, which gives its dry account of how to cut patterns into sheet metal in order to achieve various forms.

The drawing over of such a manual brings our attention to the codes of drawing, and how we understand such drawings by reference to a set of rules. Without such rules, we cannot make sense of these marks as easily, if at all. Kentridge also exploits the nature of his chosen surface, being a book

Conclusion: *The purpose of axonometric drawing*   177

after all, so that he can construct a sequence for animation. This knowing use of the surface is interesting, and increasingly an issue for artists who draw. Such artists, aware of the rules, and knowing the implications as well as the potential of breaking them, are exploring the possibilities inherent in surface as well as in the mark.

In the case of the architectural drawings presented in this volume, the use of the surface is often uncomplicated, with bounded shapes representing objects such as surfaces, columns or walls. There are cases, however, where there is some sophistication in this relationship between surface and mark. The elision of some lines by Price, where the interior angles of some cuboid shapes are suggested but not drawn, demonstrates the transformation the surface can undergo once it is drawn on. When Stirling uses both the worm's eye and bird's eye views of a building, the same blank paper can represent sky on one sheet and ground on another: there is directionality to the paper, and the introduction of a three dimensional convention means that the viewer interprets the surface as such. This is heightened further by Hejduk's subtle transfigurations across a single drawing: the status of the 'blank' paper is furtive and flittering, dependent on the contract between the viewer and the draughtsperson.

9.5 *Making* an axonometric drawing

To fully understand and exploit the differences between inscriptions, it is important to move beyond merely spatial descriptions of patterns of line and tone on surface, and to pursue a temporal understanding, that of Bergson's duration. I will be using one of my own projects to explore this, from an exhibition composed of notations, drawings, diagrams, and paintings on the theme of *Getting Lost in Tokyo*. The architectural drawings which follow are from a series of thirty episodes interpreting the process of way-finding in the metro (figure 9.2). The drawings are translations from an initial narrative (drawn as a process diagram with loops and decisions), and then a series of episodes in Laban movement notation. These described my bodily movements as I navigated the corridors and platforms of Shinjuku Station in the early 2000s; coding the movements in a symbol-based system used (controversially) for choreography. These were translated into architectural drawings, and I chose the axonometric form of drawing for several reasons; particularly its ambiguous relationship with orthographic and perspective drawings, and its capacity for deploying as a 'kit of parts' noted previously. Some objects must be hidden in order to reveal others, and an interesting series of decisions must be made whilst drawing.

Our description of axonometric drawings can be augmented with reference to my discussion of orthographic projections on the one hand and perspective drawings on the other. Orthographic projections include plans, sections, and elevations, and are the traditional tools of the architectural trade. Such drawings are taken from an objective viewpoint, and are

178 Conclusion: The purpose of axonometric drawing

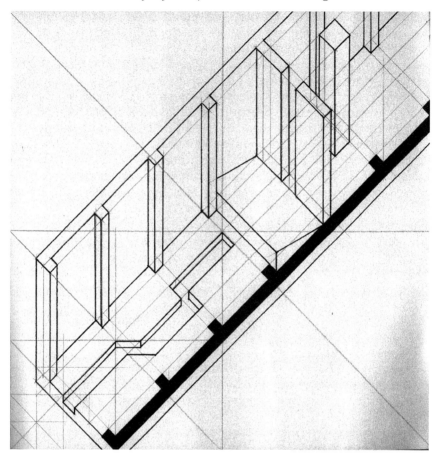

Figure 9.2 'Completed' axonometric drawing from *Getting Lost in Tokyo*.

understandings of relations within the whole, be it a floor level or specific facade. Orthographic representations can be understood as slices through an object such as a building (but are also used in medical scanning equipment, for example). A plan, then, is a horizontal slice showing floor areas, walls, thresholds, stairs, fenestration, orientation, and furnishings. A section is a vertical slice predominantly concerned with depicting the arrangements and heights of volumes. Elevations are organised along similar principles, with the same set of rules, but allow us to see and analyse the composition and harmony of the facade, the arrangement of windows, doors, masonry courses, decorative and structural elements such as the classical orders of architecture.

All the angles in such drawings are true, and this makes them particularly useful as working drawings for an industrialised building process.

Conclusion: The purpose of axonometric drawing 179

The objectivity here can be contrasted with the subjectivity of perspective drawings, which attempt to give an impression of how a building might appear from one viewing position. The representation of infinity is one of the crucial elements of perspective. By introducing the horizon line and the vanishing point, as seen from a finite viewing distance, it allows a distance of infinite length to be represented. The plan drawing, by contrast, presupposes an infinite viewing distance, but by the same token is unable to represent the infinite.[9]

The reason returning to issues addressed more fully in the introduction is that it underpins the choice of axonometric drawing for this project. This convention shares many qualities of both perspective projection and orthography—it is ambiguous with regard to subjectivity, viewing distances and the truth of angles. To take my investigations further, I prepared a series of drawings which show how these axonometric drawings were prepared. The process, as an art project using parallel projection rather than an architectural one, was somewhat idiosyncratic: the aim was to expose some of the underlying processes within the convention. As such, the drawings have an abstract quality, hinting at familiar typologies such as corridors and elements like doors, but these are represented blankly, with the explicit aim of representing archetypal elements.

Figures 9.3 Establishing the centre of the square and dividing the square into four.

180 *Conclusion: The purpose of axonometric drawing*

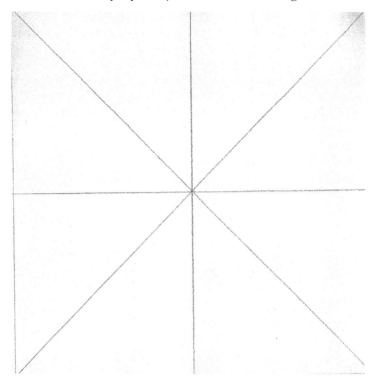

Figures 9.4 Establishing the centre of the square and dividing the square into eight.

I began each drawing with a measured square—a frame. All the drawings for the series are 25 cm square, and this is the only stage at which a ruled distance is measured, as the remaining lines are established by means of division, set square, and parallel motion. The first action we see is a drawing of a line from one diagonal corner to the other. Drawing the line from the opposite corners establishes the centre of the square (figure 9.3), allowing horizontal and vertical divisions to be made. The parallel motion[10] of the drawing board allows the horizontal centre line to be established, and the set square allows the vertical centre line to be drawn (figure 9.4) in. This divides the square into four, and I continue the process of division down towards the lower-left corner (figure 9.5). Each division is a measuring line, allowing me to project further lines according to that proportion, and with reference to the horizontals, verticals, and the frame itself.

Even though I have gone through this procedure a number of times before—the drawing is, after all, one of a series of thirty—I need each time to establish this framework by the process of division. This reminds us once again of Bergson's famous discussion of creative and speculative problems.

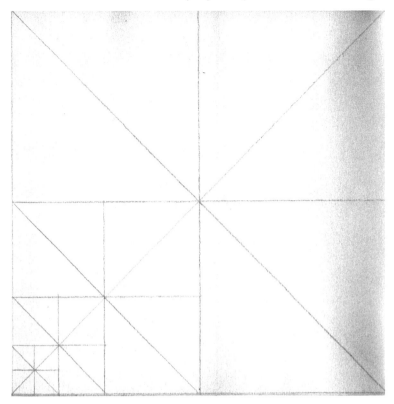

Figure 9.5 Working down to the corner.

> But the truth is that in philosophy and even elsewhere it is a question of finding the problem and consequently of positing it, even more than of solving it. For a speculative problem is solved as soon as it is properly stated. By this I mean that its solution exists then, although it may remain hidden and, so to speak, covered up—the only thing left to do is to uncover it. (1992:51)

It might seem here that we have a *speculative* problem, one that, like an idealised scientific or philosophical query, has a single correct solution that can be found as soon as the problem is stated properly. This, according to Bergson, allows the time spent on that problem to be reduced, potentially, to zero. In establishing our framework for the drawing, we achieve something already known. But although the action is repeated for each drawing, it remains essential to the process that I go through the set of gestures leaving a trace each time.

Had I been merely presented with this rather confusing jumble of red pencil lines, and told perhaps that they had in fact been drawn by another

182 *Conclusion: The purpose of axonometric drawing*

Figure 9.6 Establishing the corridor framework.

hand, would the subsequent drawing have been achievable? Would it have been possible or virtual? I maintain that the act of making these marks each time allowed me to see their purpose as measuring lines—that the *continuity* of process is, here, essential. Moreover, each line can be understood by an observer only in relation to his or her own mark-making experiences and represents more than a storyboard of the drawing process.

The aim of these initial marks is to establish a corridor (figure 9.6), with a visible entrance and threshold on the bottom left of the page, and a structure trailing off to the top right. The outside lines of this corridor are defined first, and then given a thickness by using the system of measurement-by-geometry present on each page.

This shell is itself divided into squares on its floor plan, allowing the necessary development of the translated notation of the movement found within the episode at hand. The architectural elements are then added in, as suggested by the source notations. Their placement is only made possible by the earlier process of division and measurement of the corridor floor. Once all the parts of the drawing are in place, we still have a

Conclusion: The purpose of axonometric drawing 183

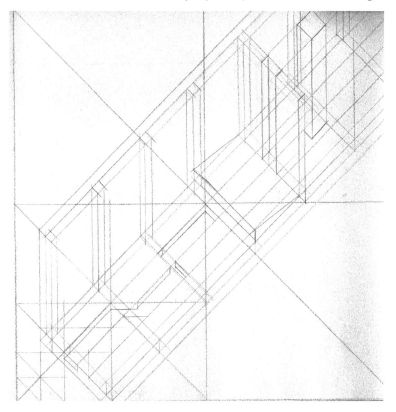

Figure 9.7 The jumble of pencil lines prior to inking.

jumble of red lines (figure 9.7). It is a jumble out of which a pattern can be found, but only with some difficulty. To this end, the relevant lines must be inked, as they contain insufficient notational force to allow another hand or eye to do the task. The process of inking has a particular logic to it, as it must work from those objects that appear nearest to the eye, according to the conventions of the projection, hence obscuring the objects behind it. It is necessary to stress once again the importance of the time enfolded within this process of drawing. While many aspects of this creative act were predictable in nature—or possible to return to Bergson's terminology—the overall effect is wholly virtual and reliant upon a particular duration of making.

By measuring the territory of the paper in this way, all the measurements are related to one another directly and form a coherent set of distances. This measurement must be completed to allow the framework of the corridor to be established—its thickness, division into stages, and other dimensions. The several steps, each checked and assessed, accumulate into the eventual drawing, although the process of making does not end there,

184 *Conclusion: The purpose of axonometric drawing*

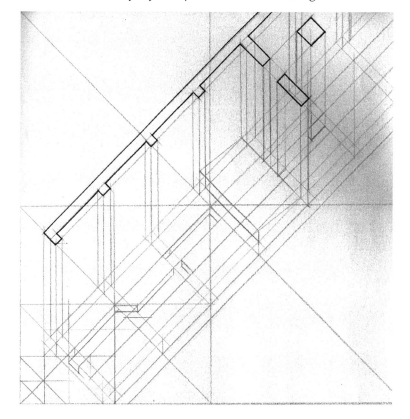

Figure 9.8 Inking lines in order.

as the drawing enters into relationships of a social nature involving interpretation, spectatorship, and ownership: those very factors that occupy so much of the attention of art historians, critics, and anthropologists.

The selection and inking of specific lines (figures 9.8 and 9.9) makes the reading of the drawing possible even whilst the construction lines remain. It is extremely difficult for an uninitiated observer to pick out which lines are intended to define the form of the corridor until the inking has taken place. The construction lines, often appreciated aesthetically by trained draughtsmen, do not aid the uninitiated observer, so the inking introduces a preferred reading to the lines, one which might elicit a response of either refusal and denial or complicity.

We can see in this example that there is a shifting relationship between speculative and creative aspects within a single practice. In this relatively simple example there are several points at which such shifts occur. Similar shifts can be exploited by practitioners in a variety of disciplines, such as architecture, fine art, or anthropology. There is a real difference, for

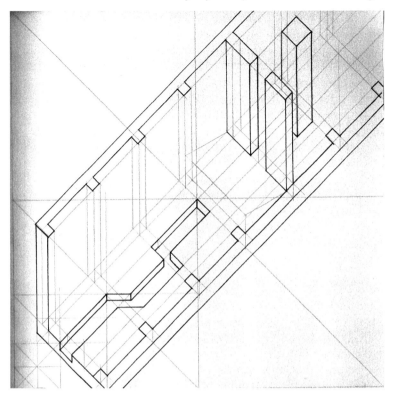

Figure 9.9 Selective inking.

example, between photography and drawing or notation, which can be characterised in terms of duration, virtuality, and possibility. In a photograph, many of the decisions are made in the moments before the shutter is released. Up to that point, the photograph is virtual, becoming reduced (and not in a negative or judgmental manner) to the possible once the shutter begins the camera's mechanical, optical, and chemical or digital work.

> I said to myself, time is something, therefore it acts. What can it be doing? Plain common sense answered: time is what hinders everything from being given at once. It retards, or rather it is retardation. It must therefore be elaboration. Would it not then be a vehicle of creation and of choice? Would not the existence of time prove that there is indetermination in things? Would not time be that indetermination itself?'
> (Bergson 1992:93)

The virtual aspect persists longer in a gestural, autographic drawing[11] or even notation, where creative choices and decisions are made throughout

186 *Conclusion: The purpose of axonometric drawing*

the process of making. I would, however, be wary of taking on Bergson's sometimes judgmental position towards possibility, as it seems to me that it plays an equally important part in creative activity. To champion the virtual and the unknowable is to miss the point that the *possible* and known actions are also necessary for the creative act to take place. It is very important to understand why this rather counterintuitive statement might be true. Similarly to the discussion of constraints within fine art practice, the known procedures act as a scaffold for the more open-ended marks. This scaffold allows both the process to continue and for it to be understood by an external reader, it gives them the reference information required to interpret the content of the drawing. The process of making the drawing also involves this reading whilst writing; placing oneself within knowable procedures not only supports the more spontaneous or arbitrary acts of flair, but grounds them in what is useful, understandable, materially possible.

9.6 Conclusion

Making an axonometric drawing is a deliberate form of words which establishes the drawing as something made, a process undergone, rather than always to be understood as a completed and finalised image. This book contends that there is a continued utility to the production of such drawings, and that this purpose is underlined by the ways in which both I and the architects studied in the preceding chapters have used the convention.

This book grew out of an interest in axonometric projection dating back to my time as an architecture student. I experimented with drawing a great deal, often working on vast perspectives drawn with pastel and chalk, showing colour and depth; organised as a sequence of spaces and eventually drawn up using the more conventional tools of plan, section, and elevation. I frequently used the 'wrong' projection, exploring the ways in which architectural drawings can convey spaces and atmospheres. A fourth-year project for what was built as the Dundee Contemporary Arts Centre by Richard Murphy was designed by my younger self as a kit-of-parts; tutored by David Grierson and Iain Gilzean under the intellectual leadership of Per Kartvedt, the school of architecture at Strathclyde was influenced strongly by Cedric Price's social conscience and, naturally following this, his approaches to design. The kit in question demanded representation in axonometric drawing, proposed as an overhead rail from which a variety of partitions and elements could be hung, the interior of the structure could be reconfigured swiftly and comprehensively. Idiosyncratically enough, I chose to present these, and a later housing project, as acrylic paintings rather than inked drawings.

I returned to drawing during my PhD research into inscriptive practices: cutting across a range of approaches including notation and diagramming,

Conclusion: The purpose of axonometric drawing   187

the previous extracts from *Getting Lost in Tokyo* demonstrated not that I sought to explore axonometric drawing so much as the drawings were a pragmatic response to the problems I had set myself. This project was rather more reflexive than prior works, and began to open a series of enquiries into the nature of drawing which sustain my research to this day. Assessing the temporality of the drawing process allows people to step back from pictorial understandings based in their status as images or spatial arrangements and brings the process of their becoming into sharp focus. This brings with it a series of implications, such as the interplay between speculative and creative elements in the process of drawing; the role that these play in producing meaning is not hierarchical as each process brings something essential to the overall practice.

Each of the architects outlined within this volume made use of parallel projection in different ways, sometimes subtle and often strikingly so.

James Stirling and JJP Oud are the most conventional of the five architects, but show remarkable sophistication in their approaches to drawing. Oud's place as a fallen star of the Modern movement, almost written out of the official histories of the movement on account of his return to ornament later in life affords a discussion of the movement's trajectory in microcosm. Starting as a student of early Dutch modern architecture from Dudok and Berlage, Oud becomes an associate of De Stijl without fully signing up to its agenda. Oud's practical and sensible design is taken up by the developing International Style, with particularly detailed housing schemes showing Oud's interest in architecture at a range of scales. This shows us the capacity of parallel projection for working with the scope of architecture, as it allows Oud to produce complete schemes which include furniture and fittings, detailed kitchen designs challenging the established ways of doing things, through the spatial planning of varied apartments and up to the level of city blocks with urban design sensitive to the existing context. This totality of vision presents his projects as complete and coherent, ready to be constructed and inhabited. This was an important part of selling the modern project in architecture to a sometimes sceptical audience: a believable version of new ways of living and organising space to balance the excesses of the other members of De Stijl.

Stirling's trajectory takes us from the postwar modernism of the United Kingdom towards the Postmodernist movement, mirroring Oud's earlier journey from abstraction to ornament. The drawings produced by Stirling's offices in partnership with James Gowan and then Michael Wilford are a testament to the architect's belief in the power of drawing to communicate. Drawings were public-facing documents, describing an elaborated intention for a space, and this had to be produced with the equivalent to verbal rhetoric. Stirling's drawings were convincing, in both the sense that they were realisable pieces of architecture, but also drawn arguments or even debates. He draws the viewer in by making the drawings more elaborate

188   Conclusion: The purpose of axonometric drawing

than they really need to be: rewarding the attention of the reader with rich detail and intricate features.

The early career of Peter Eisenman uses drawing more explicitly as a theoretical instrument, a device for exploring the possibilities of architecture without the reference to earlier precedents as in Stirling, as Eisenman sought a purely autonomous architectural language. This is controversial, and continues to be so. This is a testament to the fundamental nature of the questions being asked by Eisenman, and to an extent can be appreciated (hopefully) without always agreeing with his position. You might feel that the present volume is rather uncritical of the aims of each of the architects and their relative successes and failures, but that is not the aim. Exploring the possibilities of an underappreciated form of drawing is our goal here, and unpacking the ways in which the selected practitioners have used it presents us with an open question: how might we do things differently? Is another theory made with axonometric and oblique possible? The story of Eisenman's abandonment of the axonometric drawing in favour of procedural computing is outside the scope of the present volume, but it does present the question of what his theory said then as opposed to what it does now. Sequence is important in Eisenman's drawings, and is too often dismissed in the study of architecture. Eisenman walks us through his argument in drawing after drawing, missing out steps from this condenses his work too far and reduces the work of process to a single, final image: the result of transformational procedures.

Each architect's career develops significantly, but this is most apparent when looking at the distance travelled by John Hejduk. Starting from a similar position to Eisenman, Hejduk moves in a completely different, perhaps opposite direction towards his poetic, soulful, and obscure later works. The rules of the drawing are questioned and manipulated in Hejduk's early works, deliberately angling the drawing to show less rather than more, to hide and not reveal. This is consistent with the compact nine-square-problem houses where the densely packed enclosures produce a claustrophobic condition in the open Texas contexts he was designing for. The elongation of these houses along a wall element persist with this orientation denying the totalising view of parallel projection, preferring to show how the walls block and obstruct. Of all the architects represented, Hejduk is the one most present on his own drawings: we can be reasonably certain of the architect's own hand in these, given his position as an educator and occasional architect; but more than this, there is the autographic mark as Goodman would describe it. The wicked games of the diamond houses which flatten space demonstrate the hand of the architect as a kind of marginalia takes over the later works, dominated by Hejduk's visions of angels and other religious figures whilst confronting the aftermath of the holocaust. These are highly personal inscriptions which sometimes result in structures, sometimes poems, and sometimes remain as sketchbooks: serial in nature, multiple rather than

Conclusion: The purpose of axonometric drawing   189

single. Hejduk continues to open the rules of the conventions up, with sheets using multiple projections at once, symbolising transubstantiation and other transformative acts. Hejduk shows some of the ways in which a drawing convention designed to show more, to describe a totality, can express its opposite. This suggests that this quality of parallel projection is a spectrum from hidden and closed drawings to the most open x-ray representation. This can be manipulated in order to communicate the draughtsperson's intention more precisely.

A more down-to-earth concern for people is central to Cedric Price's architecture; and this shows through in his drawings for projects which continue to hold an influence today despite the relatively small number which were built. Price's drawings are animated, both sequentially and with the presence of people doing things. The relatively light touch architecture was not to be appreciated empty and from afar like the photography of professional architectural periodicals: the buildings were animated by people and their agency within the space. Price was interested in buildings which went together, were adapted whilst in use, and were finally dismantled, demonstrating how this ought to happen with his drawings. Price's drawings do not seduce with the sophistication of Stirling's; they do so with their deceptive simplicity. He allows the readers of the drawing to produce their own meanings much of the time, a process entirely consistent with his architecture, predicated on handing power to the building's inhabitants and users. One of the processes of reading a parallel projection is to project yourself into the spaces depicted, negotiating the rooms and thresholds. Price gives us some space to project further details of that space as well as making sure we are not alone: that the architecture is inhabited and social, consistent with his joyful approach to serious issues.

My current research involves the use of drawing as a methodology. These projects are explorations of contexts outside the scope of conventional architectural theory and history: urban festivals and marketplaces understood as architecture produced with a minimum of material means, or in a way designed to be ephemeral and temporary. Describing these instances has drawn on my background in social anthropology as well as architecture, but my aim is to find a method of research which is explicitly architectural. An all too obvious answer is to use drawing as a method of inquiry, something which academics and practitioners have been engaged with for some time, but in a way which is not recognised by the contemporary academic establishment, where the written word is of primary importance, even in a discipline such as architecture or a topic like architectural drawings. James Elkins identifies this problem with his book *On Pictures and the Words That Fail Them*[12]. The title is important to note, for fairly obvious reasons, elaborated in Elkins's engagement with Nelson Goodman where he discusses graphic marks as being *replete* as opposed to the *attenuated* and *discrete* marks in writing alphabetically (1998:10). Elkins is interested in

190   Conclusion: The purpose of axonometric drawing

the marks omitted and elided from our accounts: the smears and accidents, the errors which are all part of the process.

> By omitting marks, or herding them into broad categories of 'surface,' 'gesture,' or 'handling,' art historical accounts of all sorts make it possible to leap from recalcitrant, 'meaningless' smears and blotches of a picture to the stories it seems to embody' (Elkins 1998:46)

To extract the most from the drawings studied, it became clear to me that redrawing them was useful and important. This redrawing has the dual role of informing me about the original works, and this understanding equips me with a larger set of questions to answer verbally. The aim is not to oppose or privilege one form of understanding over the other, but there needs to be a stronger defence of drawing *even in a volume about drawing* as a valid research method. The drawing and writing for this book are in dialogue with one another, each able to provide understanding in different ways; hopefully presenting a model for future research including redrawing, copying, and distillation of key features into further drawings.

To conclude, I return to the question of the *purpose* of drawing in parallel projection. Notwithstanding the particular form: oblique, axonometric, isometric, or any of its variations; it is clear that the convention we use when drawing has a significant influence over the way we are able to articulate a design. Contemporary architectural practice is dominated by the use of digital models which can be displayed according to any standard form of projection: orthographic, perspective, or parallel; sometimes simultaneously. This has clear benefits to an integrated design process and allows for practices which move seamlessly from one modality to another, but the parallel projection is increasingly removed from this process and relegated to a presentational tool. I would argue that this is a missed opportunity and that there is good cause to reinstate axonometric and its family to a primary place within the design process. The clarity of working with a single projection for a period allows certain aspects of a scheme to be resolved fully; clearing away the bigger picture of the orthographic projections, a sequence of spaces can be programmed which make sense in themselves, has a clarity of image in the mind of a building user, and the manner of their construction explored fully. Collapsing the space between the design process and the working drawings has implications. There are very good reasons for the increased efficiency possible with digital methods, but there are losses at the same time. As Bergson suggests, the quality of the time spent on a creative problem is essential to how it is solved: it cannot be rushed or collapsed in the manner of a mathematical equation, as the statement of the problem is folded into the process.

The architects shown here used parallel projection for more than the finalised drawings, the public facing renderings. They used these drawings

Conclusion: The purpose of axonometric drawing 191

to develop their ideas, resolve issues, and to explore the possibilities. Elkins reminds us that:

> A mark can also be a shimmering thing at the edge of analysis: one instant it will seem to be solid and homogeneous, and then it will resolve into parts, or exhibit a determinate structure. If the panel had nearly invisible lines. It would have been one example: another is Seurat's experiments. I would call this Pliny's theory, since a literal reading of the text yields it as a consequence. Because painted and drawn marks routinely operate at the limit of resolution of the eye, barely perceptible forms are another universal mode for graphic marking. Their indistinctness is not always meant to be resolved, and so 'shimmering' is something that graphic marks do—it is part of their way of accepting and declining determinate meaning. (1998:44)

The density of meaning possible through drawing defies verbalisation at times, as these marks held in a constellation of relationships with one another can hold tensions and uncertainty, closer to poetry most obviously in the case of Hejduk, but also in the case of the quotidian beauty of Oud or the social conscience evident in Price. These 'syntactically dense' (1998:10) marks allow the draughtsperson to describe forms by recategorising regions of a surface: lines which enclose territories on paper. Understanding the way in which knowledge is produced through drawing is essential to the history and future development of architecture, as our tools of expression are thinking tools: providing us with a set of conditions which are possible to describe and others which are deemed outside the scope of the discipline. If we are to abandon parallel projection in favour of other methods of design, we must be sure that the new processes are more appropriate to the production of architecture today, that the aspects of space, time, and social life depicted are superior to the tools they supersede, and that we do not accidentally relegate a family of useful and relevant drawing conventions to the status of a historical artefact when we still have a need for them.

Notes

1. See Scheer (2014), for more on this idea of the death of drawing.
2. See Gell (1999).
3. This section is adapted from Lucas (2006).
4. See Tschumi (1994) for more on this.
5. See Lucas (2006:37–103).
6. See Lucas (2004, 2008a, 2008b) for more on the *Getting Lost in Tokyo* project.
7. Notwithstanding examples such as Francis Bacon, who exploited the unprimed canvas in his work, or that of William Kentridge, whose use of appropriately sourced (rather than arbitrarily found) objects such as drawing manuals or maps inform his drawing and printmaking practices.

192 *Conclusion: The purpose of axonometric drawing*

8. For more on Gilles Deleuze's (2003) reading of Francis Bacon, see Lucas (2006:103–120).
9. This property of perspective is also considered in relation to my series of paintings, *Finding Places in Tokyo* (see Lucas 2006:83).
10. The parallel motion being the horizontal bar on a drawing board which allows the drawing of parallel lines on the horizontal. With the use of a set square, vertical and angled lines can also be ruled accurately.
11. As opposed to the mechanical drawing of the draughtsman, for example.
12. Elkins, J. 1998. *On Pictures and the Words That Fail Them.* Cambridge: University of Cambridge Press.

References

Alberti, Leon Battista. 1988. *On the Art of Building in Ten Books*. Rykwert, J., Leach, N. & Tavernor, R. (Trans.). Cambridge, Massachusetts: MIT Press.

Alonso-Rodríguez, Miguel Ángel & Calvo-López, José. 2014. "*Prospettiva Soldatesca*: An Empirical Approach to the Representation of Military Architecture in the Early Modern Period" in *Nexus Network Journal: Architecture and Mathematics*, Vol. 16 (2014), pp. 543–567.

Archer, B. J. (Ed.). 1980. *Houses for Sale*. New York: Rizzoli.

Aureli, Pier Vittorio. 2011. "Revisiting Cedric Price's Potteries Thinkbelt" in *Log*, No. 23 (Fall 2011), pp. 97–118.

Awan, Nishat; Schneider, Tatjana; Till, Jeremy. 2011. *Spatial Agency: Other Ways of Doing Architecture*. London: Routledge.

Baker, Geoffrey H. 2011. *The Architecture of James Stirling and His Partners James Gowan and Michael Wilford: A Study of Architectural Creativity in the Twentieth Century*. London: Routledge.

Barthes, Roland. 1977. *Image Music Text*. London: Fontana Press.

Baudrillard, Jean. "The System of Collecting" in Elsner, J. & Cardinal, R. (Eds.). *The Cultures of Collecting*. London: Reaktion Books.

Beckett, Jane, et al. 1978. *The Original Drawings of J. J. P. Oud*. London: The Architectural Association.

Bedford, Joseph. 2010. "Stirling's Rational Facade: Self-Division within the Reading of Garches and Jaoul" in *Architectural Research Quarterly (ARQ)*, Vol. 14, No. 2, pp. 153–164.

Benjamin, Walter. 1969 [1923]. "The Task of the Translator" in Benjamin, W. 1999. Illuminations. London: Pimlico.

——————. 1997 [1933]. "On the Mimetic Faculty" in *One-Way Street and Other Writings*. London: Verso, pp. 160–163.

——————. 2008. *The Work of Art in the Age of Mechanical Reproduction*. J. A. Underwood (Trans.). London: Penguin Great Ideas.

Berger, J. 2011. *Bento's Sketchbook*. London: Verso.

Bergson, Henri. 1992. *The Creative Mind: An Introduction to Metaphysics*. Andison, M. L. (Trans.). New York: Citadel Press.

——————. 2001 [1913]. *Time and Free Will: An Essay on the Immediate Data of Consciousness*. New York: Dover Books.

——————. 2002. *Key Writings*. London: Continuum.

Booker, Peter Jeffrey. 1967. *A History of Engineering Drawing*. London: Chatto & Windus.

194 *References*

Boon, Marcus. 2010. *In Praise of Copying*. Cambridge, Massachusetts: MIT Press.

Browne, J., Frost, C. & Lucas, R. (Eds.). 2018. *Architecture, Festival & the City*. London: Routledge.

Bryon, Hilary. 2008. "Revolutions in Space: Parallel Projections in the Early Modern Era" in *Architectural Research Quarterly*, Issue 3–4, Vol. 12, pp. 337–346.

Bryson, N. 2003. "A Walk for a Walk's Sake" in de Zegher, C. (Ed.). *The Stage of Drawing: Gesture and Act: Selections from the Tate Collection*. London & New York: Tate & The Drawing Center.

Buchli, V. 2013. *An Anthropology of Architecture*. London: Bloomsbury.

Cain, Patricia. 2013. *Drawing: The Enactive Evolution of the Practitioner*. Intellect Books.

Camerota, Filippo. 2004. "Renaissance Descriptive Geometry" in Lefevre, Wolfgang. in *Picturing Machines 1400–1700*. Cambridge, Massachusetts: MIT Press, pp. 175–208.

Caragonne, Alexander. 1995. *Texas Rangers: Notes from an Architectural Underground*. Cambridge, Massachusetts: MIT Press.

Choisy, Auguste. 2018 [1899]. *Histoire de l'Architecture*. Paris: Hachette Livre-BNF.

Cohen, Jean-Louis. 2012. *The Future of Architecture since 1889*. London: Phaidon.

Colquhoun, Alan. 2002. *Modern Architecture*. Oxford: Oxford University Press.

Cox, Rupert (Ed.). 2008. *The Culture of Copying in Japan*. London: Routledge.

Daniels, I. 2010. *The Japanese House: Material Culture in the Modern Home*. Oxford: Berg.

Deleuze, Gilles. 1992. *Cinema 1: The Movement Image*. London: Athlone Press.

——————. 1994. *Cinema 2: The Time Image*. London: Athlone Press.

——————. 2003. *Francis Bacon: The Logic of Sensation*. London: Continuum.

Deleuze, G. & Guattari, F. 1988. *A Thousand Plateaus: Capitalism & Schizophrenia*. London: Athlone Press.

Difford, Richard. 2014. "Conversions of Relief: On the Perception of Depth in Drawings" in *The Journal of Architecture*, Issue 4, Vol. 19, pp. 483–510.

Eco, U. 1989. *The Open Work*. A Cancogni (Trans.). Cambridge, Massachusetts: Harvard University Press.

Eisenman, P., Graves, M., Gwathmey, C., Hejduk, J., Meier, R. et al. 1975. *Five Architects*. New York: Oxford University Press.

Eisenman, Peter. 1982a. "Editor's Preface" in Rossi, Aldo. *The Architecture of the City*. Cambridge, Massachusetts: MIT Press.

—————— 1982b. *House X*. New York: Rizzoli International, pp. 34–168.

—————— 2001. *Diagram Diaries*. London: Thames & Hudson.

—————— 2003. *Giuseppe Terragni: Transformations Decompositions Critiques*. New York: The Monacelli Press.

—————— 2004. "Cardboard Architecture" in *Eisenman Inside Out: Selected Writings 1963–1988*. New Haven: Yale University Press, pp. 28–39.

—————— 2006 [1963]. *The Formal Basis of Modern Architecture*. Zurich: Lars Müller Publishers.

—————— 2008. *Ten Canonical Buildings 1950–2000*. New York: Rizzoli.

Eisenstein, Sergei M. 1946. "How I Learned to Draw (A Chapter About My Dancing Lessons)" in de Zegher, C. (Ed.). 2000. *The Body of the Line: Eisenstein's Drawing*. New York: The Drawing Center.

—————— 1949. *Film Form*. London: Faber and Faber.

—————— 1991. *Writings Volume 2: Towards a Theory of Montage*. London: BFI Books.

References   195

Elkins, J. 1998. *On Pictures and the Words That Fail Them*. Cambridge: University of Cambridge Press.

Emmons, Paul. 2014. "Demiurgic Lines: Line-making and the Architectural Imagination" in *The Journal of Architecture*, Issue 4, Vol. 19, pp. 536–559.

Evans, Robin. 1995. *The Projective Cast: Architecture and Its Three Geometries*. Cambridge, Massachusetts: MIT Press.

Flusser, V. 2014. *Gestures*. Minneapolis: University of Minnesota Press.

Gandelsonas, Mario. 1982. "Introduction. From Structure to Subject: The Formation of an Architectural Language," in Eisenman, Peter (Ed.). *House X*. New York: Rizzoli, p. 28.

Gell, Alfred. 1998. *Art and Agency: An Anthropological Theory*. Oxford: University of Oxford Press.

———————— 1999. "Vogel's Net: Traps as Artworks and Artworks as Traps" in *The Art of Anthropology: Essays and Diagrams*. London: London School of Economics Monographs on Social Anthropology, Athlone Press, pp. 187–214.

Giedion, Siegfried. 2008 [1940]. *Space, Time & Architecture: The Growth of a New Tradition*. Cambridge, Massachusetts: Harvard University Press.

Goffman, Erving. 1959. *The Presentation of Self in Everyday Life*. London: Penguin Books.

Goodman, Nelson. 1978. *Ways of Worldmaking*. Indianapolis: Hackett Publishing.

Gunn, W (Ed.). 2009. *Fieldnotes and Sketchbooks: Challenging the Boundaries Between Descriptions and Processes of Describing*. Frankfurt: Peter Lang Publishers.

Hardingham, Samantha. 2005. "A Memory of Possibilities" in *Architectural Design*, Issue 1, Vol. 75, p. 16.

———————— (Ed.). 2017. *Cedric Price Works 1952–2003: A Forward Minded Retrospective*. London & Montreal: Architectural Association & Canadian Centre for Architecture.

Hays, K. Michael (Ed.). 1996. *Hejduk's Chronotopes*. New York: Princeton Architectural Press.

———————— 2015. "Encounters" in Amistadi, L. & Clemente, I. (Eds.). 2015. *Soundings 0/1: John Hejduk*. Florence: Aión Edizioni, pp. 23–43.

He, Weiling. 2005. "When Does a Sentiment Become an Architectural Concept? Otherness in Hejduk's Wall House 2" in *The Journal of Architecture*, Vol. 10, April 2005.

Hejduk, John (Ed.). 1971. *Education of an Architect: A Point of View*. New York: Cooper Union & Museum of Modern Art.

———————— 1985. *Mask of Medusa: Works 1947–1983*. New York: Rizzoli.

———————— (Ed.). 1988. *Education of an Architect*. New York: Rizzoli.

———————— (Illus.). 1991. *Aesop's Fables*. New York: Rizzoli.

———————— 1995. *Architectures in Love*. New York: Rizzoli.

———————— 1997. *Pewter Wings Golden Horns Stone Veils*. New York: Monacelli Press.

———————— 1999. *Lines No Fire Could Burn*. New York: Monacelli Press.

Hejduk, Renata & Williamson, Jim (Eds.). 2011. *The Religious Imagination in Modern and Contemporary Architecture: a Reader*. London: Routledge.

Herdt, Tanja. 2017. *The City and the Architecture of Change: The Work and Radical Visions of Cedric Price*. Zurich: Park Books.

196   References

Hodder, Ian. 2012. *Entanglements: An Archaeology of the Relationships Between Humans and Things*. Chichester: Wiley-Blackwell.

Houdart, S. & Chihiro, M.. 2009. *Kuma Kengo: An Unconventional Monograph*. Paris: Editions Donner Lieu.

Huizinga, Johan. 1950. *Homo Ludens: A Study of the Play Element in Culture*. Boston: Beacon Press.

Hvattum, Mari. 2013. "Crisis and Correspondence: Style in the Nineteenth Century" in *Architectural Histories*, Issue 1(1), Vol. 21, pp. 1–8.

Ingold, Tim. 2000. *The Perception of the Environment*. London: Routledge.

——————— 2011. *Being Alive: Essays on Movement, Knowledge and Description*. London: Routledge.

——————— 2013. *Making: Anthropology, Archaeology, Art and Architecture*. London: Routledge.

——————— 2015. *The Life of Lines*. London: Routledge.

Jencks, Charles. "A Note on the Drawings" in Stirling, James et al. (Ed.). 1981. *James Stirling: Architectural Design Profile*. London: Academy Editions/St Martin's Press, pp. 50–55.

Jordan, Brenda G. & Weston, Victoria (Eds.). 2003. *Copying the Master and Stealing His Secrets: Talent and Training in Japanese Painting*. Honolulu: University of Hawaii Press.

Kaji-O'Grady, Sandra. 2012. "Formalism and Forms of Practice" in Crysler, C. Greig; Cairns, Stephen; Heynen, Hilde (Eds.). *The Sage Handbook of Architectural Theory*. London: Sage Publications.

Kauffman, Jordan. 2018. *Drawing on Architecture: The Object of Lines, 1970–1990*. Cambridge, Massachusetts: MIT Press.

Kentridge, William. 2004. *Cyclopedia of Drawing*. Valence: Art3 Art Contemporain.

Küchler, Suzanne. 2002. *Malanggan: Art, Memory and Sacrifice*. Oxford: Berg.

Lawrence, Snezana. 2003. "History of Descriptive Geometry in England" in *Proceedings of the First International Congress on Construction History*, Madrid.

Libeskind, D. 1985. "Stars at High Noon: an Introduction to the Work of John Hejduk" in Hejduk, J. 1985. *Mask of Medusa*. New York: Rizzoli, pp. 9–22.

Loos, Adolf. 1998. *Ornament and Crime*. Riverside, California: Ariadne Press.

Love, Timothy. 2003. "Kit-of-Parts Conceptualism: Abstracting Architecture in the American Academy" in *Harvard Design Magazine*, No. 19, Fall/Winter 2003, online at http://www.harvarddesignmagazine.org/issues/19/kit-of-parts-conceptualism-abstracting-architecture-in-the-american-academy [accessed 14th August 2008].

Lucas, Raymond. 2002. *Filmic Architecture: An Exploration of Film Language as a Method for Architectural Criticism and Design*. Unpublished MPhil Thesis, Glasgow: University of Strathclyde.

——————— 2006. *Towards a Theory of Notation as a Thinking Tool*. Unpublished PhD Thesis, Aberdeen: University of Aberdeen.

——————— 2008. "Getting Lost in Tokyo" in *Footprint, Delft School of Design Journal*, Issue 2. http://www.footprintjournal.org/issues/current.

——————— 2009. "Gestural Artefacts: Notations of a Daruma Doll." in Gunn, W (Ed.), *Fieldnotes and Sketchbooks: Challenging the Boundaries Between Descriptions and Processes of Describing*. Frankfurt: Peter Lang.

——————— 2017a. "Threshold and Temporality in Architecture: Practices of Movement in Japanese Architecture" in Bunn, S. (Ed.). *Anthropology and Beauty: From Aesthetics to Creativity*. London: Routledge, pp. 279–291.

——————— 2017b. "The Discipline of Tracing in Architectural Drawing" in Johannessen, C. M. (Ed.). *The Materiality of Writing: a Trace-Making Perspective.* London: Routledge, pp. 116–137.

——————— 2018. "Threshold as a Social Surface: The Architecture of South Korean Urban Marketplaces" in Simonetti, C. & Anusas, M. (Eds.). 2018. *On Surfaces: Contributions from Anthropology, Archaeology, Art and Architecture.* London: Routledge (forthcoming).

——————— 2019. "Home and What It Means to Dwell" in Lucas, Ray (Ed.). *Anthropology for Architects.* London: Bloomsbury (forthcoming).

Lucas, R. Miller, M. Clarke, J. & McGuire, N. 2017. "All Drawings Are Failures" Illustrated interview transcript in Clarke, J. (Ed.), *Koryu. Aberdeen: Knowing from the Inside.* Open access PDF available at: https://knowingfromtheinside.org/files/#about

Luscombe, Desley. 2013. "Illustrating Architecture: The Spatio-Temporal Dimension of Gerrit Rietveld's Representations of the Schröder House" in *The Journal of Architecture*, Vol. 18, No. 1, pp. 22–58.

——————— 2014. "Architectural Concepts in Peter Eisenman's Axonometric Drawings of House VI" in *The Journal of Architecture*, Vol. 19, No. 4, pp. 560–611.

Lynch, K. 1960. *The Image of the City.* Cambridge, Massachusetts: MIT Press.

Marks, Laura. 2000. *The Skin of the Film: Intercultural Cinema, Embodiment and the Senses.* Durham, North Carolina: Duke University Press.

Maxwell, Robert. 1998. *James Stirling/Michael Wilford.* Basel: Birkhäuser.

McGregor, James. 2002. "The Architect as Storyteller: Making Places in John Hejduk's Masques" in *Architectural Theory Review*, Vol. 7, No. 2, pp. 59–70.

Merrill, M. 2010. *Drawing to Find Out: Designing the Dominican Motherhouse.* Zurich: Lars Müller Publishers.

Moneo, Rafael. 2004. *Theoretical Anxiety and Design Strategies in the Work of Eight Contemporary Architects.* Cambridge, Massachusetts: MIT Press.

Monge, Gaspard. 1798. *Géométrie Descriptive, Leçons Donées aux Écoles Normales.* Paris: Baudouin.

Moore, Charles & Allen, Gerald. 1976. *Dimensions: Space, Shape & Scale in Architecture.* New York: Architectural Record Books.

Moravcová, Vlasta. 2014. "History of Descriptive Geometry with an Emphasis to the Boom of Descriptive Geometry in Austro-Hungarian Empire in the 19th Century" in *Technical Transactions/Czasopismo Techniczne*, 1 NP (7), pp.160–176.

Nancy, Jean-Luc. 2013. *The Pleasure of Drawing.* New York: Fordham University Press.

Napier, John. 1993 [1980]. *Hands.* Revised by Tuttle, Russel H. (Ed.). New Jersey: Princeton University Press.

Nakamura, Fuyubi. 2007. "Creating of Performing Words? Observations on Contemporary Japanese Calligraphy" in Hallam, Elizabeth & Ingold, Tim (Eds.). *Creativity and Cultural Improvisation.* Oxford: Berg.

Pallasmaa, Juhani. 1996. *The Eyes of the Skin.* London: Academy Editions.

——————— 2009. *The Thinking Hand.* London: John Wiley & Sons.

Pérez-Gómez, Alberto & Pelletier, Louise. 1997. *Architectural Representation and the Perspective Hinge.* Cambridge, Massachusetts: MIT Press.

Pink, S. 2004. *Home Truths: Gender, Domestic Objects and Everyday Life.* Oxford: Berg.

Price, Cedric. 2003. *Re: CP.* Basel: Birkhauser.

198 References

Rancière, J. 2009. *The Emancipated Spectator*. London: Verso.

Reeser Lawrence, Amanda. 2012. *James Stirling: Revisionary Modernist*. New Haven, Connecticut: Yale University Press.

Reinhartz-Tergau, Elisabeth. 1990. *J. J. P. Oud Architect*. Rotterdam: Uitgeverij De Hef/Museum Boymans-van Beuningen.

Roccasecca, Pietro. 2008. "Sebastiano Serlio: Placing Perspective at the Service of Architects" in Carpo, Mario & Lemerle, Frédérique (Eds.). *Perspective, Projections & Design: Technologies of Architectural Representation*. London: Routledge.

Rowe, Colin & Koetter, Fred. 1978. *Collage City*. Cambridge, Massachusetts: MIT Press.

Rowe, Colin. 1986. *The Mathematics of the Ideal Villa and Other Essays. Cambridge, Massachusetts: MIT Press*.

Rufford, Juliet. 2011. "'What Have We Got to Do with Fun?': Littlewood, Price and the Policy Makers" in *New Theater Quarterly*, Vol. 27, No. 4, pp. 313–328.

Satter, Todd Jerome. 2012. "James Stirling's Architecture and the Post-War Crisis of Movement" in *Deleuze Studies*, Issue 1, Vol. 6, pp. 55–71.

Scolari, Massimo. 2012. *Oblique Drawing: A History of Anti-Perspective*. Cambridge, Massachusetts: MIT Press.

Scheer, David Ross. 2014. *The Death of Drawing: Architecture in the Age of Simulation*. London: Routledge.

Sheets-Johnstone, M. 1999. *The Primacy of Movement*. Amsterdam: John Benjamins Publishing Company.

Søberg, Martin. 2012. "John Hejduk's Pursuit of an Architectural Ethos" in *Footprint: Architecture Culture and the Question of Knowledge*, Spring 2012, pp. 113–128.

Somol, R. E. 2001. "Dummy Text, or the Diagrammatic Basis of Contemporary Architecture" in Eisenman, Peter (Ed.). *Diagram Diaries*. London: Thames & Hudson, p. 7.

Spier, Steven. 2005. "Dancing and Drawing, Choreography and Architecture" in *The Journal of Architecture*, Vol. 10, No. 4, pp. 349–364.

Stamm, Günther. 1984. *J. J. P. Oud: Bauten und Projekte 1906 bis 1963*. Mainz: Bei Florian Kupferberg.

Stirling, James. 1996 [1975]. *James Stirling : Buildings & Projects, 1950–1974*. London: Thames and Hudson.

———— 1994. *James Stirling : Buildings & Projects, 1975–1992*. London: Thames and Hudson.

Sudnow, David. 2001. *Ways of the Hand: A Rewritten Account*. Cambridge, Massachusetts: MIT Press.

Tafuri, Manfredo. 1976. "'European Graffiti' Five × Five = Twenty-five" in Caliandro, Victor (Trans.). *Oppositions*, Vol. 5, pp. 35–73.

Tarkovsky, Andrey. 1987. *Sculpting in Time*. Hunter-Blair, K. (Trans.). Austin: University of Texas Press.

Taussig, Michael. 1993. *Mimesis and Alterity: A Particular History of the Senses*. London: Routledge.

Taverne, Ed & Broekhuizen, Dolf. 1995. *J. J. P. Oud's Shell Building: Design and Reception*. Rotterdam: NAi Publishers.

Tschumi, Bernard. 1994. *Event Cities*. Cambridge, Massachusetts: MIT Press.

Unwin, Simon. 2007. "Analysing Architecture Through Drawing" in *Building Research & Information* Vol. 35, No. 1, pp. 101–110.

Van Sommers, Peter. 1984. *Drawing and Cognition: Descriptive and Experimental Studies of Graphic Production Processes*. Cambridge: University of Cambridge Press.

Van Zijl, Ida. 2010. *Gerrit Rietveld*. London: Phaidon.

Vesely, Dalibor. 2004. *Architecture in the Age of Divided Representation: The Question of Creativity in the Shadow of Production*. Cambridge, Massachusetts: MIT Press, p. 86.

Vidler, Anthony. 2008. *Histories of the Immediate Present*. Cambridge, Massachusetts: MIT Press.

Wiekart, K. 1965. *J. J. P. Oud: Art and Architecture in the Netherlands*. Amsterdam: J. M. Meulenhoff.

Wilson, Frank R. 1999. *The Hand: How Its Use Shapes the Brain, Language, and Human Culture*. New York: Vintage Books.

Wittkower, Rudolf. 1988 [1949]. *Architectural Principles in the Age of Humanism*. London: Academy Editions.

Yanagi, Soetsu. 2003 [1972]. *The Unknown Craftsman*. Tokyo: Kodansha International.

Yaneva, Albena. 2009. *Made by the Office for Metropolitan Architecture: An Ethnography of Design*. Rotterdam: 010 Publishers.

Index

Allen, Stan 95, 103
allographic 2, 7, 155; *see also* autographic, Goodman, Nelson
Ambasz, Emilio 16
analysis 1, 15, 24, 25, 34, 66, 68, 71, 73, 101, 103–108, 114, 143, 157, 167–170, 191,
anthropology 2, 6, 20, 73; *see also* graphic anthropology
Archer, B. J. 17
autographic 2, 7, 28, 96, 137, 155, 185, 188; *see also* allographic, Goodman, Nelson
axonometric projection 3, 19, 23, 31, 34, 39, 68, 76, 84, 100, 136, 143–144, 147, 166, 171, 186

Bachelard, Gaston 17
Baker, Geoffrey 36
Banham, Reyner 121, 134
Barthes, Roland 138n5
Baudrillard, Jean 159
beaux-arts 13
Bedford, Joseph 39
Benjamin, Walter 7,9–10, 93
Bergson, Henri 2, 20, 83, 88–91, 114, 143, 152, 162, 167–173, 177, 180–186, 190; extensity vs intensity, 90; speculative vs. creative problem, 114, 119 n. 19, 152, 169–171, 180–181, 184, 187; virtual vs. possible, 167, 169–171, 182–186;
Berlage, Hendrik Petrus 14, 44–46, 49, 60, 187
bird's eye 31–33, 177
Bollnow, Otto Friedrich 90–91
Boon, Marcus 9
Bryon, Hilary 5, 76
Bryson, Norman 172, 175–176

Cain, Patricia 7, 154
Cairns, Stephen 34
calligraphy 6–7
Canadian Centre for Architecture (CCA) 2
cartoon 121–122, 137, 138n4
Choisy, Auguste 6, 76, 102
CIAM (Congrès Internationaux d'Architecture Moderne) 45
clarity 18, 31, 67, 71, 78, 89, 125, 134, 165–166, 190
collage, 19, 24, 29, 34–35, 39, 85, 107–108, 134,
compostion 18, 24–25, 29–30, 32, 34–36, 39, 44, 49, 57, 60, 62, 64, 67–68, 71, 73, 85, 96, 102, 105, 107, 113–114, 125, 147, 152, 166, 172, 178
Cox, Rupert 8

dance 8–9, 88, 91, 153, 155
De Stijl 14, 16, 19, 29, 43–50, 67–69, 71, 108, 132, 147, 187
Deleuze, Gilles 2, 33, 41 n. 11, 83, 86, 135, 153
diagram 1, 7, 76, 78, 84, 103–106, 108, 133, 137, 154, 166, 170, 173–175, 177, 186
Difford, Richard 70
down axonometric, *see* bird's eye
draughtsperson 2, 19, 21, 27, 32, 67–68, 91, 98, 142, 144, 152–154, 157, 177, 184, 189, 191
Dudok, Willem Marinus 14, 44, 49, 187
duration 30, 167–168, 170–171, 177, 183, 185
Dürer, Albrecht 5

Eisenman, Peter 1, 4, 14–19, 24–25, 47, 66, 74, 78, 100–119 (Chapter 6), 133, 148, 166, 171, 188; analysis 24–25, 34, 101, 103–105; diagrams, 103–106, 108; el/L shape, 100, 110, 114; Guardiola House, 111; House II, 15–16, 106, 113; House III, 114–117; House VI, 111; House X, 19, 100, 107, 111, 113, 116; House 11a, 111–112; parametricism, 100, 111–112

Eisenstein, Sergei 22n18, 98n1, 135, 137

Elkins, James 77–78, 98, 189–191

Emmons, Paul 69–70

enchantment 19, 27–28, 32, 39, 166

entanglements *see* Hodder, Ian

Evans, Robin 25, 30, 158

failure 47, 143–148, 152, 157, 188

Five Architects 15–16, 100; *see also* New York Five

Flusser, Vilém 157

Frampton, Kenneth 15

Gadamer, Hans-Georg 47

Gandelsonas, Mario 107

gaze 31, 40–41 n. 10, 73, 79, 84–86, 153

Gehry, Frank O. 17

Gell, Alfred 6, 27–28, 166

Gesamtkunstwerk 47–50

Giedion, Siegfried 44–46

Girouard, Mark 25

Goodman, Nelson 2, 7, 12, 137, 155, 188–189

Gowan, James 15, 23, 187,

graphic anthropology, *11*, 144, 154, *156, 173*

Graves, Michael 15

Gregotti, Vittorio 16

Grosz, Elizabeth 169

Guattari, Félix 83, 86

Gwathmey, Charles 15

haptic 83–84, 86

Hardingham, Sarah 121, 126, 128, 133–134, 137

Hays, K. Michael 78, 84, 95

He, Weijing 71–73

Hejduk, John 2, 4, 14–16, 19, 28, 34, 39, 64–82 (Chapter 4), 83–99 (Chapter 5), 102, 106, 115–116, 132, 137, 164–166, 177, 188–189, 191; Compass Houses, 64; Diamond Houses, 66; Fraction Houses 64; mask/masque, 73, 85, 94–95; nine-square problem, 19, 64–66, 102, 106, 132, 188; poetry, 15, 21, 71, 74, 80, 83, 91, 92–95, 96; Texas Houses, 19, 64, 66, 71, 96, 188; Wall Houses, 19;

Herzog & De Meuron 17

Hodder, Ian 106–107

Houses for Sale (exhibition, catalogue) 17

Hvattum, Mari 47

hybridity 165

image 4, 15, 27–28, 33, 36, 46, 84, 88–90, 107, 114, 129, 133–135, 140–163 (Chapter 8), 167, 169, 172, 186–188, 190

indication 65, 69, 122, 124, 129, 135, 137,

Ingold, Tim 1, 7, 11, 12, 81n14, 89, 95, 106, 142, 153–154, 159, 164, 167; with Hallam, Elizabeth, 89

isometric drawing 3–5, 17, 30, 43, 67, 70–71, 79, 83–84, 91, 120, 129, 155, 165–166, 190

Isozaki, Arata 16, 133, 137

Jencks, Charles 34, 35

Katsura Rikyu, Kyoto 80, 81n12

Kentridge, William 190

kit of parts 24, 36, 50, 66, 121, 125, 130, 171, 177, 186

knowledge production 1, 20, 83, 85, 86, 141, 155, 164, 167, 191

Koetter, Fred 35

Koolhaas, Rem 17

Krier, Leon 25, 40n4

Küchler, Suzanne 6

Laban notation 22n18, 91, 155, 177

Lacan, Jacques 84, 85

Lasdun, Denys 15, 29

Le Corbusier 6, 15, 23–25, 29, 34, 39, 45–46, 55, 73, 78, 102, 104, 126; Maison Jaoul, 23

Lefevre, Liane 5

Libeskind, Daniel 73–74, 137, 148

linguistic analogy; In Eisenman, 15, 66, 100, 102–103, 109; In Hejduk, 94

202 *Index*

Littlewood, Joan 122, 125–127
Loos, Adolf 44, 49
Luscombe, Desley 68–69, 117

making 1–2, 4–8, 10–12, 16, 20, 22,
 86–87, 89, 92, 94–98, 117, 121, 135,
 137, 141–142, 148, 152–154, 157,
 164, 166, 167, 182–187
malleability 166
mark 2, 4, 42, 69, 77–78, 98, 122,
 137, 144, 148, 152, 155, 157,
 159, 167, 172–177, 182, 186,
 188–191
Meier, Richard 15
Mies van der Rohe, Ludwig 16, 45,
 78, 104
mimesis 6–13, 19
model 7, 16, 19–20, 24, 29, 45, 48, 53,
 71–72, 87, 89, 101, 106–107, 112,
 116–117, 141–143, 153, 155, 159,
 164–166, 190
Mondrian, Piet 14, 46, 48, 67, 78
Moneo, Rafael 17–18, 34
Monge, Gaspard 5
montage 66, 114–117, 134–135,
 137, 153
Moore, Charles 16
movement 30, 33, 39, 41n11, 69,
 87–89, 100–102, 121, 132, 135, 142,
 154–157, 164, 177, 182
Murray, Peter 137

Nakamura, Fuyubi 6–7
Namdaemun Market 144, 155–156, 175
Nancy, Jean-Luc 158
Napier, John 141–142
New York Five, the 15, 66, 100

oblique drawing 3–5, 17, 43, 51, 74,
 76, 83–84, 91, 93, 95, 155,
 188, 190
occlusion 2, 19, 41n11, 64–82
 (Chapter 4), 137, 165
orlo 77–78
Oud, J. J. P. 4, 14, 16, 19, 43–63
 (Chapter 3), 187, 191; Bijdorp
 Workers Housing, 45; Cafe de
 Unie, Rotterdam, 14; Metz &
 Co. Furniture, 50, 51; Rotterdam
 City Hall, 52–53; Second
 Liberal Christian Lyceum, 57;
 Shell Building, 14, 44–46, 56;
 Wiessenhof, 45, 48, 55

Palladio, Andrea 19, 66
parallel projection 2–6, 11, 13, 17–19,
 20–21, 30, 39, 43, 67–68, 72, 74,
 76, 78, 91, 93–94, 96, 108, 117,
 120–121, 124–125, 131, 134, 137,
 155, 165–167, 171, 176, 179–180,
 187–191
Pask, Gordon 127, 129, 139n12
Pelletier, Louise 30, 114, 158
Pelli, Cesar 16
Perez-Gomez, Alberto 30, 114, 158
perspective drawing 4–6, 30–31, 38,
 54, 68–69, 71–74, 78–79, 81, 83–85,
 94–95, 114, 117, 155, 158, 165–167,
 177, 179, 186, 190
physiology 27, 141
planometric drawing *see* axonometric
precision 93, 114, 137, 142,
 157–158, 165
promenade 30, 36, 39, 68, 73, 115, 118
Price, Cedric 4, 14–17, 20, 66,
 120–140 (Chapter 7); 171, 177, 186,
 189, 191; Fun Palace, 14, 20, 120,
 122, 125–128, 134; Generator, 125,
 129, 131; In House drawings, 121;
 In Head drawings, 121; In Action
 drawings, 121; London Zoo Aviary,
 120; Potteries Thinkbelt, 20, 120,
 125, 128–129; soirees 122, 132

Ranciére, Jacques 153
Reeser Lawrence, Amanda 23–25,
 28–29, 40n4,
reserve 168, 175
reverse angle *see* worm's eye
Rietveld, Gerrit 14, 44, 48, 68,
 132; Red and Blue Armchair, 48;
 Schröder House, 68, 132
Rossi, Aldo 17, 100–101
Rowe, Colin 15, 17, 28, 30, 35, 38–39,
 66, 103, 105

Sanja Matsuri 11, 149, 150, 155–156
Satter, Todd Jerome 33–34, 39,
scale 7, 12, 19, 43–63 (Chapter 3), 87,
 106, 117, 121–122, 127, 134, 158,
 164, 166, 187
Schechner, Richard 8
Schinkel, Friedrich 15, 36;
 Altes Museum, 36
Scolari, Massimo 5, 113
Scott Brown, Denise 17
Semper, Gottfried 47

Index   203

seriality, series 1, 7, 16–17, 19–20, 23, 27,
    29, 43, 53, 64–67, 73–74, 78, 83–84,
    92–95, 100, 106, 111, 114–118, 127,
    142, 144, 152, 155, 169–170, 172,
    177, 179–180, 187–188
Serlio, Sebastiano 70
Sheets-Johnstone, Maxine 88
Siza, Alvaro 17
skill, skilled practice 7, 9, 13, 20,
    22n16, 31, 142–143,
spectator 32–33, 40n10, 94, 133,
    153, 184
Stirling, James 4, 13–15, 17–19, 23–42
    (Chapter 2), 66, 105, 115, 118, 166,
    177, 187–189; Latina Library, 26;
    Leicester Engineering Building,
    18, 24–25, 28–29, 33, 40n4, 105;
    Olivetti HQ, 31; Staatsgalerie
    Stuttgart, 30, 34, 36, 38–39
Stirling, Wilford & Associates 15,
    26–27, 40n4, 187
Sudnow, David 6, 89
Summerson, John 16
surface 16, 23–24, 29, 34, 35, 46,
    58, 68–69, 78–79, 102, 114, 125,
    154, 152, 154, 158, 161, 164–168,
    172–177, 190–191

Tafuri, Manfredo 66
Tarkovsky, Andrey 135, 153

Taussig, Michael 10, 12–13,
Terragni, Guissepi 10, 100, 103–104
tolerance 137, 148
trap see Gell, Alfred
Tschumi, Bernard 18, 73, 148, 168

Ungers, O. M. 16
Unwin, Simon 6
up axonometric, see worm's eye
van Doesburg, Theo 14, 44, 46, 49,
    67–69, 147; Contra-Constructions,
    46, 69

van Eesteren, Cornelis 14, 147
van Sommers, Peter 142–143
Venturi, Robert 17
Vesely Dalibor 47, 162
Vidler, Anthony 28, 30
volume, volumetric 3, 18, 23–25,
    29–30, 36, 57–58, 66, 80, 85, 98,
    100–103, 106, 114, 125, 155, 158,
    165, 177, 178

Wilford, Michael 15, 26–27,
    40n4, 187
Wittkower, Rudolf 66, 105
worm's eye 3, 19, 23, 30–36, 37,
    76, 177
Wright, Frank Lloyd 25, 44–45, 49